The Connecticut Yankee
in the Twentieth Century

**Contributions to the Study of
Science Fiction and Fantasy**

The Connecticut Yankee in the Twentieth Century

Travel to the Past in Science Fiction

BUD FOOTE

Contributions to the Study of Science Fiction and Fantasy, Number 43
Marshall B. Tymn, Series Editor

GREENWOOD PRESS
New York • Westport, Connecticut • London

Library of Congress Cataloging-in-Publication Data

Foote, Bud.
  The Connecticut Yankee in the twentieth century : travel to the
past in science fiction / Bud Foote.
     p. cm.—(Contributions to the study of science fiction and
fantasy, ISSN 0193–6875 : no. 43)
  Includes bibliographical references and index.
  ISBN 0–313–24327–1 (alk. paper)
  1. Science fiction, American—History and criticism.   2. American
fiction—20th century—History and criticism.   3. Science fiction,
English—History and criticism.   4. English fiction—20th century—
History and criticism.   5. Time travel in literature.   6. History
in literature.   I. Title.   II. Series.
PS374.S35F66   1991
813′.0876209—dc20   90–38418

British Library Cataloguing in Publication Data is available.

Library of Congress Catalog Card Number: 90–38418
ISBN: 0–313–24327–1
ISSN: 0193–6875

First published in 1991

Greenwood Press, 88 Post Road West, Westport, CT   06881
An imprint of Greenwood Publishing Group, Inc.

Printed in the United States of America

The paper used in this book complies with the
Permanent Paper Standard issued by the National
Information Standards Organization (Z39.48–1984).

10 9 8 7 6 5 4 3 2 1

In memory of
Lewis Ford Foote

and for

Margaret Flint Foote

Ruth Anne Quinn Foote

William Lewis Foote III
James Murray Foote
Anna Kathleen Foote
Joseph Nathaniel Foote
Samuel Joshua Foote
Lewis Ford Foote II

Caryl Lucia Foote

my past, my present, my future

CONTENTS

PREFACE

Life being all too short, I have not tried to read every piece of fiction in English dealing with travel to the past; nor have I referred to most of those I have read. What I have included are those things I have found useful; I make no pretense to exhaustiveness. Since my interest is in ideas rather than in bibliographic or textual criticism, I have used those editions that were at hand or easily available, in spite of my awareness that editions of science fiction are often fleeting and temporary things. Because I hate endnotes and publishers despise footnotes, I have referred in the text to the list of Works Cited at the end of the book. When I have cited such standard works as *The Decline and Fall of the Roman Empire* or *A Connecticut Yankee in King Arthur's Court*, unless there is a particular reason, I have mentioned chapter number only; and when, in passing, I have nodded respectfully at the travels of Gulliver, the wake of Finnegan, or the afterlife of Dante, I have generally trusted the common culture of the community and spared myself, the reader, and the typesetter.

When no confusion can result, I have used commonly understood short forms in text and works cited: *SF* for science fiction; *ASF* for *Astounding Science Fiction* and its later avatar *Analog Science Fact/Science Fiction*; *Amazing* for *Amazing Stories*; *F&SF* for *The Magazine of Fantasy and Science Fiction*; *IASFM* for *Isaac Asimov's Science Fiction Magazine*; and, according to whim and rhythm, *Yankee* or *Connecticut Yankee* for *A Connecticut Yankee in King Arthur's Court*. ("Yankee" refers to Hank Morgan, "*Yankee*" to the book.)

There turns out to be no space for an extensive and annotated bibliography of SF about travel to the past, articles about SF about travel to the past, and the like; I have saved all that material and am in the process of compiling an additional (bibliographic) volume on the subject.

I am greatly indebted to many people and groups of people: to the College of Sciences and Liberal Studies at Georgia Tech, which has supported science fiction courses there since 1971, which has made possible a good deal of the thought and reading which have gone into this book; to its former Dean, Les Karlovitz, lately and too-early dead, a mathematician who loved the work of Mark Twain; to the English Department and the members thereof, who have been consistently tolerant of what must have often seemed to them a harebrained and maverick operation; to the Georgia Tech students in my science fiction classes, who have over the years been consistently stimulating; to Elizabeth Evans, former Head of the English Department, for encouragement and support; to A. D. Van Nostrand, another former Head of that department, and to Ken Knoespel, Acting Head, for careful and thoughtful readings and questionings; to Marshall Tymn, for the impulse to produce the book in the first place; to my colleagues in the Science Fiction Research Association, the International Association for the Fantastic in the Arts, the Popular Culture Association, and the South Atlantic Modern Languages Association, who have listened with critical patience to chunks of this material which I have inflicted on them at otherwise learned meetings; to the Georgia Tech Foundation, which afforded me released time to work on this project and assisted with the purchase of the computer on which I have composed these lines; to Forrest J. Ackerman for permission to use his unparalleled collection; to Mark Stevens of Atlanta's Science Fiction and Mystery Book Shop, who has been a good friend and an unfailing resource; to my wife, for constant intellectual stimulation and moral encouragement; and to my children for often subjecting themselves willingly to being shooed off when the gemlike flame was burning.

The Connecticut Yankee in the Twentieth Century

Chapter 1

THREE IMPOSSIBLE THINGS
BEFORE BREAKFAST

What then is time? If no one asks me, I know; if I want to explain it to a questioner, I do not know.

—St. Augustine

What I am going to try to do in this book is not simple; and maybe some sort of straightforward statement of purpose is desirable here at the outset.

First, I am trying to address a varied audience: I should like to be read by readers of science fiction who are neither critics nor academicians, but simply people who read the stuff and like thinking about it. But I should also like to address my fellow-academicians who not only read science fiction, but also teach it or write criticism about it. Further, I think that I may have something to say to people interested in nineteenth- and twentieth-century mainstream literature, to amateurs of the work of Mark Twain, and to people whose interest is in the history of ideas and perceptions.

Attempting to shotgun such a varied flock is sure to result in irritating everyone, from time to time. If I make things as clear as I may to non-science-fiction-reading Twain-lovers, then I shall appear to my colleagues in science fiction to be belaboring the obvious and rechewing ancient cabbage; if I pause for remarks about the state of science at a given moment for the benefit of folk whose expertise is in American literature, I shall appear to my scientific colleagues to be dishing up very old soup indeed. Conversely, there will be times when, to one reader or another, I shall seem to be skimming too lightly over knotty and perplexing problems. I pray pardon: it is the disease of the dilettante.

My subject is likewise complex, and it takes me a while to close in on it. Travel to the past, for reasons I shall get to in frightful detail in a bit, does not seem to belong within the field of science fiction—at least as I understand the definition—but rather to fantasy. And yet I find such travel all over the place in works labeled science fiction; and indeed, I somehow feel, in the teeth of the definitions, that it belongs there. I am trying to find out why.

Furthermore, travel to the past seems to me to be subversive of all fiction, all morality, and all human significance. That would ordinarily be enough to put me off. It does not, and I want to know why.

Travel to the past of the kind I am discussing first appears in Mark Twain's *Connecticut Yankee in King Arthur's Court*. But in our century, the idea has been used again and again and again. Why, I ask, did the idea wait until 1889 to find voice? And how do we account for the fact that Mark Twain is that voice?

This book, then, is by way of being a detective story; and like every detective story, it must look at a lot of evidence before, at the very end, the Great Detective uncaps a beer and grumbles, "I suppose you wonder why I've called you all here this evening." Patience.

SCIENCE FICTION AND CREDIBILITY

For a little while there, many of us thought we could tell science fiction from fantasy. Although Hugo Gernsback's editorial choices did not always harmonize with his original didactic purposes; although the *Astounding* of John Campbell included many a story whose fantastic elements belied the editor's scientific and engineering background; and although every story by people trained, like Isaac Asimov, in science did not train its sights on science; nevertheless, as the 1930s and 1940s passed, SF tended to adhere more and more closely, if not to current scientific thought, at least to science which could be reasonably extrapolated from the thought of the then present.

If evidence be needed for this point, it exists in plenty, both anecdotal and textual: Cleve Cartmill's "Deadline" and the bad moments it gave the FBI; Larry Niven's *Ringworld* inspiring engineers to calculate that the magnificent artifact of the title was unstable; Arthur C. Clarke's *2020* having to take into account the astronomical information new since the publishing of *2001*; Clarke again, appealing to *Science*, *Komsomolskya pravda*, and *Acta Astronautica* to establish the credibility of his spacehook in *The Fountains of Paradise*; and Poul Anderson and Hal Clement, in "The Creation of Imaginary Worlds" and "The Creation of Imaginary Beings," respectively, going into great and non-fictional detail about how to avoid nasty letters from readers overly cognizant of the sciences.

Science fiction of this sort, we may conclude, is a long way from much of the improbable space opera of the 1920s. We need to qualify this conclusion just a bit. First, there are certainly writers operating today who feel free to commit Barsooms in happy disregard of much that is currently believed about physics, geography, chemistry, and biology; but most such writers are operating somewhere on the fringes of the field, creating motion picture scripts, TV series, or Rhodan-style latter-day space opera. Second, the New Wave of the 1960s and early 1970s certainly blurred the lines of distinction among SF, fantasy, and mainstream fiction, and the results of that blurring are still with us today; indeed, many respected writers and critics have asserted that the traditional distinctions among those categories have become useless. Third, a convention gains credibility as it is used; the readers of Michael Moorcock's *Dancers at the End of Time* trilogy in the 1970s did not require, in the interests of credibility, the lengthy descriptions of a time machine and the didactic disquisitions on the nature of time which were needed by the readers of H. G. Wells in the 1890s. Finally, as physics in our century has become more and more fantastical, the implications of post-Heisenberg science have begun to filter into the lay understanding, and that process has made the line between fantasy and SF ever more difficult to define.

Let me nevertheless hold to the older commonsense definitions of science fiction and insist that (as Robert Heinlein has noted) science fiction is imitative of reality in somewhat the same way mainstream mimetic fiction is—not of things past or present, but of things to come, or which might come. To the extent that it is not, it moves toward fantasy.

A degree of credibility, then, is at the heart of science fiction, just as implausibility is at the core of fantasy; and the more easily results can be replicated in experiment—that is, the "harder" the science—the "harder-core" will be the resulting science fiction. Borderline areas, of course, will always give the would-be definer trouble, but there cannot be much doubt that Clement's *Mission of Gravity* is hard-core science fiction, and therefore offers a very different sort of intellectual and aesthetic experience from that of J.R.R. Tolkien's *Lord of the Rings*. In the one, we are in a rationally contrived universe, in which laws of cause and effect operate in expected and credible fashion, and to which we can logically get ourselves from our own here-and-now. In the other, we experience a Middle-Earth which, while it bears some resemblance to our own world, presents us with giant spiders that should collapse of their own weight, wizards with magic wands, rings of invisibility, and cave-dwelling goblins, the source of whose vitamin D is never documented. While both share in the sense of wonder, and both rely, as has often been noted by critics, on a rhetoric which distances the reader from the action, still part of the experience of SF is in its real external possibility; the corresponding experience in fantasy is in a reality which is internal and psychological.

Suspension of disbelief, then, is less demanded of the reader of science fiction than of the reader of fantasy; indeed, anyone who has discussed science fiction with a group of students at all knowledgeable in science or engineering will testify that a good deal of their time is spent in checking the science and engineering of the author with handbooks and pocket calculators. And to the extent the author has not made a viable case in his extrapolation from the current state of the art, to that very extent the SF pleasure of that sort of student, and of that sort of reader, is lessened, whatever the fantasy pleasure may be.

Clearly, then, many readers bring to SF a sophisticated set of expectations and a contemporary notion of the cosmos as now understood by the scientific community, however evanescent they may know that understanding to be; and part of our pleasure in Clarke's *Fountains of Paradise* or Frederik Pohl and Jack Williamson's *Wall Around a Star* comes from the sense that the artifacts in question, however mindboggling, are consistent with a reasonable extrapolation from current science and technology. Gandalf is not.

THREE IMPOSSIBLE THINGS

And yet, as Peter Nichols notes in "Imaginary Science" in *The Science Fiction Encyclopedia*, at the very core of this same science fiction that has often so stridently insisted on credibility are four elements which are—at least in terms of our current understanding of the universe—the most outrageous fantasy:

• antigravity;
• faster-than-light (FTL) travel;
• invisibility; and
• time travel to the past.

This last, he says, constitutes a subgenre "which has always been one of sf's most ebulliently creative aspects" (306).

Well, antigravity and invisibility are a bit old hat, and there was more of those two in the science fiction of the 1920s and 1930s than there is now; and I suspect that one reason is that too many readers now find them over-fantastic. Let's leave them out of our meditations; and let's add to the list another notion, travel to parallel universes, so that our list of things that are still all over the place in current science fiction, but do not seem by any stretch of logic or imagination to belong there, will read thus:

• FTL travel;
• time travel to the past (which would, of course, include return to the present after a trip to the future); and
• travel to parallel universes (or alternate universes or, to use H. Beam Piper's handy term, to *Paratime*).

All three of these are quite fantastic; each of us is far more likely to encounter unicorns in the supermarket, goblins in the men's room, or fairies at the bottom of his garden than he is to travel away from the Earth at eleventy-seven times the speed of light, or back to the fourteenth century, or sideways in time to a Pennsylvania in which gunpowder is a religious secret.

Please understand that whenever I write "impossible," I understand it to be followed by "at our present state of knowledge, which is sure to change," and then allow me to say that if *anything* is impossible, these three things are.

But are we, in fact, allowed to hold that there is anything which is clearly impossible? In *A Step Farther Out*, Jerry Pournelle summarizes a lecture delivered in 1975 by Professor Stephen Hawking, generally regarded by his peers and the public as a Newton- or Einstein-caliber thinker; in that lecture, developing a line of thought which has since become familiar, Hawking states that singularities—that is, areas where anything can happen, no rules apply, and cause-and-effect ceases to exist—are not only to be found inside the event horizons of black holes, decently veiled where they cannot possibly be observed, but must eventually be emitted from those black holes, producing the "naked singularity" which would make total hash of all physical laws. Pournelle summarizes the effect of Hawking's equations thus:

Western civilization assumes reason; that some things are *impossible, that's all*, and we can know that; that werewolves don't exist, and there never was, never could be, a god Poseidon, or an Oracle that spoke truly; that the universe is at least in principle discoverable by human reason, is *knowable*.
That, says one of the men we believe best understands this universe, is not true. It's not very probable that Cthulthu will emerge from the primeval singularity created in the Big Bang, or that Poseidon will suddenly appear on Mount Olympus, but neither is *impossible*; and for that matter, this world we think we understand, which seems to obey rational laws we can discover, isn't very probable either. . . . (184)

Several years have passed since this lecture, and as far as I know nobody has yet refuted Hawking's equations, though there have been quibbles and qualifications, some of them from Hawking. As a result of his best-seller, *A Brief History of Time*, Professor Hawking and his ideas have become media phenomena; if the notion of the emitted singularity is not refuted for another two or three decades, it is likely that it will become a common given in the minds of science fiction readers; and if that happens, then the line between science fiction and fantasy will sag in the middle and gently dissolve.

For the moment, however, and particularly when one deals with that vast area between the very, very tiny and the very, very large, the old rules of cause-and-effect and reason seem to work for most people, and seem to remain—whether or no they are ultimately true or provable—the givens of science fiction and the way one distinguishes that field from fantasy. Logic—that very logic which gave rise to Hawking's equations—seems to tell us that in any universe of which we can conceive, some things must be possible and others not possible. A universe in which nothing was possible would be static—either the timeless universe preceding the Big Bang or the ultimate entropy, equally timeless, which some foresee at the end of our universe. Conversely, a universe in which everything was possible would be ultimately chaotic and incapable of being understood by any intelligence, however vast. And therefore, if science and its stepchild science fiction are to exist at all, some things must be possible, others not. To be sure, as the state of our understanding changes, and presumably improves, our judgment of what is possible and what is not will change; but the principle seems to remain sound.

If, then, we may say that some things are not possible, do the three notions mentioned above—FTL travel, travel to the past, and travel to alternate universes—fall into that category of Impossible Things?

Faster-than-Light Travel

Take FTL travel first: it is true that the physicists of the tribe have devised a mathematical fiction called the *tachyon*, which, if it exists, *must* travel faster than light. Greatly simplified, the logic runs like this: in the universe we observe, we postulate the existence of *tardyons*, particles which must travel more slowly than light, and *luminons*, which always travel at precisely the speed of light. The more energy one puts behind a tardyon, the faster it travels and the heavier it gets; but as one approaches the speed of light, vast increases in energy are required to accomplish minuscule increases in speed. Only an infinite amount of energy—which is not available to us in this universe—will suffice to bring a tardyon to the speed of light.

Now, given the existence of tardyons and luminons, the principle of symmetry—which involves, after all, certain unprovable assumptions about the nature of the universe—would suggest the existence of tachyons, particles which would *always* travel faster than the speed of light, and which would require ever-increasing amounts of energy to bring them *down* closer to the speed of light and an infinite amount of energy to make them travel slower than that speed.

It is a truly elegant idea, but apparently incapable of proof or disproof. After all, if a particle has negative mass and is traveling faster than light, trapping the silly little thing becomes a truly difficult business. Furthermore, if our ideas about the relationships of space and time are correct, the tachyon would travel not only faster than light but *backwards in time*, which would make its validation an apparent impossibility.

Nevertheless, tachyon-based FTL drives have begun to appear in the literature and, because they are, however tenuously, supported by physics, are less improbable than their predecessors (the use of black-hole singularities without being pulled apart by gravity, the earlier space-warp or subspace FTL drives, and the even earlier FTL drives which were accepted by the readers with very little scientific basis at all). Still, given the difficulties involved, FTL drives seem, at very least, to be a long way from the hard core of science fiction.

Travel to the Past

You will have noted in the discussion of the tachyon above that FTL travel also implies travel backwards in time, or at least the possibility of sending a message backwards in time. In *Timescape*, Gregory Benford, himself a physicist, has carefully and intelligently used tachyons for just that purpose. Nevertheless, the notion that the past might be changed by intervention from the present still flies in the face of most theology, philosophy, and common sense. Philosophers ancient and medieval, pagan and Christian, all agree that even God cannot change the past.

In Christian tradition, undoing the past would seem to violate the very ground rules of creation. The whole notion of Christian forgiveness of sin is based on the notion that, while an evil cannot be undone, and perhaps cannot even be forgotten, it can nevertheless be forgiven, which is to say that the doctrine of repentance and forgiveness comes as a softening and humanizing of the unalterable physical principle that one cannot unspill the milk. Even Jesus, though He was able to raise the dead, apparently could not spare Lazarus the agony of *having died*; nor does the idea appear to have occurred to Him. While God could, without violating His own ground rules, create unicorns or centaurs, cause someone to sleep for a hundred years, or even temporarily and locally reverse entropy by raising someone from the dead, changing the past would seem to shake the very fabric of His universe.

Folk tradition, likewise, is full of assertions that the past is irrevocable. While a word is yet unspoken, you are master of it; when once it is spoken, it is master of you. You can't put the toothpaste back into the tube. What is past is over and done with. Let the dead bury their dead.

In "The Theory and Practice of Time Travel," an essential article for anyone who would contemplate travel to the past, Larry Niven, in an argument which, I think, would have delighted Plato, has persuasively argued that one cannot change the past. I summarize: If time travel and changing of the past is possible, then over centuries, people will repeatedly change the past. But if the past is repeatedly changed, and there is no historical inertia which causes events to tumble back into their original channel, then eventually a time line will come into being in which travel to the past is *not* invented. And if there *is* a historical inertia, then the easiest way for it to operate is for time travel never to be invented. In either case the result is the same: time travel to the past and changing the past is (will be/has become) impossible. Q.E.D.

Travel to Parallel Universes

Just as FTL travel might produce travel backwards in time, so travel to the past might well produce parallel universes. If I went back to Hastings in 1066 and then-and-there frustrated the attempted invasion of England by William the Bastard, I would then have created a history (often referred to in SF as a *time line*) in which England would remain Anglo-Saxon. Our present time line might then wink out of existence, of course; but if it did not, then the two lines of history would coexist in parallel fashion. One might then leave our present and travel sideways in time to encounter the other present, the England that might have been, except for Hastings.

That sort of parallel-universe structure depends, of course, on travel to the past; and if the latter is impossible, so is the former. However, two other parallel-

or alternate-universe scenarios exist in the literature, neither of which depends on travel to the past.

The first is the what-if story. If Cleopatra's nose had been shorter, or Grant had been drunk at Appomattox, or Alexander had not overindulged on a given evening in 324 *B.C.*, what would the world of today be like? And what would have happened in history in the intervening years? In *Alternative Histories: Eleven Stories of the World as It Might Have Been*, Charles G. Waugh and Martin H. Greenberg collect a number of stories in this genre, and Gordon B. Chamberlain contributes an essay which does essential work of definition and distinction. In this subgenre, no scientific or pseudo-scientific rationale is given for the alternate history: no time traveler goes back to generate a new time line, and the time line of which we are a part seems not to exist. There is no movement from one time line to another. This sort of fiction properly belongs, it seems to me, in the category of fantasy rather than that of science fiction, except that if this sort of story is well done, the historical logic, the reasoning, the rationality of it are all very like those of time travel fiction.

The second scenario which does not involve travel to the past is this: a myriad of parallel universes exists all the "time." Nothing except the Big Bang (or God) brought them into being. While the number of such possible universes would be very large indeed, it would not be infinite. In *The Number of the Beast*, Robert Heinlein, for reasons best known to himself, sets the number at six to the sixth power of six, which would come to some ten million sextillion universes (in our local group, he hastens to add; the total number would be much larger). We ought to be able to arrive at a rough approximation of the number, should anybody care to try; we have a rough knowledge of the size of the universe and its age, the size of a subatomic particle and how quickly it can move from one particle-sized piece of space to another, and the amount of matter/energy in this universe. Assuming that the four forces and the speed of light remain constant— as surely they should in any universe resulting from our Big Bang—then anyone who cares to take the trouble ought to be able to calculate all the possible universes resulting from our Big Bang, each universe differing from its nearest neighbor perhaps only in the differing placement of one electron for one nanosecond. John Allen Paulos (15–16) has made a start on this calculation.

Now, this sort of parallel universe may have some basis in science, some physicists asserting that at any moment of "decision," both "choices," the one taken in our time line and the other one, are equally real. Thus all possible time lines would exist in parallel. Fred Alan Wolf, in *Parallel Universes*, goes so far as to assert that quantum theory makes such parallel universes not only possible but necessary.

However, like the notion of tachyons, these lines of speculation seem to admit neither of experimental proof nor of experimental disproof; and, as I have said before, the admission of such ideas into science breaks down the barrier, which is still a useful one, between science fiction and fantasy.

For our purposes, and in our terms, then, all three ideas—FTL travel, travel to the past, and travel to parallel universes—may be said to be as impossible as anything can be. I have arranged them in this order because the first seems to lead logically to the second, and the second to the third; awkwardly enough, it is with the middle one, travel to the past, that I shall mainly be concerned in this book, dealing with the others only summarily, and as they are implied in, or imply, travel to the past.

THE PROBLEM OF IMPOSSIBLE THINGS IN SCIENCE FICTION

If, then, these three ideas, related as they are, are all, at least within our somewhat restricted meaning of the term, impossible, then *what are they doing in science fiction*? The first, travel faster than light, is perhaps the easiest to explain; it is there, in spite of its impossibility, mainly because it is a necessary plot convention. After all, without FTL travel we cannot have interstellar trade, or interstellar empires, or interstellar anything else, except for very, very long one-way voyages, either via suspended animation or via generational starships. Without FTL, we are in the position of a savage with a rowboat planning trans-Pacific adventuring: it is possible, maybe, but risky, and nobody is likely to do it very often or with any great expectation of return, either physical or financial.

And in science fiction we *need* interstellar trade and interstellar empires. Science fiction writers like history. Some of them know a whole lot about history: Fred Pohl wrote a biography of Tiberius, and Sprague de Camp wrote three first-rate historical novels, and Fletcher Pratt did more books on history than he did SF and fantasy put together, and Asimov's *Foundation Trilogy* is Gibbon all over again. Furthermore, the "future history," which spreads over several novels or short stories, is a science fiction staple: Anderson, Heinlein, Pournelle, Niven, Asimov, Stapledon, Le Guin, Blish, and Piper are some of the names which come to mind. Science fiction authors are prone to see the interstellar future in terms of the mundane history of the past; and therefore, that future history must have kings and dictators and trade and empires—and therefore FTL travel. Never mind about the logic of the matter.

No such necessity accounts for the widespread presence of travel to the past and to Paratime. Travel to the *future* is reasonable enough: we do it all the time, second by second; and every time we sleep, our consciousness takes a several-hour-long leap into the future. It is no wonder that the Rip Van Winkle scenario has a respectable, if dateable, past in our literature.

But nothing, nothing except dream and memory, stands in relation to travel to the past as sleep does to travel to the future. Travel to the past takes all customary notions of cause and effect, flings them down, and dances upon them. It plays hob with the laws of thermodynamics. It is full of I'm-my-own-grandpa paradoxes. Common sense will have none of it. Even our language, as Niven wittily observes in "The Theory and Practice of Time Travel," is ill equipped to handle the matter:

We'd need a basic past tense, an altered past tense, a potential past tense (might have been), an excised future tense (for a future that can no longer happen), a home base present tense, a present-of-the-moment tense, an enclosed present tense (for use while the vehicle is moving through time), a future past tense ("I'll meet you at the bombing of Pearl Harbor in half an hour"), a past future tense ("Just a souvenir I picked up ten million years from now") and many more. We'd need at least two directions of time flow: sequential personal time, and universal time, with a complete set of tenses for each.

We'd need pronouns to distinguish [you of the past] from [you of the future] and [you of the present]. After all, the three of you might all be sitting around the same table someday. (112)

Niven is, of course, here speaking of a time travel which is totally unrestricted, in which one may at will depart from the present, go to the past, jump to the future, and return to the present. All travelers to the past are not so privileged; the Connecticut Yankee, like many another traveler since, went into the past by accident with no evident prospect of returning to the present. But to the extent that time travel is unrestricted, I can make the argument that it, like its cousin, travel in Paratime, not only does not belong in science fiction; it does not belong in fiction at all.

For, consider: if one can change the past and then return to the present, then one is no longer stuck with the consequences of one's actions; if the traveler can return at will, doing and redoing an action until he gets it right, then no particular action has any importance at all. I could kill my brother and get any pleasure I could out of the act, and then, thinking better of it, I could return in time and prevent myself from doing it. Thus, as far as I am concerned, I am a murderer; but as far as the practicalities of the matter are concerned, I am innocent. And my still-living brother is unharmed. (If one has lusted in his heart, we are told, he is guilty, but presumably not as culpable as the adulterer. If time travel were available, presumably so would be an intermediate state: one in which one has committed adultery and then returned to frustrate the attempt.)

In fact, the time traveler has had his cake and eaten it too. And that is subversive of all morality and of all possible moralities.

In its extreme form, Paratime is still more destructive of morality. If, as this line of thought would have it, *every* possibility coexists—if *every* yes/no, on/ off, hither/yon option, down to the subatomic level, generates another possibility line, and if each of these lines is absolutely as real as any other, then we are left with two options: either all existence and all choice are mere illusion, and in that case—as in Twain's *Mysterious Stranger*—nothing anyone can do, no choice anyone can make, has any more importance than the choices I make in a dream; or, on the other hand, in some sense all possible time lines are truly real, and therefore no choice can have any possible meaning.

For, consider: in this continuum, let us suppose, I save a drowning man at great risk to myself and am therefore accounted a hero. But in a nearby contin- uum, I not only did not save him, but shoved him in and stood on his head while he drowned. If I give my body to be burned, it profiteth me nothing; for in a nearby chunk of Paratime I have knocked my youngest son on the head and given *his* body over for burning. No virtuous act in this time line is without its accompanying crime in another; conversely, every this-time Dachau has its that-time Club Med. And therefore no action can have any significance whatsoever. Q.E.D.

Now, if all morality has been subverted, so has the importance of character. If I return to the past and alter it, then (in some scenarios) I generate an alternate time line, in which there is another version of me. If Paratime exists, then all possible versions of me exist anyhow. Some are saints, some are solid citizens, some are torturers for hire, and each one is just as real as any other. And therefore no quality of character can have any more meaning than any other: if in one continuum Falstaff is fat, brilliant, and self-protective, no matter. In another he is more slender and stupid and heroic than Hotspur.

The destruction of the significance of action, and therefore the trivialization of plot, is similar. Plot, like morality, depends upon acts having consequences. "Lear and Cordelia have been reconciled and are tragically dead—but this is no more true than the fact that they are still estranged and alive" is not a plot line calculated to wring the emotional withers of any reader. Moby Dick has demolished the *Pequod* and Ahab, and I alone am left to tell thee—but only in this particular continuum.

It is only fair to point out that not everyone agrees with this view. In response to a letter about his Paratime novel *The Coming of the Quantum Cats*, Frederik Pohl wrote me this:

I don't really think that paratime impairs the working of cause-and-effect crime-and-punishment morality—after all, if you sin in paratime A you will suffer the consequences in paratime A, even though your counterpart in paratime B may not be penalized. In a theological sense, though, you raise an interesting point. (Is there a separate heaven for each paratime?...) (9/13/86).

Similarly, in *The Proteus Operation*, James Hogan has a character answer the problem of parallel-worlds morality; one may stop genocide in one time line, but

a virtual infinity of universes exists in which it happens anyway.... You are saying that it's pointless to try and change one world for the better if you can't change all of them. But by the same logic, you could argue that it's pointless for people to change themselves for the better if it doesn't change the whole world. (369)

Agreed. But if somewhere, somewhen, another one of me is knocking himself out to be virtuous without thought of reward, it still seems silly for me thus to inconvenience myself in this continuum, since all of us are equally real. By the time one gets well into Heinlein's *Number of the Beast*, the uncomfortable feeling creeps over one: if *all* things are true and possible, then nothing makes a damned bit of difference.

It may be objected that the theater of the absurd has managed to make dramatic material out of a scenario in which character is unimportant and significant action cannot exist: and I think that is true. But it should be noted that it can be done only by dramatic grandmasters like Samuel Beckett and Tom Stoppard. At the top of his form, Edward Albee can make it work, but at other moments, as with *Box*, the result is something through which it is truly difficult to sit. And it now appears that the theater of the absurd is on the wane, and that plot has returned to the stage. One can make only so much drama out of the principle that dramatic action is impossible.

And yet, in spite of the fact that travel to the past flies in the face of all common sense, demonstrably does not belong in science fiction, and probably is subversive of the very groundsills of *all* fiction, we find it throughout the literature. Indeed, it is one of the most common fantasies we have. Those of us who love history indulge ourselves in this way all the time: if I cannot sleep, I lie up in bed replanning the first century of the Roman Empire, improving upon the work of Augustus Caesar, one time using only the technology of his own age, another time considering what I could add from my own time to make the empire last longer and serve more people better.

My students confirm that the fantasy is near-universal, particularly among young males. In the South, it has been said, nearly every young boy has revised the Civil War in his mind, giving Lee the victory at Gettysburg by pointing out to him the wisdom of occupying Little Round Top. Similarly, most of us have rewritten verbal encounters which we lost with "If I had only said..."

In "The Theory and Practice of Time Travel," Larry Niven (110–11) points out the connection between this fantasy and the Three Wishes story in which the wisher, frustrated as always by the result of his wishes, speaks the third one: "I wish I'd never *had* a fairy godmother!" He goes on to ground the whole subgenre in the child's prayer, "Please God, make it didn't happen." Then it is not hard to see how this infantile wish lingers on into adulthood as "if only... if only."

THE FOUR QUESTIONS

And if it is such a common fantasy, then why does it wait until the nineteenth century to appear in literature?

To be sure, *visions* of chunks of the past have come to literary heroes before: Odysseus talks with the shades in Hades, and that is a kind of vision of the past. After all, the dead appear in our dreams all the time as if alive, and that is either—according to one's taste—an intimation of immortality or a vision of time past. Similarly, Marlowe's Faust conjures up a vision of Helen, for reasons better comprehended than justified, and by dragging a person (or a vision) from the past into the present, he has had a vision of the past. Moses and Elijah, after long sojourns in the afterlife, show up at the Transfiguration, and to the onlookers it must have been a vision of the past. And if and when Arthur or Karageorge or Barbarossa waken and charge out to redeem their nations, then that too will likewise resemble a vision of the past. All these are old, all these are traditional. But nowhere does anyone in this early literature *go* from the present to the past.

And yet, it seems to us, they *must* have thought of it; surely, like us, they did if-onlys. If only I had been in Jerusalem on the first Good Friday with a dozen picked men; if only I had put my strongest fighting men on the right wing instead of in the center; if only I had been able to keep the Trojans from bringing that damned horse in through the walls. From that sort of thought, it seems to us only a step to "If only I could go back and change it." But nobody seems to have thought that way, at least from the evidence of the literature. To assert that they did not, I realize, is to propose a change in the quality of human consciousness of the magnitude which Julian Janes thinks took place in the ninth or tenth century B.C., or else to suggest that our ancestors would have rejected such an idea out of hand. Not even realistic enough for fantasy, they would have thought. All experience, all common sense, all morality, all religion would have made the whole idea unthinkable.

Or, perhaps, the concept of time which they held was one which simply would not admit of such a notion. At any rate, nobody seems to have come up with the idea—not Homer, not Dante, not Nicholas of Cusa—nobody.

Until the nineteenth century.

It arrives in two stages. The first traveler to get snatched into the past seems to appear in 1838 in an anonymous piece in the *Dublin University Magazine* called "An Anachronism, or Missing One's Coach." Five years later we get another in Dickens' *Christmas Carol*, and then another the next year in Poe's "Tale of the Ragged Mountains." But none of these travelers does anything to change that past and thereby his present; it does not even occur to them. As far as they are concerned, the presents from which they departed are immutable. Scrooge, to be sure, does permit himself an "I wish…," but even this seems to refer to things he wishes he had done in the past very close to his present. At any rate, he does not attempt to break out of the shell he and the Ghost of Christmas Past seem to be in and tell the young Scrooge to shape up. He does, however, ask the Ghost of Christmas Yet to Come whether the future can be changed, whether his vision of his own death is of a future which must be or of one which is only probable; and as he leaves that vision, he seems to operate in the faith that the future, if not the past and present, is mutable. But he never asks that question about the past.

On September 18, 1881, as Sam Moskowitz points out, the first time machine appears in the New York *Sun* in Edwin Page Mitchell's "Clock That Went Backward." A Leyden professor and two of his students go back to 1574 and the siege of Leyden; the professor, at any rate, seems to inhabit the body of an ancestor and do exactly what that ancestor did. There is an echo here of the Poe story, and a hint of the what-is-written scenario of later time-travel fiction; but neither here nor anywhere else does any time traveler attempt to change the past.

Until the *Connecticut Yankee*.

The book began innocently enough, with no thought of breaking new literary ground, or so it seems from Twain's *Notebooks*. Late in 1884 Twain wrote

Dream of being a knight errant in armor in the middle ages.

Have the notions & habits of thought of the present day mixed with the necessities of that. No pockets in the armor. No way to manage certain requirements of nature. Can't scratch. Cold in the head—can't blow—can't get at handkerchief, can't use iron sleeve. Iron gets red hot in the sun—leaks in the rain, gets white with frost & freezes me solid in winter. Suffer from lice and fleas. Make disagreeable clatter when I enter church. Can't dress or undress myself. Always getting struck by lightning. Fall down, can't get up. See Morte DArthur. (111, 78)

In the five years which separated these notes from the publication of the *Yankee*, H. G. Wells re-invented the time machine in "The Chronic Argonauts," a fact not likely to be known to Twain. At any rate, neither in this story nor in the 1895 *Time Machine* version does the time traveler go to the past—although, to be sure, he does return from the future to his present. At the very end of *The Time Machine*, it is true that the narrator speculates (103) that the traveler may have "swept back into the past, and [fallen] among the blood-drinking, hairy savages of the Age of Unpolished Stone," or into earlier ages of dinosaurs; but still, as in "Missing One's Coach," Poe, Mitchell, and Dickens, there is no notion of changing the past. Nor does it occur to the time traveler to go two weeks into the future and bring back the racecourse results.

In 1888, Edward Bellamy published *Looking Backward*, a time travel romance right enough, but one grounded in the ancient sleeper-awakes scenario. In the Preface to the Norton *Yankee*, Allison R. Ensor speculates that this book might have been a possible influence, in that Julian West travels to a utopia "of the kind which the Yankee sought to establish in King Arthur's realm," but I think that stretches things a bit. The Yankee seeks to establish no society more advanced than the one he left in Connecticut in the 1880's. He hasn't the imagination.

Looking back at Twain's notes, we can see that a good many details from them show up in the *Yankee*, all right (Chapter XIII), but it is not the nineteenth-century man-in-armor who gets hit by lightning. It is Merlin's tower (VII) and with it the whole of Malory's sixth-century English civilization (XLIII).

And, in spite of Twain's original notes, the story as he finally wrote it is *not* a dream. If evidence is needed, it comes at the beginning of Chapter I. Hank has caught sight of a town and asks whether it is Bridgeport; Sir Kay replies that it is Camelot. "Camelot—Camelot," says Hank to himself. "I don't seem to remember hearing of it before." But if one is to dream of a place, one *must* have heard of it before; and therefore Hank's Camelot is not a dream.

A number of other changes have taken place between notes and book, as well as between one draft and another. The time traveler, originally bearing the innocuous name of Robert Smith (*Notebooks* III, 244n.; California *Yankee*, 494–510) has metamorphosed into Hank Morgan. The fact that this name recalls those of the famous pirate, Henry Morgan, and of Morgan le Fay, has been pointed out by Alice Kenney; just as important, perhaps, is the association with the name of the then swiftly rising J. P. Morgan. (A fellow robber baron, Jay Gould, served as the model for the slave-driver in the illustration preceding Chapter XXXVI.) At any rate, the time traveler who, in 1884, was the passive victim of the inferior technology of the sixth century, has, by 1889, been changed into a man who will take every advantage of the inferiority of that technology to feather his own nest.

Here is a time traveler who, once he gets oriented, is not satisfied to observe; he jumps in like an entrepreneur, with a good eye for the main chance and a full consciousness of the uniqueness of his opportunities and his situation. He is the first.

As I have said, we have it on the authority of philosophers ancient and medieval that undoing the past is impossible even to God. Our ancestors seem to have been reluctant even to imagine those things which God Himself could not accomplish. Every other sort of foolishness seems to have shown up in literature at one time or another; but travel to the past and the change of that past seems to have been a sort of megafoolishness which nobody could even think of or, if they could, could not take with sufficient seriousness even to make fiction out of it.

Until the *Yankee*, Mark Twain, Hartford, 1889. And here are the Four Questions I promised you:

- Why America?
- Why 1889?
- Why Mark Twain?
- And why, given all that can be said against it, does travel to the past appear throughout science fiction from Twain down even to the present day?

Documenting the first appearance of an idea in literature is a risky business; after all, no human person can read all the literature there is. Attempting to establish the reasons for such an appearance is still riskier and still more tentative. Mark Twain is dead, and—for the moment, and in this continuum—we cannot ask him about it; and if we could and did, likely he would not remember or never would have known himself; and if he did know, given his character, likely he would lie about it and take vast pleasure in our credulity. Let me rush in, however, where angels fear to tread.

Chapter 2

TIME TRAVEL: DEFINITIONS, PROBLEMS, RULES, LIMITS

Ne tot mençunge, ne tot veir,
Ne tot fable, ne tot saveir,
Tant ont li contéor conté
Et li fabléor tant fablé
Por lor contes embeleter
Que tot ont fait faible sembler.

Not all lies nor yet all veritable,
Not all fables nor all verifiable;
So many tales tellers recounted,
So many fables fablers mounted
To make each story admirable
That they have made all seem a fable.

—Wace

FOUR WAYS OUT OF THE PRESENT

Except in rare moments of felicity, our own times and our own ages fit us ill. "I want to be grown up," says a five-year-old, and we look at him and wonder. Does he want to be a great big five-year-old, or does he want it to be fifteen years from now, or does he want to be twenty *right now*?

We adults sigh and perhaps, later in the evening, think the archetypal thought of middle age: "Oh, to be eighteen again, and know what I know now." Do we want to be eighteen *now*, or do we want to be back in the year in which we were eighteen the first time? No great matter: both we and the five-year-old are after the same things, I suspect—power, maturity without age, money, sexual prowess, and shortcuts.

There you have the two most common directions out of the present: to the future and to the past.

But sometimes both we and the five-year-old wish for a world unlike the one we are in: "I wish I were a turtle," says the five-year-old, and "I wish I were a violinist," says the adult. "If only bees were *pretend*," complains the recently stung child; "If only God had omitted radioactivity," muses the threatened adult. And there we have the germ of Paratime.

And at still other times, oppressed with intimations of mortality, the five-year-old will deplore the passage of time. "I don't *want* today to go away," he will say, or "I don't *want* to be six; I want to stay five." Time should only stop where it is; the passage toward entropy should cease; and we say with Faust to the moment at hand, "Stay a while, thou art so fair." Or at least "Stay a while; thou art a good deal fairer than that which is likely to come after."

And thus we come to the last direction out of the present, a journey toward a state in which time does not run any more, in which it is a still pool rather than a running river. And this fourth way out of the present may be the oldest of them all. Sometimes it goes by the name of Great Time.

GREAT TIME

The native Australians, according to J. B. Priestley (138–43), have a concept they call Great Time; and in Great Time, they say, things do not happen one-thing-after-another as they do in common time, but all things happen at once.

It is in the Great Time that the ancestors and the souls of those yet to be born dwell; it is to the Great Time that the shaman goes while in mystic transport or the believer goes in the ecstasy of worship; it is from the Great Time that all virtue, all bravery, all heroism derive and are distributed to the faithful.

Great Time, in short, is the Bosom of Abraham. The idea fits well enough with modern physical theory, which tells us that without matter to define it, there can be no space; and without space, there can be no time. Therefore there can be no *before* before the Big Bang; the same holds true for the other end of the history of Creation as we now understand it, no matter which of two scenarios turns out to be true. If, in the first scenario, there is a good deal more matter in the universe than has hitherto been observed, then in the far future gravity will cause the universe's expansion to cease, contraction to begin, and the universe to contract (Freeman Dyson says in 10-to-the–11th years [Pournelle, 309]) into a single dimensionless point; at the moment of this Big Smoosh, space, and therefore time, will end and Great Time will set in. In the alternate scenario, the matter we see is the matter we get. In that case, even farther in the future (Dyson says in 10-to-the–10th-to-the–76th years) we will reach a state of total changelessness; and since the direction of time flow is in the direction of increasing entropy, at that moment time will stop. In either scenario, there is no *after* after the end.

In similar fashion, we may locate Great Time in space, both outside the event horizon of our universe, fifteen or twenty billion light years away, and inside the event horizons of black holes. In neither case is there any possible way to observe what is going on, and in both cases, likely the temporal cause-and-effect rules we all know and love do not operate. Great Time, then, is not only (as in the Ptolemaic system) outside the horizon of our universe, but scattered throughout its interior in various-sized chunks, some of which may be subatomic in size and bouncing through us at this very moment. I refer you to Stephen Hawking's *Brief History of Time (96–97)*. It is tempting to imagine what medieval scholarship would have made of such a universe.

Only from outside the realm of matter and time and space, as Dante well knew, can all time be perceived as a single timeless instant; the virtuous ancestors, many believe, are there, and the Source of all virtue, and the Origin of the wisdom of the prophets. Christians are not so far from the viewpoint of the native Australians.

This idea, Priestley suggests, may be even older than the idea of travel to the future. This position, however odd it may appear at first blush, has a certain intuited credibility: the idea of the passage of time may well have come later than the idea of the gods. Suppose the gods to live in a state where no one grows old and sickens and dies, a state in which no time passes. Our near-animal ancestors may well have seen things in this way; after all, it would appear that our animal cousins have no consciousness of the passage of time. If early prehumans lived in a world with no sense of time, then so would their gods have done; and when primitive humankind began to grasp the idea of the passage of time, then the idea of the timelessness of the gods might well have adhered.

After all, the passage of primitive humans was slow in the extreme; tens and hundreds of generations might go by with no great change in the circumstances of life, or of technology, or of ideas or attitudes. The notion of any future beyond the life of the individual—likely short enough—would be a long time coming. The faster the change—for better or for worse—in the life of a people, the more different (threatening or attractive) the future will appear. No major change occurring, the idea that the past or future might be different, and therefore an attractive destination for a voyager in reality or in fantasy, is not likely to have occurred to anybody.

By its very nature, Great Time is not likely to become the subject matter of many narratives; after all, a narrative is inevitably involved in things happening one after another. Even Dante, knowing full well that in one sense the souls of the blessed are all in the timeless presence of God outside the Chinese-box system of the Ptolemaic universe, nevertheless for the purposes of his narrative has to encounter them in the various planetary spheres and allow them to move, and talk, and react, as if they were still in space and time.

One does, of course, encounter in both science fiction and mainstream literature the occasional moment of mystic insight which results in an expression of Great

Time. But such moments are, of necessity, fleeting. The only narrative I can think of in which, as in Great Time, everything happens at once, is *Finnegans Wake*.

Especially science fiction, which is a literature of process as much as it is a literature of ideas, seems unlikely to make much out of Great Time. There are, however, a few intimations of it both in the *Yankee* and in subsequent science fiction: In *New Worlds for Old*, David Ketterer notes that in his last delirium Hank Morgan says, "A bugle?... It is the king! The drawbridge, there! Man the battlements!—turn out the—" and asks

Are we not justified in hypothesizing the adjective "apocalyptic" before bugle, in identifying "the king" as God rather than Arthur, and, in completing the phrase as "turn out the light," recall, a final time, the episode detailing the extinction of the sun... ? (232)

It is a tempting, if tenuous, reading; and the more tempting because, if we accept it, then all four ways out of the present are there in the first book of its kind, the *Connecticut Yankee*: travel first of all to the past; then to the brief alternative history generated by Morgan's actions in the sixth century; third, back to the nineteenth century through Merlin's triumphant meddling; and finally to Great Time with Morgan's death. In any case, Twain seems to have flirted with the idea; in a rejected passage (California *Yankee*, 757) Morgan speaks with a messenger from the Recording Angel, who emphasizes that from his point of view, past, present, and future are all one.

The problem of identifying Great Time in science fiction is further complicated by the fact that it often resembles other ways out of the present; indeed, insofar as one in Great Time partakes of the perspective of the Deity, past and present and future are one. Furthermore, in some ways sojourners in Elfland like Thomas Rymer—even though, later in this chapter, I choose to treat them for thematic reasons as travelers to the future—seem to represent a folkish sort of Great Time; their stay in Faerie is like that of Moses and Elijah in Great Time, and their reappearance in common time is like those individuals' travel to the future.

To complicate things still more, very often the time traveler, particularly if his movements in time are unrestricted, feels himself a god, and acts like a god. He can double back and duplicate himself, as the young Jack Havig does when threatened by a bully in Anderson's *There Will Be Time*; he can, if he makes a mistake, go back and erase it; he is like a god, saving only his mortality. Even mortality, a time traveler in the same book hopes, may be erased, making the time traveler's godhood complete:

They're bound to find immortality, far off in the world we're building... I'm convinced. I'll tell you something.... I've been back to the close of Phase One [in the future].... This trip I learned something new. At the end, I'm going to disappear.... And likewise a number of my chief lieutenants.... Our work done, we were called to the far future and made young forever. Like unto gods. (137)

Travel unrestricted, then, both to the past and to the future, would result in a godlike state, and that state, in some senses, would be like Great Time.

Those characters in science fiction who live outside the constraints of time often show a desire to become godlike which, from a traditional point of view, could be called Faustian or even Satanic. Like the Yankee, because they have more understanding than those about them, they feel justified in all manner of behavior—manipulating, lying, killing—which, had they not the benefit of hind- or foresight, they would have to call despicable.

It is not easy, however, to make moral judgments on these matters: behavior which, in the time-bound, would be unforgivable, seems not only acceptable but often mandated for the time traveler.

For example: suppose I find myself in Austria in the early part of this century and see an opportunity to kill a young man whom I know to be Adolf Hitler. Let us suppose, for the sake of argument, that my only options are to leave him alone or kill him; I can neither reeducate him, nor convert him to Judaism, nor persuade him to emigrate to New York. At the time I meet him, he has done nothing worthy of death; but I know that unless I kill him, millions of innocent men, women, and children will die horrible deaths.

How can I kill him, when he is innocent of any capital crime? How can I not kill him, considering the future which I know but which he does not? To kill him would be a crime against Hitler; not to kill him would be a crime against humanity, but only because I am possessed of a godlike foreknowledge.

Gods, then, as the book of Job tells us, can do terrible things and accrue no guilt; and in science fiction, as soon as a mortal is free from the constraints of time, he must begin to take on the awesome moral responsibilities of a god.

Now, if Great Time is that state in which no time passes, it exists, in our physical system, either before the Big Bang or after the end of the universe, whether the latter is a Big Smoosh or a state of Absolute Chaos. Great Time, then, is in the far past and in the distant future; it also exists outside our continuum "at present," on the other side of event horizons. Similarly, when Dante has struggled to the top of the Mount of Purgatory, he has reached the sphere of the moon, which is a sort of medieval event horizon beyond which no change can take place; and if no change can take place, then time cannot really be said to exist. He has also reached the Garden of Eden, which for most of the rest of us lies far back in the days of the ancestors. But Heaven lies in the future. Dante, then, in attaining to Great Time, seems in some sense to be in past, present, and future all at once. Jumping in and out of Great Time sometimes looks like travel to the future (as in the case already cited of Moses and Elijah); sometimes it looks like travel to the past, as when God the Son appears to Abraham along with the rest of the Trinity.

If Great Time implies travel to the past and the future, as it seems to from our twentieth-century point of view, then perhaps it also implies the notion of Paratime. That extraordinary man, Nicholas of Cusa, seems to have thought that the plenitude of God's creation would make it needful that God would create everything which He *could* create. His successor, Giordano Bruno (who called Nicholas "the Divine Cusanus") likewise seems—if the 1911 *Britannica* translates him correctly—to be paddling on the shores of Paratime: " [God's] necessity is true freedom... realizing himself in the infinitely various forms of activity that constitute individual things. To the infinitely actual there is necessary the possible...." Here we stand on the very edge of the Paratime idea. It is not surprising, considering, as we have, that the Paratime idea is ultimately destructive of all morality, that both Nicholas and Bruno were accused of heresy. A cardinal and a bishop, Nicholas died in bed in 1464; less well situated as to power, Bruno was burned at the stake in Rome on the 17th of February 1600.

THE FUTURE

Travel to the future would appear to have been the second idea to occur to our ancestors; it is, as we have said, the direction we are going anyhow and does no violence to common sense. The most obvious method of going to the future is a long sound sleep: in our national literature, Washington Irving's Rip Van Winkle is the most obvious example. But poor Rip ages as he sleeps, and so the travel is a bit compromised; in contrast, Julian West, in Bellamy's *Looking Backward*, lying mesmerized in a vault under his ruined house, manages to awake at the same apparent age at which he dozed off.

That seems an improvement; but it is not by any means a new idea. It appears in the first example of the sub-subgenre I can find in western literature: the tale of the Seven Sleepers of Ephesus. Although very early sources exist in the east, the first (according to the *Britannica*, 11th edition) being the *Acta Sanctorum* of Jacob of Saurig, the earliest version in the west comes from the *de gloria martyrum* of St. Gregory of Tours, who flourished a century and a half after the Sleepers are supposed to have awakened. (His century is also the century to which the Connecticut Yankee returned.) The tale is told with his customary wit by Gibbon (XXXIII), who draws upon both St. Gregory and the *Annals* of the Patriarch Eutychius to retell a tale also told in the Quran (Sirah XVIII), of seven persecuted Christian young men who, entombed in A.D. 250, slept 187 years to find their faith triumphant.

The story spread with almost incredible speed from Bengal to Norway (where seven still-sleeping Romans, according to Paul of Aquileia, were reserved as future apostles to the Scandinavians), and this very speed would seem to indicate, first, that the mindset of the times was ready for just such a story and, second, that the story was a very early one of its kind, perhaps the first: for had many stories of Rip-Van-Winklehood been abroad, the story of the Seven Sleepers would not have raged so far so fast. The psychic need for the story would already have been filled.

Twain knew the Seven Sleepers story; he parodies it in *Innocents* XL, running in a Rip Van Winkle motif by having the sleep come about as the result of a drinking bout. In the same book (LIV) he also has fun with the tale of the Wandering Jew, a Van Winkle who does not sleep.

However unpleasant the events of the two centuries between Decius and Theodosius for the pagan armies of Rome, one can understand the appeal of the whole process for the Seven Sleepers: they move from the losing side to the winning without having to do anything to bring about the victory, just as Rip Van Winkle, bedeviled by wife and work, can sleep his wife's life away along with his own productive work years, achieving both retirement and widowhood in an apparent overnight.

Sleeping through the years or centuries has the obvious advantage to the sleeper of evading the toils of the present. It is the sort of thing which depends, one would think, at least partly on the idea of progress. If the future is likely to be less attractive than the present, then the traveler would be better off staying put. It would appear that the notion of substantial change in the human condition, and that for the better, has not been imagined for most of the history of the human race, except perhaps for the movement of the individual into Great Time. If any change *did* loom on the horizon, it was as likely as not a change for the worse in the form of plague, famine, or invading barbarians.

Homer, for example, is telling a good-old-days story about the times when men were really men and the remnants of the civilization of Crete had not totally been wiped out, days when one man could lift a stone which would take several men in Homer's present. There are some promises of better things in the Old Testament—the promise to Abraham, the promised land, the promised Messianic Age—but mainly the Old Testament shows us a gradual decline in the status of humankind, from the Adam who walked with Yahweh in the cool of the evening, to the Abraham who could entertain Him at dinner, to the Moses who was the last to speak to Him directly. And yet, strangely, as we have noted, the notion of returning to those better times seems never to have occurred to them.

A few groups, scattered here and there, might find the future promising and therefore a time it would be worth sleeping into. Barbarians about to move in on an established civilization would, it is logical to suppose, look forward to several years or decades of heated rooms, unsoured wine, and warm baths. They would, however, have reasonable hope of seeing the results of their larcenies in their own lifetimes, and so, likely, travel to the future would not occur to them. In any case, such folk do not spend a whole lot of time writing books, and so one can only speculate.

Early Christians, however, did write a whole lot of books, and it is clear that they looked forward to a world changed for the better. Not only would vast numbers of pagans get themselves converted to the True Faith and, therefore, presumably behave themselves in somewhat more mannerly fashion, but Jesus Himself would be showing up any day now to set up a new Heaven and a new Earth. Not only is Great Time out there in the future, but so are better everyday times, and thus the slumber of the Seven Sleepers makes a good deal of sense.

Throughout most of the Middle Ages, all the good times were past and gone:

the Roman Empire in the West had passed away, and with it competent civil engineering, reasonably hard money, and functioning governmental bureaucracy. Here again, as in the age of Homer, one would expect people to envy the past rather than to anticipate the future. Not until the early Renaissance do we get a clearly articulated sense that things are changing for the better. In the early sixteenth century Rabelais (*Pantagruel* VIII) makes Gargantua write Pantagruel, his son, about all the changes for the better in human thought and education since *he* was a boy; and we have the sense that the rationale for travel to the future has once again activated itself.

From that time down to our own century, the future has been a promised land for a great many people. To be sure, in Twain's own time, and before, some folk were beginning to have second thoughts about the progress represented by the industrial revolution: in 1818, Mary Shelley created the Frankenstein monster, which, whatever the emphasis of the original text, quickly became the very symbol of the threat of change for the nineteenth and twentieth centuries. In Twain's own time, the pre-Raphaelites were looking with hungry eyes on the late Middle Ages; and in 1919, for much of Europe, traditional notions of honor, patriotism, and progress crashed into a terrible and cynical despair.

As long as optimism remains, however, there will be a public ready to entertain the scenario of travel to the future. To live to a better time is only the most obvious reason for such travel to the future. There are others. First, of course, curiosity, the desire to see what will happen after one is dead. When a belief in an afterlife was strong, one could assume that the blessed could see those still stuck in time; as the belief in such an afterlife has faded, Van Winkling into the future takes its place. Further, one can stay alive longer, if not in subjective time, then across a bigger span of years. Those who at present are making provision for their bodies to be frozen, turning themselves into corpsicles, are planning their own Van-Winklehood for just such a reason. And, as we plan for interstellar space voyages, we realize that the only alternatives to the apparently impossible FTL ship and the generational starship are, first, the long sleep of suspended or near-suspended animation and, second, the time dilation which will occur when ships travel nearly as fast as light.

The idea that the future may be better and the desire to see what will happen next are not the only reasons for travel to the future: many a culture hero sleeps into the future, like the Seven Sleepers of the North, because the future may have need of him. Here is a reason for going to the future which does not depend on the idea of progress, but rather implies that the future may in some ways be worse. The mythic landscape of Europe is littered with Arthurs, Barbarossas, and Karageorges, all sleeping up in caves until their peoples shall have need of them.

In England during World War I the story was widely told, and apparently believed by some, of the appearance of a band of King Arthur's knights at a crucial moment for the English forces on the Western front. Mark Girouard documents (284) the origin of that tale as a short story in the London *Evening*

News by Arthur Machem ("The Bowmen," September 29, 1914), in which the aid came not from Arthurian knights but from St. George and Agincourt bowmen. In the hands of an apparently credulous clergy, the bowmen became angels; but the nature of a mythic hero such as Arthur is to revive himself every time a good role for him appears. Like an Arthur, a Barbarossa, or a Karageorge, the Yankee sleeps up in his cave for 1300 years after his final confrontation with Merlin, as if needed to deliver a message to the nineteenth century: "Salvation by technology won't work: I've already tried it."

The Long Sleep, as we say, seems to be reserved for great culture heroes; as we shall note later, travel to the *past* seems to be an almost Satanic attempt to take on some of the attributes of deity. It is interesting to note, however, that Van Winkling seems to partake of the divine as well: de Santillana and von Dechend cite Plutarch to the effect that "Kronos, sleeping in that golden cave in Ogygia, dreams what Zeus is planning"; and in those dreams of the God of Time are all the principles of creation, according to an Orphic fragment:

The greatest Kronos is giving from above the principles of intelligibility to the Demiurge [Zeus], and he presides over the whole "creation"... and Kronos seems to have with him the highest causes of junctions and separations... he has become the cause of the continuation of begetting and propagation and the head of the whole genus of Titans from which originates the division of beings. (134)

Even the relatively prosaic movement out of our own time represented by the Long Sleep, therefore, involves the traveler with the mythic divine and with time itself and that "division of beings" which, according to our own shamans, began with the Big Bang.

The final reason for the appeal of travel to the future rests not in the psychology of the reader but in the needs of the author. Up until the 1930s, most authors of science fiction felt the need to anchor the fantastic future in the familiar present: Verne began the 20,000-league voyage of Professor Aronnax in Nebraska in 1866. H. G. Wells started the incredible voyage of the inventor of *The Time Machine* in a Victorian drawing room, the futuristic invasion from Mars in a small English village. In 1917, Edgar Rice Burroughs found it appropriate to begin the Barsoom tales in the Arizona of 1865. In 1928, Philip Nowlan told the story of a Buck Rogers who, shortly after World War I, was entombed in a cave in good mythic fashion, only to revive in the year 2430. As late as 1937, Olaf Stapledon considered it necessary to anchor the cosmic vision of *Star Maker* in the dream of a narrator on an English hillside.

That convention often made the Rip Van Winkle sleep significant only as a way of getting the reader out of the present into the future. Of major science fiction writers in the 1920s, only Eugene Zamiatin, in *We*, plunges us into the alien future without apology. But beginning in the 1930s—Huxley's *Brave New World* is a distinguished early example—authors seem to have perceived their readership as sufficiently sophisticated to bear up under the intellectual demands of a story which *begins* in the future, even the very distant and alien future; and since then, if anyone travels from the present into the future, that travel must be regarded as thematically significant.

Sleeping, whether under the influence of little men's liquor, mesmerism, or suspended animation, is, of course, not the only way to get from the present into the future. Sleeping is the oldest method, as the time machine is the most recent; but another very old method is via a sojourn in Faerie or Elfland.

Several such stories are documented by Francis James Child in his discussion of the ballad "Thomas Rymer" (Child 37). According to Child, the historical Thomas of Erceldoune, called "Thomas Rymer" or "True Thomas," lived from maybe 1210 or 1220 to maybe 1294 or 1297. A poem bearing his name tells the tale of his three- (or seven-) day stay with the queen of Elfland, who gave him prophetic powers on his departure; on his arrival back in our customary continuum, he discovered that three (or seven) years had passed.

This bit of time travel is modest enough, compared with other similar bits from the tradition. Ogier le Danois (Holger Danske) stayed what seemed twenty years with Morgan le Fay, only to find that two hundred years had gone by; even more extravagantly, the British King Herla lived three hundred years with the King of the Dwarves, and thought only three days had passed. Tench, Child says, has a story of a monk who, entranced with the song of a bird, let three hundred years go by in three hours.

That such legends form part of the consciously understood background of SF time travel is indicated in Poul Anderson's "Time Heals," in which the about-to-be-Van-Winkled hero remembers "the old legends—the Seven Sleepers, the tales of Herla, Frederik Barbarossa, and Holger Danske—of men for whom time had stopped until the remote future date when they awoke" (167).

In spite of the modest dimensions of the Thomas Rymer story, the revelation of the slippage of time, as Child finds it in the Thornton manuscript, stanzas 55 and 56 (written possibly in 1401), comes to the modern science fiction reader as strangely familiar:

> Thomas sayde thane, with heuy chere,
>   Lufly lady, nowe late me bee;
> Ffor certes, lady, I have bene here
>   Noghte bot the space of dayes three.
> 'Ffor sothe, Thomas, als I the telle,
>   Thou hase bene here thre yere and more;

The Thomas Rymer story and its relatives will be readily recognized by science fiction readers as the ancestors of the nearly-as-fast-as-light (NAFAL) scenario, which relies on the principle that a person traveling at a speed very close to that of light will experience a time which passes much more slowly than that of the rest of the universe. A space traveler might, then, return from a voyage which, in his terms, took only a few months, to find his own time almost forgotten by the inhabitants of his native planet; thus the True Thomas scenario enters science fiction, and it has been well and often used. Ursula Le Guin's first published story, "Semley's Necklace," a typical example, is almost mythic in its construct, though hard-core in its science: Semley, a noblewoman of a primitive planet, goes on a long and dangerous journey to the starfolk in the starfolk's NAFAL ships in order to recover an ancestral treasure. Recover it she does, only to discover on her return to her home that she has paid for that triumph with all the young years she might have spent with her family. Although she is still young, they are all old or dead.

Here, as in many other time travel narratives, playing with time, in spite of the initial attractiveness of the idea and the obvious advantages to the traveler, ends in disaster. It is an old notion, reflected, as Larry Niven has pointed out, in the three-wishes and monkey's-paw stories; playing God invites the retribution of fate, or of God, or of the ground rules of the universe. Such folktales are the people's Sophocles, and many tales of time travel are similar moral fables; Brian Aldiss' short and humorous definition of science fiction, "hubris clobbered by nemesis" (*Trillion Year Spree*, 26), fits this sort of tale very nicely. One might call such narratives the story of the monkey's paw on the dial. Nobody can visit Elfland with impunity or accept three wishes without risk: one monkeys with time, likewise, at one's peril.

One may argue plausibly that the Thomas Rymer–NAFAL scenario is related to Paratime or Great Time as intimately as it is to travel to the future. It is true that, as we have said, a sojourn in Great Time may give the same results as travel to the future or the past; it is also true that we may imagine a Paratime in which time runs at a different rate, thus giving a stay there the same results as travel to the future. I choose to treat it as a species of travel to the future for this reason: just as the Van Winkle scenario is related to something familiar to us, namely sleep, so is the Rymer scenario. We all have experience with periods when our subjective experience of time changes—some days when we look at the clock and say, "Where did the day go?" and others when the afternoon takes two forevers. Thus this sort of story has a credibility which stories of Paratime and travel to the past do not, in spite of the extravagance of the methods employed. Drinking Catskill moonshine, rolling up in bed with Morgan le Fay, or being cursed by a Merlin in drag may not strike us as particularly scientific methods of travel; but the travel itself does not do to our sense of the universe the sort of violence which is done by tales of travel to the past or to Paratime.

PARATIME

If we stretch the idea of Paratime to its extreme, as Heinlein does in *The Number of the Beast*, then all fantasy, and indeed all fiction, can be included in Paratime. In some continuum or other, Heinlein suggests, the Merry Old Land of Oz exists in a fashion as real as that of the Bronx, while in others hobbits gambol happily in the Shire, Lord Hornblower sails the Pacific, and Holmes strides through the London fogs.

But to include all fantasy, and indeed, all fiction, under the heading of Paratime would be to stretch the term out of all meaning. Let us then simply define Paratime fiction as that in which a time line other than ours exists, whether or not inhabitants of one can travel to the other or others.

As has been noted before, travel to the past sometimes generates a Paratime; and no matter how Paratime comes to be, it, like travel to the past, is profoundly subversive of common sense, morality, character, and plot. The idea of Paratime seems to creep into consciousness about the same time that the idea of travel to the past does, that is, in the nineteenth century—another reason for linking the two.

Jan Pinkerton cites Edward Everett Hale's "Hands Off" as an example of early time travel to the past generating an alternate history; but in our terms, I think rather that Hale's traveler is in Great Time and is thus able to observe— but only observe—the past and the future. "I was in another stage of existence. I was free from the limits of Time, and in new relations to Space." He moves freely from one epoch to another, not interfering. Nor, when he is tempted to intervene so that Joseph may escape from the slave traders, is he allowed to do so; his "guardian," apparently an angel, takes him instead to a far distant world in which the same action is going on and allows him to interfere *there*. "Here you may try experiments.... Only these here are not His children... not conscious, though they seem so. You will not hurt them whatever you do; nay, they are not free."

Thus Hale sets up a puppet continuum in which the narrator may experiment without damage to his conscience. Less endowed with conscience, Twain's Yankee would never have reflected that the inhabitants of his past "are all conscious and all free. They are His children just as we are. You and I must not interfere unless we know what we are doing."

In the pseudo-world—close to a Paratime—however, the traveler is free to intervene; and predictably, his well-intentioned intervention has disastrous results. Without Joseph in Egypt, Egypt and Israel both starve to death and Canaan and Carthage emerge triumphant; Greece never achieves civilization, Rome goes under in the Punic Wars, and in a few centuries the human race exterminates itself.

The story is a fable, with a moral: "From what I call evil, He educes good." It is also, however, a very early example of the notion that two alternate human histories might coexist, and thus a strong hint of Paratime. Since it appeared in *Harper's* in March of 1881, Mark Twain might well have read it (we know he was reading *Harper's* at that time: *Notebooks* II, 91n), and it might well have contributed an idea to the *Yankee* which Twain began composing three years later. But in Twain's voluminous notebooks there is no hint of such an influence.

Even though Hale's story is unusual in allowing more than one history to coexist in the same framework, there was no scarcity of what-ifs at the time. Darko Suvin says that three main clusters of science fiction may be distinguished in the period 1871–85: the Extraordinary Voyage, the Future War, and the Alternative History, the last of which, "with 33 full-size books... is much the largest cluster of SF at the time." "The very first book-length uchronia," says Gordon B. Chamberlain, by "uchronia" meaning an alternative history, "is L[ouis]-N[apoléon] Geoffroy-Château's [1836] chauvinist pipe dream of Napoleon as world-conqueror" (285). The first critical discussion of alternate history, Chamberlain says (284), was Isaac D'Israeli's "Of a History of Events Which Have Not Happened" in 1849.

Although the full-blown Paratime scheme is not to appear until the fourth decade of our century, the germ of the idea is present in the alternative histories of the nineteenth; indeed, we may detect hints of it in the *Yankee* itself.

Chamberlain would disagree. "Twain's Connecticut Yankee of 1889," he says, "... visits only the past of dream... and ultimately fails to change even that"(284). This is one of the few places, I think, where his excellent analysis is flawed; for as I noted before, if the Yankee has never heard of Camelot, he cannot very well dream a dream of Arthur's court. In spite of the bizarre propulsive mechanism, the *Yankee* seems to me to be true time travel; but in order to account for its apparent contradictions, the Paratime idea has to be brought into play.

The 1879 from which Hank Morgan departs is similar to "ours" in many respects, but differs in its past: for in Morgan's continuum of origin, Malory was not a fabler but a historian (as in Anderson's *Midsummer Tempest* Shakespeare was a historian), and, while all historians lie, Malory seems to have lied no more than most.

In the past of *our* 1879, of course, if King Arthur ever existed, he was not a king, but a leader of Britons in the horrid days after the departure of the Roman legions. Arthur (or Artus) seems to have been a Romano-Briton and is sometimes given the title *dux bellorum*, sometimes *comes brittaniae*. Leslie Alcock argues persuasively that the Easter Annals (Harley 3859) are contemporary and historical rather than fabulous (45). If so, then there would be reason to credit this entry for A.D. 539: "Gueith camlann in qua arthur & medraut correurunt [the strife of Camlann in which Arthur and Mordred perished]." Geoffrey Ashe, on the other hand, identifies Arthur with one Riotimus, who may have been High King of the Britons and may have invaded Gaul in the fifth century.

In any case, if, in our continuum, Arthur did indeed exist, there could have been, in his time, neither plate armor, nor Norman surnames, nor a Souldan of Syria. Nor did an eclipse occur in 528, as it does in the *Yankee*. *Canon of Eclipses*, by Theodor Ritter von Oppolzer (Charts 80–86), has solar eclipses visible in the British Isles as follows: 458, 594, 603, 639 and 664, old style. Finally, in our universe, neither magic nor time travel work; in Morgan's 1879, one can be sent to the past by a blow on the head, and in his sixth century, the magic of Merlin works once in a great while. The *Yankee*, then, implies at least one other time line than ours, perhaps two; and, although all the 1879s of those lines are similar, their pasts are quite different.

One plausible reading of the *Yankee* would involve three continuua: the one from which Hank Morgan departs in 1879 (call it the *Malory* continuum), the one he generates starting in 528, ending about 539 (the *Morgan* continuum), and the one to which he returns about 1839 (*Our* continuum).

Begin with the 1879 in the *Malory* continuum. It is much like ours in many ways: but in it one can be thrown into the past (*Yankee* II) by a blow on the head, and in it Malory's stories are mainly history. Hit on the head, Hank Morgan returns to the A.D. 528 (II) of that same continuum; in that 528, a good deal happens which in *Our* time line would not happen until much later: medieval armor, the interdict, the use of Norman names, the presence of Islam. Further, in this 528 magic works, though rarely. And in this time line, unlike ours, a total eclipse occurred on June 21, A.D. 528, old style.

By his actions in 528, Morgan generates a new continuum, the *Morgan* time line; up until 528, it and the Malory continuum would share a common past, this line forking off as a result of Morgan's actions. Morgan founds his school shortly after his arrival (X), and by the end of his Camelot stay, some of his students (XLIII) have been there ten years. In the period 528–39, Arthurian civilization enjoys an extraordinary spurt into near-nineteenth-century technology and political theory. As in Marx's *Das Kapital*, first published in English in 1886, industrialization comes first, followed by class war led by a cadre. The lower class loses, and their leader, The Boss, is cursed by Merlin with a 1300-year sleep.

Now, the 1879 which would result from Morgan's actions would, one might think, be Our 1879; but not so. Up until the very end of Morgan's stay, Malory's narrations remain history; in Chapter XLII, the account of the King's death from the newspaper is straight out of Malory, Book XXI, Chapter IV. And in this past, as in the Malory continuum, there was a solar eclipse in 528.

This *Morgan* 1879 is never touched on in the *Yankee*, and only implied there. With a bit of work, we might make it *Our* 1879: the Dark Ages which followed the sixth century can be accounted for by the wholesale destruction of Arthurian civilization; in the confusion, both the calendar and the ancient art of magic would become confused and lost; and there would be a hole in a suit of armor and an expression "paying the shot" as the only other result of all the Yankee's efforts.

It is easier, however, to suppose a third continuum, *Ours*. In *Our* 1879, the Past According to Malory is a fable; Arthur was a Romanized Briton, and—since Morgan seems never to have looked them up on his return to the nineteenth century—Puss Flanagan and the Yankee's other friends from the Malory continuum apparently do not exist. The ex-Boss wakes in *Our* continuum and lives from 1839 or thereabouts—1300 years after his swoon in or about 539—until sometime between 1879 and 1889, at which time he meets M. T., Mark Twain's narrator, and tells his tale. By this time he would be between eighty and ninety years of age, if we don't count his 1300-year sleep. (At a time shortly before his leaving the sixth century, he and Arthur [XL] are of an age—about forty.) It is no wonder that he tires of telling his tale and turns the manuscript over to M. T.

One must assume that as a result of Merlin's magic and the physical shock of apparent death, the Yankee was moved from the *Morgan* time line to *Our* time line. One should note, in passing, how time lines tend to converge; see how very similar all the 1879s are, in spite of their varied pasts. We shall note the tendency of time lines in some fiction to converge in just a bit, when we discuss travel to the past; we should also note that, in contrast, in *The Mysterious Stranger* Twain asserts divergence of time lines rather than convergence:

If at any time—say in boyhood—Columbus had skipped the triflingest little link in the chain of acts projected and made inevitable by his first childish act, it would have changed his whole subsequent life, and he would have become a priest and died obscure in an Italian village, and America could not have been discovered for two centuries afterward. I know this.... I have examined his billion of possible careers, and in only one of them occurs the discovery of America. (VII)

The three-line time scheme for the *Yankee* outlined above is by no means the only one which can be hypothesized to account for the events of the *Yankee*: I could, for example, keep the whole thing within one time line with a what-is-written-is-written scenario in which Hank Morgan caused the hole in the suit of armor in his own present, and in which the Battle of the Sand-Belt destroyed all records and caused a historical Arthur's court to be regarded as legend. Such a reading is tempting beyond its reasonableness, simply because of the fine irony which would result: instead of bringing Camelot into the nineteenth century, Morgan would not only destroy it and cause the Dark Ages, but destroy the Round Table's very historical credibility. In such a scheme, the Yankee, on his return to the nineteenth century, might well have met his younger self. Anybody who wants to take the trouble can easily dream up half-a-dozen more; Paratime can account for *anything* in dozens of different ways.

The argument is not that Mark Twain imagined *any* of the possible Paratime explanations for the *Yankee*, or even that he was totally conscious of the possible contradictions in the work; he was, after all, in the process of inventing a whole new subgenre, and if he did not see all the implications of travel to the past, it is no wonder. Besides, one can do only so much in one book: "But if it were only to write over again there wouldn't be so many things left out," as he wrote to Howells (*Mark Twain–Howells Letters* I, 613) after finishing the *Yankee*. In 1889, the Paratime concept does not exist, although the closely related Alternate History concept is going strong; and travel to the past is in its shapeless infancy.

What I *have* been trying to establish, in this somewhat lengthy and tedious analysis of the *Yankee* in Paratime terms, is that, to account for the real difficulties of the book, it is not necessary to postulate that Morgan's adventures are a dream; that, on the contrary, the *Yankee* is genuinely a book about travel to the past, and the first of its kind at that; that the notion of Paratime is present in the *Yankee*, if only in embryo; and that that last fact is not surprising, given the plethora of alternate histories surrounding the book in the Victorian age.

Treating fiction as if it were historical, as Twain does in the *Yankee*, has of late become a popular game. The Baker Street Irregulars have long maintained a tongue-in-cheek belief that Sir Arthur Conan Doyle was the literary agent and editor of the works written by Dr. John Watson (except for two stories written by Holmes himself, two of doubtful authorship, and one which by some is attributed to his brother, Mycroft Holmes). W. S. Baring-Gould extends the joke still farther, carefully checking the birth date of Nero Wolfe to show that Wolfe, whose resemblance to Mycroft Holmes is notable, could well be the child of Sherlock and Irene Adler; he writes Rex Stout about the matter, and gets a straight-faced reply regretting that Archie Goodwin's editor is pledged to secrecy.

Further, Philip Jose Farmer gives us biographies of Tarzan and Doc Savage, as well as "the true story" of Phileas Fogg as Verne could not tell it in *Around the World in Eighty Days*, and there are even books representing themselves as having been written by characters in other books: the putative author of Farmer's *Venus on the Half-Shell* is Vonnegut's Kilgore Trout.

All such playing with the line between fiction and reality is not necessarily part of the Paratime canon; but certainly it exists on the fringes of it. As in Heinlein's *Number of the Beast*, what is fiction in one continuum may be history in another. Such a blurring of distinctions is doubtless at least partly a reflection of the abandonment of a neat cause-and-effect Newtonian universe for one of probabilities and singularities. It is reflected in the works of such mainstream writers as Pirandello, whose *It Is So! (If You Think So)* presents us with a universe in which any explanation is as true as any other explanation; whose *Six Characters* permits fictitious folk to migrate from play to play; and whose *Henry IV* drags the past wholesale into the present.

Whirl is king, having deposed Zeus.

But before ever Zeus was King, whirl reigned. In the world of Homer, the line between fiction and history was never clearly drawn; nor did any carrier of the Gospel ever consider the stories told of Jesus from the perspectives of modern history. Are we not simply returning, after a brief recess, to the perspective of our ancestors? For several centuries, it appeared that no-god would liberate us from divine whim and set the universe on a firm foundation of predictable cause and effect; now, particularly in the realms of the very-large and the very-small, but possibly also in the great middle range, it seems that no-god gives us as whimsical a universe as many-gods gave Homer. Whether in the Homeric scenario or in our own century, it is difficult to tell the real from the fictitious without a program.

THE PAST

The fiction of travel to Great Time appeals to our yearning for the timeless and the eternal; tales of travel to the future give satisfaction to our wishes for progress, long life, knowledge, or significant purpose; and stories of travel to other time lines in Paratime respond to our if-onlys or what-ifs. Travel to the past participates to some extent in all of these needs, particularly those responded to by Paratime; furthermore, more than any of the others, as we have noted, it is responsive to the Faustian or Satanic desire for godhood or near-godhood.

Results of Travel to the Past

As the literature develops in post-Twain times, several possible results of travel to the past appear, the first two of which have already been touched on in our discussion of Paratime. Of the six possibilities which I can see, five are implied in Twain's *Connecticut Yankee*, a remarkable accomplishment in a book which is the first of its kind:

Paratime Resulting from Travel to the Past

Travel to the past results in the generation of a new time line which coexists with the line from which the traveler departed, as in such works as Benford's *Timescape* and Asimov's "Fair Exchange?" The difference between the two lines may be very small, a mere matter of the presence or absence of a piece of music, a book, or a single person; or the two lines may diverge enormously, like the channels of the delta of a rivermouth. As was noted in our discussion of Paratime, this scenario is one which is a possible fit for the *Connecticut Yankee*.

Paratime Independent of Time Travel

All possible continua coexist and have equal reality and do not depend upon time travel for their generation, as in *Number of the Beast* and the Paratime tales of H. Beam Piper. Such a system not only ruins the delicate line between fiction and fact, but makes all other time travel possible and superfluous. Why go to the past, when in an alternate present everything is just as it was in our 528, except that it is *now*? Similarly, in another time line things are exactly as they will be in the future, and travel to such a line would be indistinguishable from travel to the future. There are universes, likewise, in which all the other possibilities in the present exist and are operative. Since *all* fiction is possible on one time line or another, the *Yankee* can of course fit this scenario.

What Is Written Is Written

A traveler can go to the past and act there, right enough; but he cannot change the present or generate a new time line. What he does is *already* part of his own past. Sometimes, as in Aldiss' "T," the result is frustration of the traveler's efforts; sometimes the traveler can operate only in those areas which are not matters of record, knowing that what he does is part of the past already, but a necessary part, and therefore his action is purposeful—as in Anderson's *There Will Be Time*. In our discussion of Paratime, we have noted that this scenario, too, can be made to fit the *Yankee*.

Channels Converge

The time traveler can change the past and generate a new time line, but there is an overwhelming tendency for this time line to join the traveler's original line in a relatively short time. It is as if a raft floating down the Mississippi were to launch a boat, and that boat were to drift down a different side of a long island, an image that Twain uses in Chapter XV of *Huckleberry Finn*. If the island were a small one, boat and raft would rejoin one another shortly; if it were an island several miles long, the reunion would be postponed. Each boatman might think he was in the main channel; he might even think the other had forever disappeared. But eventually the two channels will merge, and once again boat and raft will be in the same river. Like a mighty river, the passage of time has tremendous inertia; while it is relatively easy to divert the little stream that is the headwater, it is almost impossible to make such deflection have much substantial effect a thousand miles downriver. This is the scheme of such works as Damon Knight's "You're Another" and Harold MacKaye's *Panchronicon*. A short time from the traveler's action in the past, the result is the generation of a temporary alternate time line (as in "Paratime Resulting from Travel to the Past," above); a bit farther into the future, the result is nil (as in "What Is Written Is Written," above). Thus this scenario likewise fits the *Yankee*.

Changes at the Jonbar Hinges

The traveler can change the past so that his present is affected in substantive fashion, but only with difficulty and with great care in choosing the *point d'appui*, which, in the critical literature, is often called *the Jonbar hinge*. The term derives from Jack Williamson's *Legion of Time*, in which two possible future civilizations, the good Jonbar and the wicked Gyronchi (each ruled, in good pulp fashion, by a beautiful princess) are at war to decide which of them will come into real existence when the wave of the present reaches their time. The Legion of Time, made up of men who have died in their own times—since no living man can become a time traveler, a notion reminding us again of Great Time—discovers that the action which will determine which civilization comes into being occurs in 1921: the 12-year-old John Barr will either pick up a bright pebble (in which case the Bad Guys win) or he will choose a nearby discarded magnet (in which case he will become the great scientist for whom Jonbar will much later be named, and the Good Guys will triumph).

This is a fascinating and subtle notion, combining as it does the possibilities of different and conflicting theories of history. On the one hand, I might go back to a given street in Ajaccio on a given night in December 1768 and shout under a given window. Given the odds against any given sperm's reaching its desti-nation, I should be able, simply by causing a moment's inattention, to prevent the birth of Napoleon. (Someone *else* might well be born nine months later, but it wouldn't be the Napoleon we all know and love.) And that might, in accordance with the great-man theory of history, change all subsequent European history; or it might not. If the conception of Napoleon did not happen to be a Jonbar hinge, another great French military leader might well rise in Napoleon's place, thus vindicating those historians who see history as the result of great social and economic movements, quite independent of the actions of individuals. On the other hand, on the way down the street from the window of Napoleon's parents' house, I might well displace a pebble, and that action might cause the young would-have-been-Napoleon to go into the church instead of the army, and that might cause the papacy to achieve hegemony over all of Europe; and thus the accident theory of history would be vindicated. Clearly, if we assume that Hank Morgan simply did not have the good luck to land on a Jonbar hinge, this scheme will likewise fit the *Yankee*.

Great Results from Trivial Actions

Every moment in the past turns out to be a Jonbar hinge. This is a favorite scenario, emphasizing as it does the profound effects of small actions: a theme to delight almost any author. Show up in the wrong place on the battlefield of Gettysburg, Ward Moore tells us in *Bring the Jubilee*, and the South will lose the war, and all of human history will be changed from that point onward; step on a butterfly sixty million years in the past, Bradbury's "Sound of Thunder" warns, and you will return to find your democracy gone and a fascist totalitar-ianism in its place; disturb a hundred molecules two billion years ago, and, if William Tenn's "Brooklyn Project" is right, in the present the day will have thirty-three hours, the Earth seven moons, and its intelligent inhabitants slithery pseudopods.

The present from which the time traveler has come is snuffed out, and he becomes an effect without a cause: both the most isolated of isolates, and Ar-istotle's Uncaused Cause. If the traveler doesn't watch it, he may stumble into the killing-one's-grandfather paradox; or, in another equally familiar and more friendly scenario, he may blunder into becoming his own ancestor.

This is the only scenario of the six which cannot be made to fit the *Connecticut Yankee*; in that book time streams tend to converge. For it to be otherwise, it would be as if one could voyage to the headwaters of the Mississippi, drop a kitchen match into the trickle, and thereby cause the river to flow into the Atlantic. But perhaps history is not like a river, after all.

Reasons for Travel to the Past

In a lecture to the Eighth Conference on the Fantastic in the Arts (3/20/87), published in *Contours of the Fantastic*, Brian Stableford extended the argument of his book *Scientific Romance in Britain*: that SF in the United Kingdom constitutes a distinctive tradition, to be distinguished from American science fiction of the same period, not only by its relationships to earlier British speculative literature and fantasy, but by its overall tendency to be wary, not only of industrialization and technology, but of the very idea of progress.

One's first impulse is to search for exceptions to this idea. If in Great Britain we have the skepticism and pessimism of Jonathan Swift, Mary Shelley, and H. G. Wells, we also find there the optimism of Tennyson, which is, in the 1842 "Locksley Hall" at least, wide-eyed enough for any Yankee. The British Isles likewise contribute the optimistic vision of Bulwer-Lytton's *The Coming Race*, in which humanity has evolved into the Vryl-ya, who surpass us as we surpass our barbarian ancestors.

And, if the United States could contribute such optimists as Bellamy, so likewise could they give us the grim visions of Hawthorne and Poe, and the even more complex pessimism of the *Connecticut Yankee*, in which technocratic optimism ends in societal catastrophe.

Still, Stableford's generalization seems to work, in general, particularly if applied to the general public consciousness and the popular literature which appealed to it. Many things conspired to keep America relatively optimistic; she still had a frontier well into the late nineteenth century, and even the terrible War Between the States does not appear to have impacted the American consciousness in the way that World War I later did the European. One might have expected the South after the Civil War to have produced European-style scientific romance; but the South, largely unindustrialized, was not writing science fiction. And for the northern United States, the Civil War was followed by an era of unparalleled development and prosperity; and World War I was to the American popular mind not the killer of a whole generation of men, but a gallant and relatively inexpensive rescue of Noble Allies in a Good Cause.

Even so, the last important American utopia was Bellamy's *Equality* in 1897, to be followed in less than a decade by the first major American dystopia, Jack London's *Iron Heel*. Mack Reynolds' reprises of Bellamy are, as recent utopias, near-unique in science fiction, and Ursula Le Guin's 1974 utopia, *The Dispos-*

sessed, she correctly subtitles "ambiguous." Stableford's *Science Fiction Encyclopedia* article "Utopias" notes that after Hugo Gernsback's editorial career faded, few truly optimistic visions of the future occur in science fiction:

Despite Gernsback's inspiration and intentions, SF was never strongly Utopian. The early SF pulps abounded with adventure stories set in pseudo-Utopian futures where poverty and injustice, if they still exist, are nowhere in evidence, but when writers turned their attention away from adventure toward the prospects facing society as a whole doubt and pessimism were obvious.

This pessimism, he notes, resulted in reactionary utopias such as those which had been in vogue in Europe since Tolstoy:

Utopian thought in the last half century has to a large extent dissociated itself from the idea of progress and connected itself to the idea of an "historical retreat" to a simpler life.... Even the recent past has been restored, by the medium of nostalgia, to the status of a pseudo-Utopia in such novels as *Time and Again* (1970) by Jack Finney. (622–23)

A growing popular suspicion, then, that the future may not be utopian, but ambiguous at best and inhuman at worst, would furnish adequate psychic fuel for journey's to the past, as well as for historical romance, flights to worlds that never could be, and—very much as Poe's distaste for the American nineteenth century fueled his horror fiction—a growing expression of alienation in fiction of the grotesque and horrific; thus the popularity of movies like *Gone with the Wind*, and of fantastic romances (on the one hand) and the horrific constructions of Stephen King (on the other) can be seen as reflections of this rejection of the future. So can the widespread American tendency to return to simpler, and more simplistic, versions of religious thought which are associated with the American past.

(It is interesting and ironic to note that, while early Christians, looking forward to the future with hope, could create the Seven Sleepers story, many contemporary Christians look mainly to the past. Jerry Falwell's TV ministry, for example, is called *The Old Time Gospel Hour*, not by accident. And the imminent second coming, which gave early believers reason to hope for the future, seems in our time to reflect a fear of that future—although the growing chorus of "We live in the end times" doubtless is largely due to the beginning of the third millennium heaving up on the horizon. It is difficult to persuade people infatuated with numbers that, had we four fingers on each hand, we would attach the magic to 2048; if six, to 3456.)

LIMITS PLACED ON TIME TRAVEL

Had he but known it, Wells' Time Traveler could have had the power of a god, saving only his mortality. With his machine, he could voyage to the future and the past at will; he could therefore have readjusted history after the manner of a schoolma'am, doing things over and over until he got them right (uniting Morlocks and Eloi in a harmonious utopia); and he could have become The Boss in a way undreamed of by the Connecticut Yankee.

But such an unlimited power, presented in fiction, can have but two ends; either, as before noted, all action becomes insignificant, or else all action crashes into the most abominable solipsism.

Unlimited powers, however attractive and amusing they might be in real life, soon pall, therefore, as a fictional device. There you have the reason that no hero of a folktale, given three wishes, ever makes the wish for unlimited wishes— an idea that occurs to every five-year-old. Not long after Superman's creation in 1938, he had become totally unvulnerable: without really trying, he overwhelmed all obstacles. And the strip enjoyed a fantastic success for some years. Eventually, however, the whole business became boring, and the writers of the strip began to introduce elements designed to find holes in the armor of the Man of Steel: green kryptonite, red kryptonite, yellow kryptonite, and the like. If a hero cannot lose, then he is no hero. A god can be a hero only if, like Prometheus or Jesus, he is subject, like us, to suffering or death. Odysseus seems to understand this principle when he rejects Kalypso's attractive offer of eternal indolence and pleasure to return to the turbulence of his homeward voyage.

If the time traveler is not similarly hedged in, the significance of action similarly dimishes. In Heinlein's *Number of the Beast*, the at-will voyages of the heroes into one Paratime after another begin very swiftly to pall upon the reader in spite of the intellectual novelty of the exercise. Similarly, Heinlein's two earlier exercises in at-will travel to the past and future, the 1941 "By His Bootstraps" and the 1959 " 'All You Zombies' " are fascinating intellectual exercises (as is David Gerrold's 1973 reprise, *The Man Who Folded Himself*)— the first time through. Once a reader has decoded the sinuous and evasive path of the traveler back and forth through time and worked out how he can be his own grandfather, wife, child, and recruiting officer, the fun is over. If the traveler in time is not somehow limited as to what he can do, the reader rapidly loses interest: Diktor and all the other Bob Wilsons in "By His Bootstraps" may have, as Diktor says, "a great future," but Heinlein is too wise to try to inflict it on the reader.

The writers of fiction of travel to the past (and future) have therefore devised a vast number of ways to hedge in their travelers and make them less godlike. Some travelers, like the Yankee, depart from their presents unwillingly and without warning; others, like Bob Wilson, do so willingly and with preparation (in one avatar or another). Some travelers are opposed to other travelers: Time Patrolmen by temporal bad guys, the armies of Jonbar by those of Gyronchi. In some scenarios, one may go only to a given time or a given place (Asimov's "Cosmic Corkscrew," and Julian May's *Saga of Pliocene Exile*, for instance). Some time travelers are threatened by temporal pollution—change time too much and you threaten the whole fabric, as in Richard Meredith's *Timeliner Trilogy*. Some can change anything they wish in the past and have it affect subsequent history; others, like Havig in Anderson's *There Will Be Time*, only those things of which there is no record; still others, nothing—like the travelers in Anderson's *Dancer from Atlantis* and all other what-is-written scenarios. Still others, like the bad guy in John D. MacDonald's "Half-Past Eternity," find that monkeying with time involves truly hideous traps. Some can return to their own times, as the Yankee unwillingly does; others are stuck in the past, like Padway in L. Sprague de Camp's *Lest Darkness Fall*.

First, then, the literature evolves the idea of travel to the past; then it sees the possibilities of godlike action with such travel unrestricted; and finally it builds restrictions on such travel in order to preserve plot integrity.

Chapter 3

CHILDREN OF THE YANKEE: THE NOSTALGICS

If those were barbarous ages, then
Let us be barbarous again.

—Maclise

A BRIEF HISTORY OF NOSTALGIA

Only define the term broadly enough, and writers seem always to have been nostalgics. Homer, after all, was writing about a time some three centuries before his own, which age seemed to him more valiant, more civilized, more interesting, than the one in which he lived; the little bit of Greek tragedy we have left spends much more time on the distant past than on recent events (out of thirty-three surviving plays by the three great tragedians, only one, *The Persians*, is not set at least four hundred years in the audience's past); and *Beowulf*, written probably in the seventh century, deals with matters which are supposed to have occurred two centuries before.

But the simple fact that people have always liked to write about the past does not, in itself, constitute nostalgia. After all, there is a lot more distant past out there than there is recent past, and one must write about *something*. One cannot, of course, write about the present, which turns into the past as one writes; only the journal comes close. But even if we grant, for the sake of argument, that the present, for fictional purposes, stretches backward and maybe forward for ten or a dozen years, there is still a lot more distant past out there than anything except distant future. And, as noted before, only relatively recently does it seem to have occurred to anyone, prophets excepted, to write about the future. As Brian Aldiss points out in Chapter III of *Trillion Year Spree*, all the "honorable ancestors'' of SF—''the wonderful journeys, the utopias, the adventures and satires''—are strangely ''time-locked—not recognizing change as the yeast of the societies they depict.''

Nor does the perception (apparently shared by Homer and the author of *Beowulf*) that the ancestors were greater than we are, in itself, give us nostalgia. After all, when we are children we see our living ancestors as bigger and stronger and wiser and more moral than we are, and when we in our turn become ancestors, we recognize all too well our own smallness and weakness and stupidity and corruption. Furthermore, we remember that when we were young the food tasted better and people were more sexually attractive than they are now. Naturally enough: an adolescent is a combination of famine and orgy, looking for someplace to break out. The appetites of those of us who have become parents of adolescents have calmed down a bit.

In nostalgia proper, however, there is something quasi-pathological, a looking-inward and looking-backward to the large exclusion of looking outward and forward. There is but little of this tendency in Western European literature before the late eighteenth century.

In the Middle Ages, to be sure, folk like Dante looked backward with a certain wistfulness at the civilization of the Roman Empire; but Dante's unquestioned admiration of Virgil as representative of that empire is coupled with his satisfaction at being born after the day of Virgil's ''false and lying gods.'' The very name of the Renaissance, to be sure, indicates a rebirth of interest in, and knowledge about, classical culture and science; but the population explosion and resulting voyages of exploration and colonization of that period sufficed to keep people's minds largely on the affairs of the present and future. Shakespeare, whether he writes about Greeks or Romans or early Britons, is always clearly focused on the intricacies of the politics of his own time.

Interest in the past, and particularly in the medieval past, begins to pick up in the Age of Reason. The London Society of Antiquaries and the Society of Antiquaries of Scotland were formally constituted in 1717 and 1780, respectively; the American Antiquarian Society and the Kilkenny Archaeological Society (later the Royal Society of Antiquaries of Ireland) not until 1812 and 1849. It was in the eighteenth century that the fashion of building pseudo-medieval ruins on one's grounds began to appear; and it was in the middle of that century that Sir Francis Dashwood and his cronies began to meet disguised as monks and nuns in the thirteenth-century ruins of the Cistercian abbey at Medmenham.

But for most eighteenth-century folk, their own century and its values seem to have suited them well. As Mark Girouard notes, there had not been a tournament since 1694, nor an edition of Malory since 1634:

Many of the most important elements of chivalry now [in the Georgian age] conflicted with the conviction of the upper and most of the middle classes that anything that savoured of ''enthusiasm'' could and should be remodelled according to the dictates of reason. Loyalty to a king or leader, however disastrous the result, faithful love, however little

requited, readiness to fight for one's honour, however slight the slur on it, or truth to
one's word, however rashly given, were qualities which the literature of chivalry singled
out for praise, but which eighteenth-century opinion tended to consider stupid rather than
noble. (17–19)

This evaluation is borne out by the fact that in 1790, in *Reflections on the
Revolution in France*, Edmund Burke, *not* happy with the late developments in
his own century, oppressed by the spectacle of the rising middle class, could
write, "The age of chivalry is gone. That of sophisters, economists and calculators, has succeeded: and the glory of England is extinguished for ever"
(Girouard, 19). But in the backlash against the French Revolution, during the
reigns of George III and George IV, the age of chivalry came back in force; and
it was George IV who in 1820 created Walter Scott a baronet, having told Byron
eight years before that he preferred Scott to "every Bard past and present"
(Girouard, 34).

The French Revolution, the rise of the middle class, and the growth of technology all helped set the stage for the influence of Scott, which, as Girouard
shows, was considerable: art, literature, architecture, manners, and even the
details of the celebration of Christmas all seem, for the remainder of the nineteenth century, to owe a good deal either directly to Scott or indirectly to the
nostalgia for the medieval of which he was the great exemplar. Folk of good
family were painted in quasi-medieval getup; respectable country houses were
rebuilt with moats and crenelations; and a tournament, a year in the planning
and hundreds of thousands of pounds in the execution, aborted on August 28,
1839, in a sudden rainstorm, to the great delight of the Whig press.

In spite of the occasional jeers of the whiggish rabble, however, nostalgia for
things medieval—however mistakenly conceived as things Arthurian—seems to
have had an extraordinary hold on the mid-nineteenth-century mind. There is,
however, an important difference to be noted between the nostalgia of the nineteenth century and that of the post–World War I period: in the former, the values
of the past were to be imported into the present and put into practice. In England,
the mania for the medieval was at first largely associated with Tory politics;
those upper-class radicals who flirted with medievalism and those members of
the Round Table associated with *Fraser's* seem all to have moved into a Toryish
position by 1850.

One science fiction writer, Keith Roberts, has noted in "Weinachtsabend"
the connection between Scott and right-wing politics. In that alternate-history
story, native English sympathizers help Hitler to triumph in World War II: "The
English bourgeoisie, anxious to construct a rationale [for anti-Semitism], discovered many... precedents. A true Sign of the Times... was the resurgence of
interest in the novels of Sir Walter Scott."

But by the end of the century many of the "knightly virtues" seem to have
been taken up by the very middle class at whose head Burke would have flung
them; the most notable example is that of the Boy Scouts, whose founder, Sir

Robert Baden-Powell, stirred up a synthesis of Ernest Thompson Seton's Wood-craft Indians, Kenelm Henry Digby's 1822 *Broad Stone of Honor*, and the Vermont-originated Knights of King Arthur. Even in the 1940s, the *Boy Scout Handbook* was loaded with references to chivalry and with pictures of knights in armor pointing the way to scouts in uniform.

Baden-Powell, then, like Digby (and Scott, and Tennyson, and many another), saw the redemption of a bourgeous society in the acceptance of feudal values. He seems to have seen nothing wrong in playing with history in order to back chivalry up to the days of Arthur, nor in ascribing Digby's rules of conduct to that king. Or perhaps he really thought that Malory was a historian.

TWAIN'S REACTION TO NOSTALGIA FOR THE MIDDLE AGES

Early in Twain's career, in Chapter LIV of *Innocents Abroad*, his narrator, weary of touring a sordid and commercialized Jerusalem, comforts himself with the thought that his memories of the day, at some time in the future, will be uniformly pleasant—an echo, perhaps, of Virgil's *forsan et haec olem meminisse juvabit* (some day we'll remember even this with pleasure). And he makes the connection between nostalgia for the past and nostalgia for one's own childhood with a typically cynical edge:

School-boy days are no happier than the days of after life, but we look back on them regretfully because we have forgotten our punishments at school, and how we grieved when our marbles were lost and our kites destroyed—because we have forgotten all the sorrows and privations of that canonized epoch and remember only its orchard robberies, its wooden-sword pageants, and its fishing holidays.

From our point of view, the passage is a remarkable foreboding of the *Yankee*, which will take the hero *into* an epoch recently canonized by Scott and his followers and show us the sorrows and privations and the fact that the swords were not all of wood.

Because, however sentimental Twain could be at odd moments, however skeptical of his own century and its trumpeted virtues, there was in him enough of the Connecticut Yankee to see Sir Walter Scott, most notable examplar of nineteenth-century sapheadedness about the Middle Ages, as a moral and intel-lectual disaster, in spite of the fact that his beloved friend, the Reverend Joe Twitchell, was a devoted Scotian (*Autobiography* II, 224). In 1883 In *Life on the Mississippi* Twain wrote

[Scott ran] the people mad, a couple of generations ago, with his medieval romances. The South has not yet recovered from the debilitating influence of his books. Admiration of his fantastic heroes and their grotesque "chivalry" doings and romantic juvenilities still survives here, in an atmosphere in which is already perceptible the wholesome and practical nineteenth-century smell of cotton factories and locomotives; and traces of its inflated language and other windy humbuggeries survive along with it. (XL)

We may see an irony in the notion that the smell of cotton factories and loco-motives is "wholesome"; but the main drift of the passage is clear, apparently sincere, and worthy of Hank Morgan.

In *Huckleberry Finn* it is the steamboat *Walter Scott* which is wrecked (XII–XIV), and in its looting Huck and Jim find a cargo of romances which set them up for their encounter with the Duke and the Dauphin, who are not merely con men imitating royalty, but deformed versions of royalty itself. It is Scotian romances which carry off the good sense of Sally and Aleck in "The $30,000 Bequest," two otherwise practical small-towners who spend their evenings "reading romances to each other, dreaming dreams, comrading with kings and princes and stately lords and ladies in the flash and stir and splendor of noble palaces and grim and ancient castles" (3). It is Scott whom Twain parodies in "A Medieval Romance" in 1868. When (*Yankee* XI) Sandy cannot understand Hank Morgan's skepticism about her tale of four-armed monsters, as much in the spirit of literary criticism as expletive, the Yankee bellows "Great Scott!"

And it is the ugly underside of Scott's medievalism which Twain belabors in *The Prince and the Pauper* in 1882. This book was much misread in its own time and continues to be misread. In his introduction to the Penguin *Yankee*, Justin Kaplan says that, in contrast to the *Yankee*, for which Twain was much castigated by "the guardians of the genteel," *The Prince and the Pauper* was "an act of cultural fealty which they praised for having the conventional virtues of finish, refinement and delicacy." In *Mr. Clemens and Mark Twain*, to be sure, Kaplan sees *The Prince and the Pauper* as a sign of Twain's growing disenchantment with England (248); but he also asserts that Twain intended that the book should establish him as "a serious practitioner of polite, colorful literature" (276). As he notes, the reviewers of the time agreed: "the words 'pure,' 'lovely,' 'subdued,' 'delicate,' 'refined,' and 'enobling' recurred as part of a grateful appreciation of just those qualities which any conventional romancer might be expected to possess..." (279). And although Sylvester Baxter, review-ing the *Yankee* in the Boston *Sunday Herald* in December 1889 (Norton *Yankee*, 321), is not blind to that book's social satire, he refers back to *The Prince and the Pauper* as "that lovely idyll of childhood."

One can only imagine Twain's amusement. To be sure, the book has as romantic a mistaken-identity plot as ever delighted Sir Walter Scott or Frank Yerby: but all classes are cruel, aristoi and commoners alike; burning at the stake and boiling alive in oil are there, but never a tournament; the knightly rescuer of the Prince is an impoverished and humorous Samaritan who is a terrible seamster and who wants nothing better than to be able to sit down in the presence of his apparently mad guest; royal customs are seen, correctly, by Tom Canty to be an artificial drama of foolishness—as Twain wrote (*Letters* I, 490), Tom has a "gilded and worshipped and dreary and restrained and cussed time of it on the throne''; everyday life is sordid, nasty and brutal; royal blood does not give nobility, but practical experience may; in Chapter XVII the beggar Yokel delivers an indictment of his society which is just short of revolutionary; and although, at the story-book ending in which the rightful king is restored, Yokel is "put in the way of a comfortable livelyhood," Twain makes it clear that the merciful reign of Edward was brief and followed by a return to ancient barbarisms. It seems clear that, beneath the surface of a romance superficially like those of Scott, in *The Prince and the Pauper* Twain is being every bit as subversive of nineteenth-century nostalgia for medievalism as ever he was in the *Yankee*.

One great late hurrah of such nostalgia used in the interests of reaction came on the continent, during the Dreyfus affair; in triumph at the acquittal of Esterhazy in 1897, Albert de Mun, in a speech at the French Academy, found the voice of those who would repeal the French Revolution and return to the days of clerical domination: "By an irresistible evolution the ancient ideas reappear to fulfill new tasks. Our flag unfurls proudly; it shows the cross and the glorious device: *In hoc signo vinces*. Our aim is clear: this is a new revolution that puts the rights of God against those of men" (Halasz, 123–24). But Twain, like the Yankee in Chapter XIII (who calls the French Revolution "ever-memorable and blessed"), is, he says in his letter to Howells (*Letters* I, 490), "not a pale, characterless Sansculotte, but a Marat." Making due allowance for overstatement, one may at least say that Twain is not ignorant of the potential for using nostalgia for reactionary purposes, and that he sees, as the humorless Scott cannot, the realistic and unwholesome side of medieval civilization.

And, as we already have seen from the evidence of Twain's notebooks, it is a romanticized medievalism viewed with a realistic and humorous eye which is the very genesis of the *Connecticut Yankee*.

But the *Yankee* is not all satire; the hero is able, throughout his stay in Arthur's court, to see those elements which would have appealed to Scott, and which appeal to him, however much he insists on coupling them with the sordid. In Chapter I, for instance, he has a description of his approach to Camelot which includes "a distant blare of military music... a noble cavalcade... glorious with plumed helmets, and flashing mail, and flaunting banners and rich doublets and horse-cloths, and gilded spear-heads" which nevertheless winds through "muck, and swine, and naked brats, and joyous dogs, and shabby huts."

In Chapter XVII there is a nod in the direction of chivalric virtues as seen by the nineteenth century: Arthur, the king, is a man "whose word is gold." The nineteenth-century flippancies of the *Camelot Weekly Hosannah and Literary Volcano* in Chapter XXVI make The Boss a bit uncomfortable; he would prefer something a bit more dignified. In Chapter XXIX, the king's knightly honor leads him to behave as well in the smallpox hut as could be asked of any Eagle Scout. The *Connecticut Yankee* is not without traces of Scott-like admiration for the Middle Ages, and at the end the Yankee, displaced into his own time, dies of, or at least with, homesickness for the sixth century.

NOSTALGIA IN LATER TIME TRAVEL FICTION

In the literary descendants of the Yankee, however, nostalgia is often much more pronounced. It is not, however, the medieval nostalgia of the nineteenth century, which hoped to import chivalric values into a mercantile and industrial age; it is a nostalgia which sees the modern world as hopelessly corrupted and would escape to a happier historical period.

Often the nostalgia is not the overt motive for the traveler's journey in time; it simply precedes an accidental and unexpected transport to the past. In de Camp's *Lest Darkness Fall*, for example, at the very beginning a friend of the traveler is complaining that in his world there is "nothing big, nothing new," and the traveler seems silently to agree. In Le Guin's "April in Paris," the hero, Professor Barry Pennywither, is in Paris longing for the Paris of François Villon when he is snatched back into 1482, where he can be something besides "an unsocial, unmarried, underpaid pedant, sitting... alone in an unheated attic in an unrestored tenement trying to write another unreadable book." By great good luck, such heroes become fulfilled Miniver Cheevys.

Ray Bradbury

One of SF's great nostalgics is Ray Bradbury. Almost without exception, his visions of the future are menacing; almost without exception, any positive vision is either of the past or partakes of the past. Bradbury does not often write of travel to the past, but when he does it works out as one might expect. In "The Dragon," a railroad train driven by men whose main concern is making their schedule thunders across a tenth-century moor where gallant knights attempt to kill it and are brutally slain on the tracks: the present impinges on the past to the past's discomfiture. The dragon "runs with sulfur and thunder and kindles the grass. Sheep panic and die insane. Women deliver forth monsters.... Tower walls shake back to dust. His victims, at sunrise, are strewn hither thither on the hills." All this takes place on a moor where there "is no Time, is only Forever... no man's place... no year or time at all." It is a godless place: when one knight sees the train and breathes "Lord!" the other replies without hope, "Yes, let us use His name." In his working notes for the *Yankee*, Twain had had a quite similar idea:

Picture: The first locomotive tearing along, & priests, people & steel-clad knights breaking in every direction for the woods.... Priests "casting out" this devil with due & awful ceremony.... A green knight from a far country, seeking adventures, sees the locomotive coming, lays his lance in rest & charges it; air-break [*sic*] out of order. *Picture of the collision.* (California *Yankee*, 512)

In Bradbury's "Scent of Sarsaparilla," an old man finds the past in his attic and rides the attic like a time machine to a time when his wife and he could walk out on a Sunday "with your silk parasol and your long dress whishing along, and sit on those wire-legged chairs at the soda parlor... and then ride out in our 1910 Ford to Hannahan's Pier for a box supper and listen to the brass band." "Night Meeting" gives us an encounter on Mars between a 2002 Terran and a Martian from centuries before, strangely redemptive for both. In "Forever and the Earth," a future writer finds himself unable to portray his own world and uses a time machine to bring Thomas Wolfe from 1938 to do the job. In "The Exiles," Poe, Dickens, Bierce, Coppard, Machen, and Blackwood all come from the past to Mars and are wiped out by the arrival of a rocket from Earth. "Time in Thy Flight" gives us a school field trip from the future to a 1928 which the teacher finds barbarous and unhygienic, but in which the children want to stay so that they can have Halloweens and Fourths of July with fire-crackers. And in "The Fox and the Forest," in a familiar scenario, refugees from 2155, a time when the world was "like a great black ship pulling away from shore of sanity and civilization, roaring its black horn in the night, taking two billion people with it, whether they wanted to go or not, to death, to fall over the edge of the earth and the sea into radioactive flame and madness," are tracked down and apprehended in 1938.

Jack Finney

A nostalgic perhaps even more committed than Bradbury is Jack Finney, who has written about time travel again and again, and always with the apparent conviction that western civilization peaked in the Midwest in the 1890s.

Finney was born in 1911, early enough to have a sense of pre–World War I America. But it is not to 1911 that the narrator of "The Third Level" wishes to return; it is to the time when Finney's (and the narrator's) grandfather was an adult: 1894. (We are meant, I think, to be reminded of Orwell's 1984.) There are supposed to be only two levels to Grand Central Station; but the narrator has found a third, a fact which worries his psychiatrist. From the third level, which has clerks in green eyeshades working underneath gaslights, the narrator is sure that he and his wife can depart for any 1894 destination they wish; he wants Galesburg, Illinois, the city in which Finney went to college:

It's a wonderful town still, with big old frame houses, huge lawns and tremendous trees whose branches meet overhead and roof the streets. And in 1894, summer evenings were twice as long, and people sat out on their lawns, the men smoking cigars and talking quietly, the women waving palm-leaf fans, with the fireflies all around, in a peaceful world.

Why were "summer evenings...twice as long"? Not, surely, because people worked shorter hours. And daylight saving time hadn't yet been invented. Two things come to mind which have the effect of subjectively lengthening time: a low rate of change, and childhood. "I went to school there," Charley the narrator tells us later in the story. The contented adults, seen only in the evenings, and the fireflies, both argue that this is a child's vision. What follows is an adult's perspective: "To be back there with the First World War still twenty years off, and World War II over forty years in the future... I wanted two tickets for that." An adult's perspective, but a childish wish: to be far enough back in time so that one would be too old for combat by World War I, and to take one's wife with him. To be an adult, in fact, with none of the responsibilities—a dream of Eden, or of an adult childhood. Charley tries to buy two tickets, but the ticket agent will not accept his 1940s money; he gets out fast: "There's nothing nice about jail, even in 1894."

Now, *there* is a strange perspective; from all accounts, as disagreeable as contemporary jails can be, they were much, much worse in 1894. I see no auctorial irony here; Finney's attitudes throughout his fiction are sufficiently consistent to make it likely that he shares the infantile escapism of his character. (I regret that the words "infantile escapism" have such thoroughly pejorative connotations; Jesus of Nazareth suggested that being in some ways infantile might be not only desirable but necessary to the complete human, and His follower C. S. Lewis has sane and positive things to say about escapism in his essay "On Science Fiction.")

Charley buys old-style currency at a coin dealer's the next day and spends his idle hours searching for the third level, which, at the end of the story, he has not yet found. His friend Sam, however, disappears, and a letter from Sam turns up in Charley's grandfather's collection of first-day covers:

I've been here two weeks, and right now, down the street at the Dalys', someone is playing a piano, and they're all out on the front porch singing, "Seeing Nellie home." And I'm invited over for lemonade. Come on back, Charley and Louisa. Keep looking till you find the third level! It's worth it, believe me!

Charley discovers that Sam had bought $800 worth of old currency before disappearing: "That ought to set him up in a nice little hay, feed and grain business."

Inflation is, of course, one of the great symbols of the going-to-Hell of the modern world. When I fill my gas tank and grumble, "Jesus, I've bought *cars* for less than that," even though I remember full well what hourly wage I was making at that time, I am complaining, it seems to me, about the devaluation of a whole system of standards which I learned as a boy; I am complaining, in fact, about the uncomfortable business of having to adjust to change. The twice-as-long-as-now summer evenings of 1894, at least as seen from the perspective of fifty years later, would take a long, long time to change. Time passes slowly for the child. And supposing a child blessed with prosperous middle-class parents who can afford a piano and a front porch and whose tipple is lemonade, a child might well see the world as a sane and orderly place: a place, in fact, where

Charley's friend Sam would have to find a new line of work. (Sam was Charley's psychiatrist.)

"Of Missing Persons" is not a time travel story, but the echoes are so strong as to deserve attention. The narrator, another Charley, finds a travel bureau which, it has been hinted to him in a bar, offers more than the usual. Charley fits a mold, that of the typical time traveler, which we will begin to recognize as we go along:

I'm a young guy who works in a bank; a teller. I don't like the job; I don't make much money, and I never will. I've lived in New York for over three years and haven't many friends.... I see more movies than I want to, read too many books, and I'm sick of meals alone in restaurants. I have ordinary abilities, looks and thoughts. Does that suit you; do I qualify?

What he wants, he tells the travel agent, is escape.

From New York, I'd say. And cities in general. From worry. And fear. And the things I read in my newspapers. From loneliness.... From never doing what I really want to do or having much fun. From selling my days just to stay alive. From life itself—the way it is today, at least.... From the world.

Now, what Charley is seeking in the travel agency is precisely what believers used to anticipate in the afterlife, in Great Time. And it is what they looked backward to in Eden: a time when men did not work and women did not suffer the travail of childbirth—a time, in fact, when adults did not have to bear the burdens of adulthood.

What the travel agent offers Charley is just such an Eden, but it is apparently on another planet rather than back in time: it is "a whole land of unspoiled, unharmed forests, where every stream [runs] pure," but which nevertheless has electricity, washing machines, vacuum cleaners, and modern bathrooms and medicine. The technological infrastructure necessary for such conveniences is never seen. Everybody is very nice, and sometimes natives of Verna offer entry visas to natives of Earth. Charley backs out of the deal after paying for his ticket—it costs everything you have on you, reminiscent of the story of Jesus and the rich young man—and spends the rest of his life being sorry for it.

Certainly, the tale has a strong echo of the fairy story: in the most ordinary corner of New York, in a place most people would ignore, there is a gateway to Faerie, or Elfland, or Tolkien's Lothlorien—a Thomas-Rhymer place in which time passes differently—where all is well and one is released from the burdens of time and adulthood. But the deal offered Charley also recalls the Eden story: you have a chance, and it will involve total commitment, and you have only one chance. There is no second chance at Eden.

Here we come close to one possible reason for the rise of the notion of travel to the past in the nineteenth century: it was a century in which accepted chronologies, and with them accepted matters of religion, were crumbling. If the world were not a mere six thousand years old, if Adam and Eve had not lived in Eden in 4004 b.c., then perhaps nobody had ever *had* an Eden; if there was no Eden behind us, perhaps there was no Paradise in front of us; if the Creator had taken millions and millions of years to evolve the human race, then perhaps Jesus was not coming again soon. The old doctrine was cozy and comfortable in a short span of time, as the Ptolemaic universe was a comprehensible enclosed egg: In six days, we are told in Talmud, God created the world, on the seventh He rested. But a day of God is equal to a thousand years (Psalm 90:4). Hence the world will last for six thousand years of toil and labor; then will come one thousand years of Sabbath rest for the people of God in the kingdom of the Messiah.

The opening up of the great span of the past needed by the new sciences likewise opened up a great span of the future; and the attempt of William Miller to close that span in 1843 and again in 1844, and the enthusiasm of his followers, can be seen as an attempt to shut human consciousness off from that vast and frightening expanse of future time.

As all the world knows, the relationship between Mark Twain and the Deity deteriorated as time passed; beginning in conventional unthinking respectable Presbyterianism, he seems to have thoroughly unchurched himself in the west; and, as Justin Kaplan says in *Mr. Clemens and Mark Twain* (IV), he seems to have got religion for just a bit in order to get Olivia and respectability. "I believe in you, even as I believe in the Savior," he wrote her in fine Twainish ambiguity. After his marriage he backslid in fine fashion for the rest of his life, ending with the perception that the most reprehensible human was morally superior to the God of the Bible.

If there is no Eden in the future, then it must be in the past; and everybody's Eden tends to be in his own childhood, or a time which echoes his delusions about his own childhood. Malory himself has the same sorts of delusions about sexuality past that many a child has about his parents:

Right so fareth love nowadays, soon hot soon cold: this is no stability. But the old love was not so; men and women could love together seven years, and no licours lusts were between them, and then was love, truth, and faithfulness: and lo, in likewise was used love in King Arthur's days. (XVIII, 25)

Twain, in spite of his professed affection for "Old Malory," and in spite of flirtations with the memories of his own childhood in *Tom Sawyer*, was too much the realist, as noted above, to buy nostalgia as a substitute for Heaven. Bradbury and Finney are not.

One reason, then, for the emergence of travel to the past as a major theme in the late nineteenth and twentieth centuries: *as Eden disappears from the historical past, and the millennium (and Heaven) from the future, then travel to the past appears to fill the psychic void.* Past time may be no substitute for Great Time, but it is better than no escape at all: because, as we have noted, for many people the future looked even worse.

Finney dramatizes the point in "Such Interesting Neighbors," in which, a century or so in the future, things have gone to pot to such an extent that the 1950s seem Edenic by contrast:

Everyone working twelve, fourteen hours a day, with the major part of a man's income going for taxes, and the rest going for consumers' goods priced sky-high because of war production. Artificial scarcities... and hanging over everything, killing what little joy in life is left, is the virtual certainty of death and destruction.

When travel to the past is invented, it hits like television in the 1950s, and everybody starts taking vacations in the past. They they stop going back. In two months, the world is emptied. "And that, my friends, is how the world ends. On the edge of a precipice, with one foot over the edge, it stops, turns, and goes back, leaving an empty earth of birds and insects, wind, rain and rusting weapons." That is the well-known post-holocaust scene without benefit of holocaust; the human race has no future. It has ducked back into the past and pulled the covers up over its face.

The history of nostalgia over the past two centuries would seem to indicate either that things have, indeed, been getting worse, or that, just as likely, nostalgia is singularly ahistorical and undiscriminating: In Twain's time, folk were nostalgic for the Middle Ages; in our time, Bradbury and Finney are nostalgic for Twain's time; and in Finney's future, folk are nostalgic for our time.

Upon occasion, Finney's nostalgia becomes so strong as to endow the past with a power to preserve itself in the present. In "I Love Galesburg in the Springtime," the same Galesburg, Illinois, to which Charley wished to return in "The Third Level" begins to defend itself against polluters: would-be factory builders get run down by ghostly streetcars, and he who would cut down Galesburg's elm trees is subject to be run down by a 1916 Buick. Treasured old buildings which catch on fire in the middle of the night get saved by horse-drawn fire engines.

Similarly, in "I'm Scared," things from the past appear in the present and things from the future likewise. The narrator's explanation is the psychic power of nostalgia:

Haven't you noticed... on the part of nearly everyone... a growing rebellion against the *present*? And an increasing longing for the past? I have. Never before in all my long life have I heard so many people wish that they lived "at the turn of the century," or "when life was simpler,"or "worth living," or "when you could bring children into the world and count on the future," or simply "in the good old days." People didn't talk that way when I was young! The present was a glorious time! But they talk that way now.

In the presence of the everyday and often frustrating present, the laundered and edited past takes on awesome power.

Second dictum, then, about the popularity of travel to the past: *as belief in progress fades, the future is not only vast but distasteful; and the impulse to avoid it draws the consciousness to the past.*

(Seen from this point of view, science fiction—even space opera—set in the future is not the real escapism; belief in a future, and particularly in future progress, is belief in the present and in the importance of present action as contributory to that progress. Rejection of the future is rejection of the present, and that is true escapism.)

We have already noted that trees and buildings in Galesburg seem to have powers to bring back the past. In ''Second Chance,'' an automobile, a 1923 Jordan Playboy, has similar time-binding powers, just as in ''Where the Cluetts Are,'' the building of a house to 1880s plans and specifications brings the 1880s into the present for the inhabitants of the house.

As we have noted before, the temptation to monkey with the past is like the temptation of three wishes; and the prevailing folk wisdom is that taking the genie's offer of three wishes is just asking for trouble. But in many of Finney's stories, the decision to change the past is taken casually, almost offhandedly, as if the changer were possessed of godlike insight and self-confidence. One of the problems we have with the Yankee is that he operates with the same hubris, both in his behavior toward the sixth century and his unself-conscious threatening of everything between the sixth century and the nineteenth.

In Finney's ''Second Chance,'' the narrator and the author blithely assume that the prevention of a wreck and two deaths in the past is an unmixed good, as the foolish narrator in Hale's ''Hands Off'' assumes the saving of Joseph from the slavers would be. Similarly, in ''The Face in the Photo,'' the narrator, the inventor of a time machine, sends escaping criminals (into whose identity he has not cared to inquire too closely) back into the past; and when a police officer devises a way to punish them in that past and will not heed the narrator's pleas for mercy, the narrator sends him back to become a cop in San Francisco, 1893, with never a qualm nor a thought that he may be endangering his own present.

In Finney's most important and complex piece of fiction, however, he does rather better at tackling moral issues; and he does considerably better at documenting the real ugliness of the past which he nevertheless longs for. In *Time and Again* Finney has written the best-achieved novel of our century about nostalgic travel to the past.

It is clear, from Finney's introduction to *Forgotten News*, that he shares both the nostalgia for the 1890's and the aversion to the mid-twentieth century which characterize the narrator of *Time and Again*, Si Morley:

Some several years ago I was thinking of writing a novel—which I did, eventually, calling it *Time and Again*—whose central character would somehow be able to do what I've always wanted to do: visit the nineteenth century. Physically, literally, go back in time to a New York of the last century, and walk around seeing the sights.... in the century before the world went bad.

In *Time and Again*, Si Morley is fascinated by the 1880s Bad Guy, Jake Pickering, because

Jake is such a *villain*! It's the first time I've ever even used the word, but it's what he is, all right. Complete. In everything he does. He's a complete man of his times, and I guess I'm also smiling because in spite of everything I like him. (380)

Si's creator shares his enthusiasm: in the story of the murder of Harvey Burdell in *Forgotten News*, he is delighted with the characters, "as strange a lot, as malevolent, eccentric and amusing, as any I could ever hope to come across," and in another story he finds "the kind of powerful personality peculiar, it seems to me, to the nineteenth century... a wonderful varied time."

The past, particularly the late nineteenth century, is *realer* for both Finney and Morley than the present. Morley says of the people on the streets

Today's faces are different: they are much more alike and much less alive.... There was... an *excitement* in the streets of New York in 1882 that is gone.... They were... interested in their *surroundings*.... They carried with them a sense of purpose.... They weren't *bored*, for God's sake! Just looking at them, I'm convinced that these men moved through their lives in unquestioned certainty that there was a reason for being. And that's something worth having, and losing it is to lose something vital. (218–19)

In *Forgotten News*, Finney says likewise:

I believe their faces are also different from ours; that you can see this when you study the old photographs. Faces different because the people are different.... Even greater than the differences in what they know are the differences in the way they see the world and in the ideas that move them; their faces are formed by their own times.... (102)

Time and Again is filled with such pictures, drawings and photographs not only of the people of the 1880s but of their surroundings; and the reader is obviously expected to share the delight of the author and his narrator in the seeing.

Finney's narrator, Si Morley, is, like so many of Finney's characters mentioned above, an ordinary sort of fellow. So, typically, are time travelers in general. We can have a stab at defining the typical time traveler:

1. He is male and young-middle-aged to middle-aged: old enough to have grown bored with the present and disillusioned with his prospects, but not old enough to have become reconciled to them. (Morley, a bit on the young side, is twenty-eight.)
2. He is unmarried or estranged from his wife; he has no children to anchor him in the present. (Si is divorced—from a woman of whom, significantly, we hear very little—and has an appropriate sort of romance going with an antique-shop owner, a relationship of which clearly nothing permanent will come.)

3. He has found neither monetary reward for his talents, nor the opportunity for heroism, nor sexual fulfillment, in the present. (Si is bored to tears working as an artist in an advertising agency; he hated the army; and he gazes wistfully at the girls on Fifth Avenue, thinking what a shame it is that he will never know or speak to most of them.)

4. He has "the eye of an artist," as Ruben Prien says. (Prien is the government man who enlists Si, and his description of how Si was chosen is a useful though not exhaustive characterization of the potential time traveler.) Obviously, to take advantage of time travel, even an "ignoramus" like the Yankee must be able to pick out the colorful and describe it for the reader. (Si, as we have said, is an artist in an age which puts its artists to work designing soap wrappers.)

5. On the other hand, he is not terribly imaginative or sensitive; if he were too fine-spun, either he would have hideous doubts about his sanity upon arriving in the past, or the psychic shock *would* drive him out of his head. (Si passes a test designed to test his confidence in his own perceptions: "inner-directed," says Rossof the psychologist with satisfaction.)

6. He is an only child and an orphan with no close friends. (All true of Si. Never specified, incidentally, in the case of the Connecticut Yankee, who is attached to the present, apparently, only by a sentimental relationship with the much younger Puss Flanagan. Most later time travelers begin as isolates in their own time. Finney has Morley explain that such is the common lot of twentieth-century humans: "Like most everyone else's I knew about, [my life] had a big gaping hole in it, an enormous emptiness, and I didn't know how to fill it or even know what belonged there."

7. He is threatened by the future, either because of the way things seem to be going or because of the unpredictability of the future. (Si gets a scarf over his eyes driving down the road, and his reaction has strong symbolic overtones: "You don't know *what* to do; whether to hang onto the wheel trying to steer from memory, braking as fast as you can without skidding off the road; or whether to let go and try to snatch off the scarf before piling up" (21). Pirandello makes the same point in *Henry IV*: supposedly mad Henry, living in a fantasy life eight centuries before his time, knows full well what he is doing:

And to think that at a distance of eight centuries from this remote age of ours... the men of the twentieth century are torturing themselves in ceaseless anxiety to know how their fates and fortunes will work out! Whereas you are already in history with me.... And sad as is my lot, hideous as some of the events are... still all history... that cannot change, understand? All fixed for ever! (II,195)

8. Ordinarily, he does not have a specialist's knowledge of the period he is about to visit. That would make the game too easy. (It might also take some of the veneer off the nostalgia.) If his role is to be that of an imperialist, he often has, however, some specialized technical knowledge which will stand him in good stead: like the Yankee, he is a skilled mechanic, or like the traveler in Dean McLaughlin's "Hawk Among the Sparrows," a fighter pilot, or like Anderson's traveler in "The Man Who Came Early," a soldier. If, on the other hand, he is to be mainly that of a student, he is often an artist like Finney's Si Morley, an architect like the traveler in Anderson's *Dancer from Atlantis*, or a professor like the traveler in Le Guin's "April in Paris." (Si has an amateur's interest in the period, fueled by his antiquarian girlfriend, but no more than that.)

So much for the traveler before his departure. All travelers do not, of course, fit this description to perfection: some are children, some are youths, and some seem perfectly happy with their home times. But as we move through the literature we shall note how many times how much of this description fits, much as Joseph Campbell did in his explorations of the myth-hero. Though the Monomyth of Travel to the Past varies widely in the plots of its various avatars, the heroes of that monomyth have an extraordinary and suggestive consistency.

In *Time and Again*, Finney's affirmations of the validity of nostalgia come as no surprise; but it is not the easy vindication of "The Third Level." Morley turns a hard eye on political corruption, child abuse, police brutality, poverty, smallpox, and many other shortcomings of New York in the 1880s. Racism, sexism, and the plight of underdeveloped nations Si largely ignores: that the "wonderfully variegated" world still contains veiled Turkish women and Zulus who "were still happy cannibals" he can observe with satisfaction as aspects of an "unbulldozed, unpaved, unpolluted world" (208). Note the uncritical sentimentality of this last phrase, a sentimentality shared, on the evidence, by the author. Anyone who has ever moved a large amount of dirt with a shovel can testify to the blessings of the bulldozer; anyone who has ever walked an unpaved road in mud-time can appreciate pavement; and to regard the nineteenth-century urban environment as unpolluted is to ignore horse droppings, flies, and the soot of thousands of coal fires. It is fashionable to regard the twentieth century with nausea: but nausea, like its cousin nostalgia, is a bourgeois luxury. We know that Orwell is only playing at being down and out in Paris and London when he discards a glass of milk because a fly has dropped into it. When Finney feels nostalgia for the past, his narrator does not envision himself a beggar, a homeless waif, or a house servant: he is a comfortable bourgeois, who sees the bulldozer not as the end of inhuman human labor, but only—and equally truly— as a spoiler of the beauties of nature and a symbol of the end of a picturesque human heterogeneity. But it must be remembered that the great sentimentalizers of nature are not those who wrestle with it, but the prosperous urbanites, beginning in the eighteenth century, who can view it from a safe distance or play at it in disinfected fashion in the gardens of Versailles. It was Asimov, ever the realist, who in "The Good Old Days" disclaimed any nostalgia for "the days when one could get good cheap servants," for, he said, odds-on, he would have been one of the servants.

The project which sends Si back to the 1880s is government-sponsored, and he is at one point scheduled to try for the Dakota Apartments in Manhattan in 1894; he insists, however, on 1882, because he wants to watch the mailing of a letter, a mysterious and enigmatic letter which is said, in a note added later, to have caused "the Destruction by Fire of the entire World" (72). And here is another motive for the traveler, related to that of the nostalgic: *the desire to find out what really happened—the motivation of the scholar*. We shall treat of this in more detail when we get to "April in Paris."

Note also *the Destruction by Fire of the entire World*, an apocalyptic notion indeed; David Ketterer has noted the apocalyptic nature of much of science fiction, and has particularly cited the example of the Battle of the Sand-Belt in the *Yankee*, which results in the destruction of a whole society by electricity and gunpowder. Ironically, though Si Morley will be present at "the Destruction of the entire World," the "World" in the scrawled note turns out to be the old *New York World* building, burned in "the Great Fire of Park Row," an historical event, on January 31, 1882. More importantly, it will be Si who will destroy a whole future.

The method by which Si gets back into 1882 is treated in great detail by Finney, first, one supposes, because of the need for credibility, a need which here is satisfied by detail of process rather than by intrinsic scientific plausibility, and second, because the method itself appeals: it is systematic nostalgia, nostalgia given scientific or pseudo-scientific rationale. Rejecting a high-tech present, Si can move into the past without benefit of time machines developed in that present. Si moves into the Dakota, a building still (at this writing) facing Central Park in the west seventies. His food is delivered by the boy from Fishborn's market, and it is organically grown and packaged as it would have been in 1882; he receives it dressed in 1882 clothing, and pays with 1882 currency. He reads the paper, a newly printed *Evening Sun* for the date in 1882, and the "current" *Leslie's*. And eventually he walks out of the building into 1882.

He loves it. On his third visit, he rents a room from a lady who is skeptical about his lack of local references; he successfully jokes his way into her good graces by confessing that he is "an escaped convict, an active counterfeiter, and occasional murderer," (148) all of which is, in a sense, true. He *has* escaped from his own time, in which he found himself a prisoner, he *is* counterfeiting his identity in the past, and he *will* cause a friend of his in the twentieth century never to be born—murder of a sort.

A fellow-boarder, Jake Pickering, older and obese, "a fine figure of a man," is in love with Julia, daughter of the house; of course, Si likewise falls in love with her. They discover that the letter in question relates to blackmail, and that the attempt at blackmail causes the death of the blackmail victim and the burning of the old *World* building. They tangle with a corrupt police inspector, and to save their lives, Si brings both of them back to the twentieth century.

Finney knows the tradition and the literature, and knows full well that the native of the past, brought into the present, is supposed to be knocked over by the technology of our time. He has fun thwarting expectations based on his readers' knowledge of that tradition. Julia easily accepts airplanes, "auto mobiles," and electric lights as logical extrapolations from her own time; she has read about some of those things in Jules Verne. Though she is impressed by television and by men on the moon, what really impresses her the most, and that not favorably, is the change in women's fashions and the unprintable words one can find in print in 1970.

Si does not want to keep her there, and she does not really want to stay. The last good times to be alive, Si thinks, were in Julia's home time; the world of his own time is ghastly:

Julia, we're a people who pollute the very air we breathe. And our rivers. We're destroying the Great Lakes.... We've made bombs that can wipe out humanity in minutes.... In Asia we burned people alive, we really did.... (378)

They go back to 1882 and stay there.

The question of altering the present by acting in the past has been brought up before this point in the book; indeed, such alteration is at the heart of governmental interest in time travel. Some members of the project think that nothing one does in the past can affect the present, or that it can affect it only minimally—the "twig-in-the-river" theory—but Dr. Danziger, the scientist at the heart of the project, digs in his heels, fearing that the potential damage can be enormous. This is not the first or the last time that time travel projects in the literature echo the atomic experiments of our own time; as H. Bruce Franklin points out in *War Stars* (174), William Tenn's 1948 "Brooklyn Project" is one in which America's leaders

try to outdo the Manhattan Project by bending time itself into the ultimate weapon that "our democratic hands" can manipulate; unaware that they are thus transforming the entire course of the planet's evolution, they metamorphose into fanatical amoebalike blobs while insisting "Nothing has changed!"

The government man overrules Morley's objections to the proposed tampering with time "Because you don't turn back. Not ever.... Risk? Yes... certainly. But who did that ever stop?" Nobody there, of course, sees the irony in *you don't turn back*; turning back into the past is exactly what they are preparing to do. They decide that Si must destroy Pickering's life, in order to prevent his becoming an advisor to President Cleveland; that act should, they think, make Cuba into an American possession in the 1890s. "My God," says one, "to correct mistakes of the past which have adversely affected the present for us—what an incredible opportunity." Translated: to avoid taking responsibility for past actions—what an incredible temptation for any government, or any child.

Can Si destroy a man's life? he asks them. "The man's long dead," they tell him. But he won't be when *I* face him, Si notes; Si, unlike the government men, is no temporal imperialist, for whom all out-timers (like all natives for spatial imperialists) are Not Quite Human. "I just don't think *anyone* has the godlike wisdom," he says, "to actually rearrange the present by altering the past." If you don't, they tell him, they will send someone else to do it. He agrees, not to kill Jake, but to ruin his career; but on his return, he instead contrives to prevent the meeting of Danziger's parents. Thus he has caused the project to evaporate in his future; thus he is stuck in 1882. He does not wink out of existence as a causeless effect; but the innocent Danziger, who has pleaded with Si to stop "them," is gone.

He has accepted, then, the godlike responsibility which he is unwilling to concede to his own government; and character, writer, and reader are persuaded that his decision was necessary, and that he will live happily ever after in the past.

Clifford Simak

Born in 1904, a writer since 1931, a Grand Master Nebula Award holder since 1976, Clifford D. Simak was, until his death in 1988, the dean of SF; and he is every bit as much a nostalgic as Bradbury and Finney.

Though it is important, nostalgia is not at the center of his best-known time travel novel, *Time and Again*, with which he beat Finney to the title by nineteen years. The book has a complicated and interesting time scheme: it begins in 7991 or 7992, to which year travelers from still farther in the future arrive. In an echo of Williamson's *Legion of Time*, some come to prevent one Asher Sutton from writing a book; others come to ensure that the book gets written. Sutton gets a copy of the book from the future, apparently by accident; like many another SF invention, book, idea, and person, Sutton's book becomes an effect without a cause.

In his family papers, Asher Sutton finds a letter written in the past by an ancestor in 1987 in Bridgeport, Wisconsin; and in Sutton's reflections on the writer of that letter, the familiar note of nostalgia is sounded, not without ironic humor:

John H. Sutton, an ancestor six thousand years removed.... He was a man who... saw the sunrise against the green Wisconsin hills... if Wisconsin has any hills, wherever it may be. He felt the heat of summer... went fishing in the river...[and] would have lived closer to the Earth.... Earth would have been a living place instead of a governing place where not a thing is grown for its economic worth, not a wheel is turned for economic purpose. He could have chosen his lifework from the whole broad field of human endeavor.... (71–72)

We have seen before the notion that the future may feel nostalgia for our time, just as we feel nostalgia for Twain's time, and his time felt nostalgia for Arthur's time; either nostalgia is an unreasoning disease of all humankind, we must conclude, or, more likely, our authors see things getting ever worse and worse and worse.

The ancestor relates in his letter than ten years before he met a man whom he believes to have been a traveler from the future; that the man left behind a wonderful wrench (with bloodstains on it), a wrench which could not be duplicated in 1977; and that some time later a wanderer took employment on his farm, apparently so that he could write a book in his spare time. Harassed by temporal imperialists from the future and the present, Sutton travels back to the twentieth century to become that very traveler; and he does it with mental concentration very like that of Finney's Si Morley. Once again the motive of the student appears, only this time it is not the motive of one who would see what truly happened, but that of one who would recapture the wisdom of the past:

Man was in a hurry and he went too far, too fast. So far and fast that he missed many things... things that he should have taken time to learn as he went along... things that someday in some future age he would take time to study. Someday Man would come back along the trail again and learn the things he'd missed and wonder why he missed them and think upon the years that were lost for never knowing them. (172)

The man with the wrench was another temporal imperialist, this time from 8386, and the blood was Asher Sutton's; recovered from the assault, Sutton, of course, becomes the hired man who is writing a book. He *must*; because, in Simak's system, that which is on record is unalterable. Some small alterations in the past can be made—otherwise temporal imperialism would be pointless—but "by and large it stands."

But Asher Sutton also *likes* being a hired hand on a Wisconsin farm in 1977: "here were peace and security and a living close to nature that no man of his own age ever had experienced" (203). He stays until his ancestor can use his typewriter to write the note to him—ten years—and returns to confront another imperialist, who would replace the destiny of which Sutton has been writing with a manifest destiny for an imperialist human race directed by a giant corporation.

Asher, however, believing that the future belongs to the androids and robots as well as to the human race, gives the underground the weapons to defeat the imperialists and retires to a bucolic planet—the nearest he can get to twentieth-century Wisconsin—a planet which has been homesteaded by an old family robot.

In twentieth-century Wisconsin, there has been a brief encounter with an otherwise unexplained old wise man, a man who seems to have some knowledge of Asher's mission. The man gives his name as "Old Cliff," and is obviously Simak himself. "You ought to read Thoreau," he says to Asher. "He had the right idea, Thoreau did."

Simak likes Wisconsin. He was born there, and he went to university there, even though his profession, journalism, took him to Minnesota. Wisconsin is not only the source of virtue in *Time and Again* but, in "Project Mastodon," a place peculiarly favored by time and therefore a most desirable place for time travel:

The southwestern corner of Wisconsin... was missed by all the glaciations. Why, we do not know. Whatever the reason, the glaciers came down on both sides of it and far to the south of it and left it standing there, a little island in a sea of ice. (263)

There is a revealing characterization of the scenes of one's childhood: a little island in a sea of ice.

Except for a time in the Triassic, that same area of Wisconsin has always been dry land. That and a few other spots are the only areas in North America which have not, time and time again, been covered by water. I don't think it necessary to point out the comfort it would be to an experimental traveler in time to be certain that, in almost any era he might hit, he'd have dry land beneath him. (263)

As we have seen in Pirandello's *Henry IV*, the past is the only place where you can put your feet down solidly. Simak keeps anchoring his temporal and spatial ventures in a plain, rural, countrified Wisconsin, as if ultimate security in a vast universe of space and time were to be found in one's own childhood scenes. (In this story, interestingly enough, those who would use the power to travel in time to ensure military superiority are the winners, with the apparent approval of the author.)

"Mastodonia" is the name the travelers propose in this story for their 15,000-year-ago country. It is also the name of a 1978 novel. Simak is never one to under-utilize a good thing. The hero of that novel, Asa Steele, fits our profile of the archetypal time traveler: he is a palaeontology professor on sabbatical in the town where he was a boy; supposed to be writing a book but not; planning to quit his job, maybe, after the year is up; divorced.

He is trying to dig up what he thinks is a long-ago crashed space ship, a task which he started as a boy; but his dog keeps bringing in fresh dinosaur bones. Once Bowser comes home speared with a Folsom point. And a lady from Asa's own past shows up unexpectedly and moves in with him. Nostalgia? Old dogs, children, and watermelon wine.

It is to Old Ezra (who reminds one of old Cliff), a philosophical hermit, "a bitter-ender of a died-out breed," that Catface, an immortal alien who crashed the space ship fifty thousand years back, first reveals himself. Later, the alien informs Asa and his lady friend Rila that he is a temporal engineer and can open gates anywhere in the past.

Asa has a somewhat stuffy childhood friend who has money and is anxious to make more, and who has the skills to get the whole business organized; Rila likewise is experienced in the business world. After a hunt in dinosaur-land (not without some worriment about affecting the present), they begin to plan a safari-cum-antiques operation and, for tax purposes, set up the foreign nation of Mastodonia in the past. Crowds of people want to become imperialists, to skim off the Inca gold or beat the crowds to the South Dakota gold rush; others want to be tourists (and, as in many another story, a favorite prospective destination is the Crucifixion: odd, I would think, to want to be in on the Death of God rather than His ministry or His resurrection).

Mastodonia lies about 150,000 years back, between the Illinoisian and Wisconsin glacial periods; the names of the epochs echo the home territories of

Finney and Simak. It is more attractive to merchandisers of safaris than the twentieth century, obviously, for business reasons; "up in the twentieth century, the hunting's gone." Besides, the air is better back in the Sangamon. There is a strange mixture here of nostalgic and profiteer.

It is proposed that the past might become a new frontier for the present, that the homeless and dispossessed might go there; Mastodonia, says Rila, is out. It has already been homesteaded. Once again we have the mixture of nostalgia for the frontier and a sharp eye for the main chance, of Si Morley and the Yankee.

As a business, it collapses. As a frontier, it works. The shortcomings of the present are remedied once again by the past.

In *Our Children's Children*, the future has become frightful. Hideous extra-terrestrial invaders have landed, apparently mindless killers who mutate on demand, obvious symbols of a future which changes so fast it is incomprehensible, a future which embodies greater and greater potential for destruction. Twentieth-century America, already suffering from overpopulation, is loaded with billions of refugees from the future; as if this is not enough, some of the invaders follow, the hideous future invading the present.

New roads are to be opened as soon as possible into the more distant past; and there is no shortage of twentieth-century volunteers to go along. As in *Mastodonia*, the objective of choice is the Miocene, the period in which grass, and therefore grazing animals, first appeared. Like the Eden story and the later Babel story, this choice seems to reflect a wish to return to a pre-sodbuster, pre-urban period in which the hunting-herding ecology prevailed.

Nostalgic time travelers wish to escape a present which has become distasteful; refugees *have* to escape a present which has become intolerable. The distinction is not always crystal-clear, any more than the line between emigrants and refugees has been in the mundane continuum. "Are you a political refugee," we are likely to ask, "or are you merely starving to death?" Similarly, the difference between the nostalgic, the anthropologist, the historian, and the tourist may admit of some debate; often it is a matter of declared intention and the credentials one can produce.

It seems clear, at any rate, that what the nostalgic finds in the past is mostly *virtue*: authenticity, strength, wisdom, heroism, and a sense of proportion. These are the adult virtues as seen by a child fortunate in his parents. The nostalgic is not generally attracted by money or prosperity; indeed, people of my generation have been known to mutter about the attractive qualities of the Great Depression. In spite of his devotion to his own century and its values, Hank Morgan sometimes sees the virtues of Arthur and his court, just as, in spite of his cynicism about Scotian nostalgia, does Twain.

Chapter 4

CHILDREN OF THE YANKEE: THE INNOCENTS ABROAD

The future lies before us.

—Warren G. Harding

It is said that in the American Southwest there lives a tribe of people who insist, logically enough, that the future lies in *back* of us, where we cannot see it, and that the past is *before* us, where it is visible, and that the future flows around the stationary observer and becomes the past.

At first glance, it seems an absurd idea. A moment's thought convinces one of its reasonableness; it may take a few moments more for it to become obvious that both this image and our more customary images are equally absurd—as absurd as those of Heraclitus, St. Augustine, and John D. MacDonald. Time is *not* a river flowing in any particular direction; still less is the future out there in front of us (westerly, as I sit at my keyboard), or behind us, or to the right hand or the left, or over our heads or beneath our feet.

Even after we become conscious of these facts, it is difficult, almost impossible, to describe time and its passage in other than spatial terms. In science fiction, things are likewise: we may move *up the line* with Robert Silverberg, or *downtime* with Jack Chalker, or *sidewise in time* with Murray Leinster, but whichever way we go, we always seem to see ourselves moving spatially in one direction or another.

That time, space, and motion are all woven into the same fabric is a truism of modern physics; it is also important to note that, up until recently, most people told time in terms of space and movement: "when the sun is over the oak tree," or "when the sun goes down," or "when the big hand gets to nine and the little hand has almost got to three." With the advent of the digital timepiece, a whole generation of children is using *pattern change* rather than *movement in space* as a measurement of time, and that change may generate some interesting new perceptions of time, although both children, on and off—"when it gets dark" and "when I get hungry"—and physicists—"as entropy increases"—have used pattern change for quite a while.

If space can be used to express time, so can time be used to express space, as Mark Twain notes in *Innocents Abroad*:

All distances in the East are measured by hours, not miles. . . . In Constantinople you ask, "How far is it to the Consulate?" and they answer, "About ten minutes." How far is it to the Lloyds' Agency?" "Quarter of an hour." "How far is it to the lower bridge?" "Four minutes." I cannot be positive about it, but I think that there, when a man orders a pair of pantaloons, he says he wants them a quarter of a minute in the legs and nine seconds around the waist. (L)

The process is a bit like measuring interstellar distances in terms of light-years. Seeing space in terms of time is simply the other side of seeing time in terms of space.

THE AMERICAN VIEW OF TIME AS EMBODIED IN PLACE

But the American, I would submit, *is unique in his perception of time past or time future as embodied in geographical location*, and that fact helps to account for the American genesis of travel to the past as more than passive observer. For the American, the past and the future are places to which one may go; in the Old World, the past and the present are inextricably woven into the present. St.-Denis, in which kings of France were buried for centuries, sits in the middle of an industrial suburb of Paris.

Consider: of the American population, only Native Americans are sitting anywhere near the territory which their ancestors occupied five centuries ago; and most of *them* have been involuntarily removed from their ancestral lands, so that the attitudes, say, of contemporary western Cherokees toward north Georgia may well resemble those of Alex Haley toward his ancestral village. And so nearly all Native Americans, Euroamericans, African Americans, and Asian Americans are descended from people who came from somewhere else. And that Somewhere Else is for them, in general, their symbol for the past. Most of us, Euroamericans or otherwise, have been more or less Europeanized by our language and education; and so, for Americans, notably, the past is Europe.

But the past is not only Over the Water; it is also, because of patterns of migration and industrialization, localized in our own country. As soon as the West ceased to be a hellish forest from which red-skinned demons could erupt, it became, for Boone and his successors, the future; and it stayed that way until the closing of the frontier. One might hypothesize that a similar pattern of thought, in reverse direction, did not develop in Russia (as my Russian friends tell me it did not) because the vision of the East as frontier-future was compromised by the inhospitable nature of the land and its use of the land for purposes of political exile; and in South America, since the Spanish tended to colonize from the west, the Portuguese from the east, the future never got to lie in any particular direction. For many a contemporary North American westerner, however, as a result of historical movement, the East continues to be the past; for probably rather fewer easterners, the West is the future.

Furthermore, the North was industrialized before the predominantly agricultural South, wherefore many folk saw the Civil War as a combat between the past and the future, whatever value they placed on those directions out of the present. By extraordinary coincidence, Mark Twain was born at almost dead center of the Republic, moved in a north-south direction as a riverboat pilot, served briefly and unspectacularly in the Confederate forces, moved to the Wild West as a journalist, and eventually settled in the East as an adopted Connecticut Yankee.

Here, then, is the next way of accounting for the appearance of the *Yankee* theme when and where and with whom it surfaces: *Americans have a peculiar tendency to identify past, present, and future time with location; as one travels to the past in space, one can generate the idea of doing so in time, and Mark Twain was ideally situated, midway of two past-future geographic continua, to give utterance to such a concept.*

Sylvester Baxter, in his 1889 review of the *Yankee* in the Boston *Sunday Herald*, saw much of this clearly:

By resorting to the principle that "distribution in time" is paralleled by "distribution in space," we may solve many a problem. So there is a certain aspect of sober truth in this most fanciful tale and, just as the Connecticut Yankee went back into the days of King Arthur's court, so might he go out into the world today, into Central Asia or Africa, or even into certain spots in this United States of ours, find himself amidst social conditions very similar to those of 1300 years ago, and even work his astonishing 19th century miracles with like result. (Norton *Yankee*, 322)

THE CONNECTICUT YANKEE AS INNOCENT ABROAD

The American tourist in Europe, then, is a pilgrim to the past. One would therefore expect the American attitude toward the past to be similar to the American attitude toward Europe. Our position *vis-à-vis* the Old Country (and toward the East, the South, and the countryside) is contradictory and ambiguous. On the one hand, the Old Country is the motherland, and as such deserves our sentimental respect; on the other hand, our ancestors left the Old Country, usually under some degree of political, economic, or religious pressure, and presumably they were right in so doing. Either they were forced out because they were losers in a dispute, or holders of unpopular opinions, or unsuccessful in the local economic game, or they were transported for crimes against established order; on either count, the mother- or fatherland would deserve our quiet feelings of superiority, if not our active contempt.

You will have recognized that the peculiar mixture of feelings we have just described is very like the mingling of emotions we have regarding our own parents, who are, after all, our own pasts. One might expect these feelings to be particularly acute in the Victorian era, during which affection for parents was expected as a *sine qua non* of respectability, and during which emotional distance between parents and children was likewise expected. The ambiguous feelings about Europe, on the part of an America which was becoming adult, and about parents, would be still further echoed in the ambiguous feelings—already noted— of nineteenth-century folk about the past and the future of their century, and about the question of whether the past was to be respected or scorned.

Freud, a product of that era, was still to give all this matter a voice; but we can now see still another reason for the appearance of travel to the past at this time and in this place: *America is to Europe as child is to parent, and as the present is to the past: both these relationships were in a condition of peculiar strain at the end of the nineteenth century, and therefore both attraction and repulsion were at a high level.* The psychological component of this equation we shall deal with later, when we speak of the Oedipal qualities of the traveler to the past; let us for the moment speak of America and Europe simply as source of tourists and destination of tourists.

Mark Twain's first major book, *The Innocents Abroad*, appeared in 1869, just twenty years before the *Yankee*. In it we see American tourists as naïve admirers, as debunkers, as hostile critics, as vulgar chauvinists, and as vandals. One does not have to read very far into the *Connecticut Yankee* before one has seen Hank Morgan in all these roles.

For if the American tourist is, in a sense, a time traveler, then the time traveler is at least partly a tourist; and it should not surprise us to find many parallels between *The Innocents Abroad* and *A Connecticut Yankee*. One story appears in both, with really only minor changes: Twain, like Hank Morgan himself, had no hesitation about repeating a good "effect." The Blucher episode in the Azores (*Innocents* V), which shows the American tourist's amazement at the paltry buying power of foreign currency, as well as the power of the Yankee dollar, is closely paralleled by the 32nd chapter of the *Yankee*, in which Morgan pays for a dinner party with all the vulgarity of a rich tourist enjoying a favorable exchange rate.

Bear with me while I list other parallels between the books: difficulties with the language of the natives (*Innocents* XIX; *Yankee* XI); foreigners as belonging to the past and therefore not quite real (*Innocents* VI, XVIII; *Yankee passim*); evocation of the past through ancient sites (throughout both books); time travelers in both, Hank Morgan in the *Yankee* and, in the *Innocents*, the Wandering Jew, "that old tourist," and the Seven Sleepers (LIV, LV); the organized church as a negative force in history (*Innocents* XXV, L, LIII; *Yankee* XXII, XLI) in spite of the saintly valor of individual churchfolk (*Innocents* LV; *Yankee* XXXV); the uses of prophecy (*Innocents* XXXVIII; *Yankee* VIII, XXIV, XXXIII); the "tiny kingdoms" of old as contrasted with the vastness of the New World (*Innocents*

XLIV, LI; *Yankee* XL); old jokes presented as new in out-of-the-way places and times (*Notebooks* I, 359; *Yankee* IV); the past as morally, technically, aesthetically inferior to the present (*Innocents* XIV, XXI, XXII, XXIX; *Yankee* throughout); the past as superior to the present (*Innocents* XXXIII, XLIII, LVI; *Yankee* I, XII); the past as just about the same as the present (*Innocents* XXVI, XLII; *Yankee* XVI, XXXIII, and *Notebooks* I, 424–25); and the traveler as god-figure (*Innocents* XLV; *Yankee* VIII).

It should be further noted that, in the *Innocents*, geography, as geography books and tourist guides teach it, is the bunk (XV, XVII, XXI, XXXI, XLVIII, L), just as in the *Yankee*, history—as the books teach it—is the bunk (XVI). Twain, however, is nothing if not self-contradictory; the same Innocent Abroad who makes fun of the supposedly enchanted sword which supposedly had belonged to Godfrey of Bouillon (LIII) comes back home—to the extent that one can identify Twain with his narrator—with a supposed relic of the same man, which he apparently either accepts with a tourist's creduilty or cynically foists off on his lodge brothers:

This Mallet is of Cedar cut in the Forest of Lebanon, whence Solomon obtained the Timbers for the Temple. The handle was cut by Bro. Clemens himself from a cedar planted just outside the walls of Jerusalem by Bro. Godfrey De Bouillon, the first Christian Conqueror of that City, 19th of July 1099. (*Notebooks* I, 422n)

So reads the inscription on a gavel presented to the Worshipful Master of Twain's mother lodge. (This Godfrey of Bouillion is the same man who, according to Paul Grosser and Edwin Halperin, after taking Jerusalem and massacring the Muslims, "drove the Jews, Rabbanites and Karaites into a synagogue and burned it and all inside" (105), an act worthy of the Yankee at the end of his career.) What Twain thought of de Bouillon and his supposed relics is doubtful; but it all seems of a piece with the fact that in the *Yankee* he debunks a good deal of Arthuriana at the same time that he accepts, for the sake of the argument, a good deal of Malory as historical.

I take it that I need not whip this dead horse any longer; clearly Hank Morgan, the Connecticut Yankee, owes a good bit to "Mark Twain," the Innocent Abroad, and travel to the past is analogous to travel to the Old Country.

A visitor to a foreign land—or time—may reasonably be expected to go through the following stages:

1. Innocent amazement, willingness to believe almost anything, bafflement; corresponds to *childhood*.

2. Irritation, rejection, cynicism; corresponds to *adolescence*.

3. (Supposing the tourist to settle down in that place or time and become a permanent resident) Gradual acceptance of the values of his new society; corresponds to *adulthood*.

We may, I think, demonstrate this process working out in the *Yankee* by looking carefully at Morgan's reactions to the narrative of Malory.

If we take Malory's *Morte d'Arthur* to represent the past, which is also one's own childhood, and also the Europe of which most of us are children (or abused stepchildren or foster children), we can see that the changes in Morgan's reactions parallel the changes in attitude of the tourist we discussed a moment ago.

Twain first read Malory, it would appear, in 1884, and began work on the *Yankee* in 1886. He planned, he said (Norton *Yankee*, 296), to "leave unsmirched & unbelittled the great & beautiful *characters* drawn by the master hand of old Malory."

As Twain proceeded with work on the book, however, he seems to have discovered a number of warts on old Malory's characters; and just so does Hank Morgan, as he becomes progressively better acquainted with the universe of *Le Morte d'Arthur*.

Malory is quoted at length in five places in the *Yankee*:

1. a chapter read by Twain's narrator just before Hank appears to tell his tale (*Yankee*, "A Word of Explanation"; Malory, IV, 2);

2. a story told by Merlin at Arthur's court (*Yankee* II; Malory I, 25);

3. a report of a tournament written by a priest, a would-be columnist for Hank's newspaper (*Yankee* IX; Malory VII, 28);

4. the interminable and oft-interrupted narrative recited by Sandy as she and Hank go on quest (*Yankee* XV, XIX; Malory IV, 16–18); and

5. the report of King Arthur's death as printed in the *Camelot Weekly Hosannah and Literary Volcano* (*Yankee* XLIII; Malory XXI, 4).

Let us briefly look at them, and see how they are received.

Twain's narrator, "M. T.," meets Hank Morgan while on a tour of Warwick Castle; Morgan makes a few cryptic remarks and wanders away. That evening, in his inn chamber, M. T. listens to the rain on the window, hears the wind roar in the eaves, dreams "of the olden time" (a nostalgic who might have been included in our last chapter), and from time to time dips into "old Sir Thomas Malory's enchanting book" and feeds at "its rich feast of prodigies and adventures" and breathes in "the fragrance of its obsolete names." What he reads is straight Malory, less six short paragraphs.

The story, which has Launcelot killing two giants, freeing a castle, single-handedly defeating three knights who were about to kill Sir Kay, and finally getting up early in the morning, donning Sir Kay's armor, and leaving his own for Sir Kay, serves Twain's narrative purpose; it sets Sir Kay up as a paper tiger and makes his braggadocio after Morgan's capture just that much more ridiculous. It is probably less tedious than the average Malory chapter, and one can understand M. T.'s romantic delight in it; the "real" Camelot will serve as contrast in Morgan's narrative. Living in Camelot is less picturesque than reading about it; M. T. is like the stay-at-home who delights in reading over-inflated travel brochures.

The aged Morgan arrives, talks, and departs, leaving his journal in which, after a bit, he recounts how he was subjected to Merlin's recital of Arthur's receipt of Excalibur from the Lady of the Lake. Morgan has never heard the story before, but everyone else in Camelot has, and repeatedly:

The same suffering look that was in the page's face was observable in all the faces around—the look of dumb creatures who know that they must endure and make no moan.

"Marry, we shall have it again," sighed the boy; "that same old weary tale that he hath told a thousand times in the same words, and that he *will* tell until he dieth, every time he hath gotten his barrel full and feeleth his exaggeration-mill a-working. Would God I had died or I saw this day. . . . Perdition singe him for the weariness he worketh with his one tale. . . . Maledictions light upon him, misfortune be his dole!

Merlin tells his tale in a soft drone, and directly everyone except Morgan goes to sleep; soft snores echo around the room, and a rat comes out and sits on the king's head and nibbles a bit of cheese. "It was a tranquil scene," the Yankee reports, "and restful to the weary eye and the jaded spirit."

The tale, one complete chapter of Malory, gets this critical reaction from Hank: "It seemed to me that this quaint lie was most simply and beautifully told; but then I had heard it only once, and that makes a difference; it was pleasant to the others when it was fresh, no doubt."

A bit later on, risen to might and power, Hank commissions a priest to write up the story of a tournament in preparation for the later founding of a newspaper. Thus Hank becomes a cause of part of Malory's prose; this business of the traveler causing something in the past which is "already" a matter of record becomes a widespread game later on in the literature, but Twain does not call any particular attention to it; it is almost as if he did not notice what he was doing. The result of Hank's commission is a passage only slightly abridged from Malory, surely one of his most tedious chapters, a weary and interminable listing of combatants, collisions and brasted spears, as soporific to us as would be a baseball box score to Sir Thomas. But Hank says

Well, the priest did very well, considering. He got in all the details, and that is a good think in a local item. . . . And he had a good knack at getting in the complimentary thing here and there about a knight that was likely to advertise—no, I mean a knight that had had influence; and he also had a neat gift of exaggeration, for in his time he had kept door for a pious hermit who lived in a sty and worked miracles.

(The buncombe of Malory's supposed history, then, comes from the sixth-century equivalent of the press agent; and the hermit in the sty is but the first of a series of humans who will be identified with pigs.)

Of course, this novice's report lacked whoop and crash and lurid description, and therefore wanted the true ring; but its antique wording was quaint and sweet and simple, and full of the fragrances and flavors of the time, and these little merits made up in a measure for its more important lacks.

(Like Merlin, the priest has an exaggeration-mill; but it does not work at nineteenth-century levels. "Whoop and crash and lurid description" are ironically what gives a report a "true ring"; journalists and historians are no less liars in the nineteenth century than they were in the sixth.)

Here, then, are three Malory passages, each getting a positive reaction, each approving audience commenting on the quaintness and the romantic simplicity of the narrative. We can, however, observe some small changes in attitude toward Malory, more on the part of the author than on the part of his narrator. Twain is having fun with Hank's shortcomings; Hank is, after all, as Twain said to Dan Beard (Norton *Yankee*, 309), "a common, uneducated man . . . a perfect ignoramus . . . [with] neither the refinement nor the weakness of a college education." Hank does not, therefore, as any educated person would do, find Merlin's tale older and staler by 1300 years than do the courtiers of Camelot.

Twain here also allows Morgan to make an unconscious literary evaluation: a good story is one which stands up well under repeated reading or hearing, and Malory's story, at least as told by Merlin, does not. Hank's more or less positive reaction to Merlin's tale, then, conceals a negative judgment on the part of the author. Furthermore, part of the fun of the Yankee's reaction to his priest's news story is his elevation of the worst standards of small-town nineteenth-century journalism to the status of literary criticism. Twain, then, is beginning to make a distance between author and narrator and is beginning to cast some doubt on Morgan's positive reactions to Malory's prose; but positive those reactions remain, mainly because of what Hank and M. T. see as Malory's quaint, sweet, simple beauty.

See how like the Innocent Abroad this is; part of the time, to be sure, Twain's tourist is a skeptic, but mostly he is so admiring of the New Old World that we, and Twain, see him as perceiving the past, as memorialized and monumentalized in Europe and the Near East, with an admiration which the reader is meant to see as sapheaded and simpleminded.

"Quaint and sweet and simple" would also do as a description of Eden, and of our own childhoods. The Yankee's uncritical admiration of Malory is much of a piece with the child's uncritical acceptance of the adult world which surrounds him. It may lack the "whoop and crash" of childhood, but the characters are larger than life—indeed, they are giants—and, to a child, adult life looks simpler than childhood. (As does childhood to the adult; doubtless both are wrong.) In all three passages of Malory we have discussed, then, in spite of any minor ironies committed by the author, the reader of Malory is a child, a newly arrived tourist—uncritical, admiring, somewhat overwhelmed: an Innocent Abroad.

Read Hank Morgan's early reactions to Camelot as a whole, and you find much the same pattern; he complains, of course, about the lack of tobacco and chromos and new jokes, but in general (ironically enough, considering his own childlike posture) he sees the folk of the past as charming children. Of a tournament, he says,

It was a most gaudy and gorgeous crowd, as to costumery, and very characteristic of the country and the time, in the way of high animal spirits, innocent indecencies of language, and happy-hearted indifference of morals. . . . They had a most noble good time. (IX)

That last line is pure Tom Sawyer; where we are, is childhood. But the preceding sentence sounds like a tourist commenting on the natives of an undeveloped country: they are picturesque, to be sure, but more primitive and animal-like than we, and not, after all, quite as proper or as civilized. They really know how to have a good time on a Saturday night.

Several years pass—seven, by my count—during which Hank Morgan, as The Boss, has been right busy. Occupied as he has been with his own projects, he has found little of importance about which to complain, except for the institution of aristocracy (and the fact that he is excluded therefrom), the general state of education, and the paucity of technology. He is then, however, dragooned into going on a quest with the Demoiselle Alisande la Carteloise, whom he later nicknames "Sandy." When he questions her, her answers have the flavor of childhood, his questions the exasperation of a chapter-and-verse-seeking adult. They are both funny: she as naïve and simpleminded, but nevertheless in some ways more sensible than he; he as realistic and systematic, but misled by his assumption that papers and measurements and documentable facts are somehow an assurance of reality:

"Where is the castle?"

"It . . . lieth in a far country. Yes, it is many leagues."

"*How* many?"

"Ah, fair sir, it were woundily hard to tell, they are so many, and do so lap the one upon the other, and being made all in the same image and tincted with the same color, one may not know the one league from its fellow, nor how to count them except they be taken apart, and ye wit well it were God's work to do that. . . . "

(Remember our previous identification of space and time, and see how this speech might be switched into the mode temporal: one cannot take apart time as it flows—it were God's work to do that.)

Sandy serves as guide on the trip, and in the process Hank is forced, first, to listen to more Malory, and, second, to observe the middle depths of human folly and wickedness, both as they appear in the sixth century and as he mentally draws parallels to his own century. He sees forced labor, torture, murder, slavery, all manner of religious foolishness—indeed, the whole perpetual apparatus of the adult world. He becomes critical; he rejects; he is becoming an adolescent, very like the cynical half of the Innocent Abroad.

His reaction to Sandy's tale reflects this change in attitude toward the past; the tale is no more boring than Merlin's, and much less tedious than the account of the tournament, but Hank will have none of it:

She would be thirty days getting down to those facts. And she generally began without a preface and finished without a result. . . . I had to interrupt, and interrupt pretty frequently, too, in order to save my life; a person would die if he let her monotony drip on him right along all day. (XV)

The passage reminds me of an adolescent's reaction to a parental lecture or the narrative of a younger sibling; Hank's reaction is a long way from "quaint and sweet and simple."

The matter as well as the manner offends him; Sandy tells how three damsels spat and threw mire upon a shield, and Hank uses the occasion for a criticism of medieval manners; when in the words of Malory, she praises men of prowess, he reflects that Comanches and prizefighters would fit right in at the Round Table. Then he criticizes the prose again:

If you've got a fault in the world, Sandy, it is that you are a shade too archaic. . . . The truth is, Alisande, the archaics are a little *too* simple; the vocabulary is too limited, and so, by consequence, the descriptions suffer in the matter of variety; they run too much to level Saharas of fact, and not enough to picturesque detail; this throws about them a certain air of the monotonous; in fact the fights are all alike: a couple of people come together with great random—random is a good word, and so is exegesis, for that matter, and so is holocaust, and defalcation, and usufruct and a hundred others, but land! a body ought to discriminate. . . . and as a *picture*, of living, raging, roaring battle, sho! why, it's pale and noiseless—just ghosts shuffling in a fog.

Hank is finding that a little Malory goes a long way, as does, indeed, many a reader who sits down for a long stretch with him. His objection to archaisms is funny, of course, given that he is a walking anachronism; but I think it reflects Twain's own judgment on Malory, who seems to be rejecting the prose of his own day as he strains for an artificial antiquity. Further, the demand for precision in diction echoes Twain's comments on Fenimore Cooper and Walter Scott; Twain, like Orwell after him, sees imprecision in use of words as reflective of sloppy and very often sentimental and reactionary thinking. Finally, the examples "random," "defalcation," "usufruct," with their implied judgments on Arthur's world (and the adult world as seen by the adolescent)—the world makes no sense, it is haphazard, property is embezzled away from those who should rightfully enjoy it—are a sharper comment on feudalism than they are on the prose of Malory; and "holocaust" anticipates the later Battle of the Sand-Belt, in which Hank will attempt to destroy Arthur's century.

"Ghosts shuffling in a fog" is a good description of the past by one who has rejected it; but it also reflects the perception of the temporal or spatial imperialist who sees the people with whom he must deal as not quite real, not quite human.

It is a rich passage, and Twain seems specifically to invite "exegesis." In the mouth of Morgan, it is pretty high-flown literary criticism, for an ignoramus; but directly Hank, following the example of Merlin's audience, dozes off to sleep, and when he rouses, he is his old vulgar self, objecting only that the king's son of Ireland doesn't speak with a brogue, after the fashion of stage Irishmen of the nineteenth century.

After a merciful interruption of the narrative by their adventures at the court of the murderous Morgan le Fay, Sandy resumes; Hank's final evaluation of the narrative is that chivalry is not only self-seeking, but not too bright about the process of self-seeking, at that (a familiar reaction of adolescents to the adult world):

A successful whirl in the knight-errantry line—now what is it when you blow away the nonsense and come down to the cold facts? It's just a corner in pork, that's all, and you can't make anything else out of it. . . . when you come right down to the bed-rock, knight-errantry is *worse* than pork; for whatever happens, the pork's left, and somebody's benefited anyway; but when the market breaks, in a knight-errantry whirl . . . what have you got for assets? Just a rubbish-pile of battered corpses and a barrel or two of busted hardware. Can you call *those* assets? Give me pork, every time. (XIX)

(And pork is what he gets: the demoiselles whom he set out to rescue turn out to be a herd of swine. Twain is, of course, having Quixote-like fun with the romantic propensity to turn the everyday into the miraculous; but he is also continuing a line of comparison between humans and animals. You remember that the hermit lived in a sty like a pig and that Merlin's listeners were compared to dumb animals; Beard's illustration at the head of Chapter XX shows Queen Victoria caricatured as a pig; and in a rejected passage (California *Yankee*, 681), Twain says that George II "and the great majority of the other English monarchs" are "mere pork.")

Hank here sounds like an adolescent addressing the adult world: all your noble pretensions are just a cloak for self-interest, and you're not even very good at serving yourselves. The bloom is off the rose; the feet of clay of the noble Arthurian past are out there for anyone to see; Hank has uncovered his father's nakedness; and the tourist has begun to see the inconveniences of the foreign country. The natives are not only ignorant, but also rapacious.

Before he encounters the last passage from Malory, however, Hank undergoes one more period of growth and change. Incognito, he travels about the kingdom with Arthur. The standard popular picture of King Arthur is that of a venerable and bewhiskered father-figure; indeed, only archetypal father-figures like Arthur end up not dead, but sleeping in caves, once and future kings. But Twain is at some pains to have Hank note later (XL) that he and Arthur are about of an age, some thirty-seven at the time of the trip. As we'll note in more detail when we come to discuss the traveler to the past as Oedipal hero, one of the attractive things about time travel as psychomyth is that it gives the son and the father the opportunity to confront each other at the same age. In this trek about the kingdom, Hank both instructs Arthur in the ways of Arthur's own culture and is himself instructed by the experience.

During the voyage, Hank, on the one hand, becomes more and more disillusioned with mankind in general and medieval civilization in particular; his experiences are even more dismal and grim than the ones he had on the voyage with Sandy. Not only does he see slavery and brutality, but he also suffers from it. (There are echoes of *The Prince and the Pauper* here, and not only in the scene in Chapter XXXVIII in which the true king is jeered at as a crazy beggar; the disguises, the inability of one class to understand another, all are out of the same tradition.) On the other hand, Hank learns love and respect for Arthur, who, in spite of the limitations of his humanity and of his age, turns out to be capable of learning (he decides, after being enslaved, to abolish slavery [XXXV]); to be a worthy adversary or ally in a rough-and-tumble fight (XXIV); and to be a man of true courage and nobility of soul. Entering a hut full of smallpox victims in spite of the Yankee's cautions, Arthur says,

"It were shame that a king should know fear, and shame that belted knight should withhold his hand where be such as need succor. Peace, I will not go [away]. . . . ''

[The king] came forward into the light; upon his breast lay a slender girl . . . dying of smallpox. Here was heroism at its last and loftiest possibility. . . . this was challenging death in the open field unarmed, with all the odds against the challenger, no reward set upon the contest, and no admiring world . . . to gaze and applaud; and yet the king's bearing was as serenely brave as it had always been in those cheaper contests where knight meets knight. . . . He was great, now; sublimely great. (XXIX)

Now, in the speech of the king, we hear the noblest echoes of Malory; and in the comments of the Yankee, a correspondingly elevated Victorian prose.

Having learned that there is, after all, something to be said for Father, for the king, for the Middle Ages, and for the past, Hank marries and settles down. The name of the daughter Sandy bears him, Hello-Central, comes out of the ties he still has to his home time, just as a given name strange to the natives might be given by an immigrant from another country; but in the begetting of his daughter Hank Morgan has become not only part of the adult world, but part of the past, part of Malory.

He has already replaced Merlin (a bad-father-figure) as wizard, although it will be Merlin (emblematic of the dark side, the old side, of his own nature) who will eventually destroy him; now he must become the good father as well, replacing Arthur. He has already taken over Arthur's power; now he is ready to take the mythic place of Arthur, fighting against impossible odds in a dubious cause, ultimately arriving at the Rip-Van-Winklehood reserved in medieval European tradition for the greatest of culture-fathers.

But first Arthur must die. Clarence brings Hank a newspaper story out of Malory, an echo of that earlier story written by Hank's priestly reporter. Hank had read that earlier report with the naïve eyes of a new tourist or a child, seeing it as quaint, but lacking in "whoop and clash." Now, however, he reads Malory and the past with the calm eye of an adult who has become part of the culture, or of a tourist from another country who has settled down and become part of a new culture: "That is a good piece of war correspondence, Clarence; you are a first-rate newspaper man."

Like the Innocent Abroad, and like his other tourist Hank Morgan, Twain went through the same changes of attitude toward Europe (and, by extension, the past). During his first visit to England, in 1872, he was lionized and responded with proper admiration: "He went to a stag hunt and dined with a direct descendent of the Plantagenet—'Why it had all the seeming of hob-nobbing with the Black Prince in the flesh!' " (Kaplan, *Mr. Clemens*, 173) But by 1886 he could say of Henry Stanley, "In this day . . . when it is the custom to ape and imitate English methods and fashions, it is like a breath of fresh air to stand in the presence of this untainted American citizen" (175). Infatuation followed with disillusion, you see, just as in the *Yankee*; and, as in the *Yankee*, there is final reconciliation shortly before death: in 1907, "forty years to the day since the start of his first voyage to the Old World . . . he sailed on his last" (453). And on this last voyage he was fêted by George Bernard Shaw, Max Beerbohm, and Sir James M. Barrie; and at a royal garden party at Windsor, acted out something like the dreams of Hank Morgan and Miles Herndon: "The Queen commanded him to keep his hat on—she was afraid he might catch cold" (454). Moreover, he accepted an honorary degree from Oxford on June 26 of that year, and for the rest of his life "cherished and flaunted" (455) the scarlet robe that went with it.

Similar were his changes of attitude toward France. In 1869, France was "a bewitching garden" (*Innocents* XII); through his middle years, Twain nourished an abiding contempt for the French; but by 1896 he could glorify the nation in the person of its greatest heroine in *Personal Recollections of Joan of Arc*.

THE TOURIST IN SEARCH OF MANA THROUGH TIME-BINDERS

Twain calls the Innocents Abroad "pilgrims," as we have noted, again and again; his book is subtitled *The New Pilgrims' Progress*. Most tourists, I suppose, partake a bit of the pilgrim; and the pilgrim is always in search of mana. Things and places and people all can have this magic, and a mundane pilgrim finds mana in the connections things have with the past.

Mark Twain may make fund of his Innocent weeping over the supposed grave of Adam, but, as we have noted, Twain himself seems to have found mana in a tree supposedly planted by Godfrey of Bouillon. We seek it in museums: such-and-such an axe or crown or book belonged (or so it is supposed) to whichever great warrior or king or warlock, and something of his might and power seems to remain therein. In the Middle Ages, items belonging to saints, or remnants of their bodies, had enormous mana. Babe Ruth's bat, or Louis Armstrong's horn, look to the naked eye very like any other bat or horn; but for the believer they are charged with the power to bring some of the past into the present.

Holy objects (relics, religious art) or places (cathedrals, graves, places of martyrdom) accomplish a seeming removal to the past, I suppose, aided by the perception of their participation in Great Time. In more mundane fashion, living things which operate on a different schedule from our human pace engender similar thoughts. In the midst of a redwood grove, one's thoughts are not only of vegetable majesty, but of the time spanned by these living things; similarly, in Anderson's *Corridors of Time*, the hero finds himself in 1827 B.C. and thinks "the General Grant Tree [is] a seedling." In a world in which the Minos rules in Crete and Mohenjodaro is a going concern, it is somehow comforting to him to know that something is alive that spans the gap from "then" to "now." The General Grant Tree, then, is (like the mana-bearers sought by the mundane pilgrim) a *time-binder*; in the same book, churches and dolmens serve similar functions for the traveler. In *Innocents*, Twain says,

We went to see the Cathedral of Notre Dame . . . and gazed long at its . . . stony, mutilated saints who had been looking calmly down from their perches for ages. The patriarch of Jerusalem stood under them in the old days of chivalry and romance, and preached the third Crusade . . . and since that day they have stood there and looked quietly down upon the most thrilling scenes, the grandest pageants, the most extraordinary spectacles. . . . I wish these old parties could speak. They could tell a tale worth the listening to. (XIV)

Clearly the Innocent's Notre-Dame, like Finney's Dakota, is a time-binder. In Le Guin's "April in Paris," the fact that Jehan Lenoir in 1482 and Barry Pennywither in 1961 occupy the same apartment in the same building and share the same view of Notre-Dame is one of the things which makes Pennywither's time trip possible. Paris is clearly one of those cities where many events intersect, at which, if time travel were possible, one would expect it to occur; as L. Sprague de Camp observes in *Lest Darkness Fall*,

History . . . is a tough web. But it has weak points. The junction places—the focal points, one might say—are weak. The backslipping, if it happens, would happen at these places . . . places like Rome, where the world-lines of many famous events intersect. Or Istanbul. Or Babylon. (6)

Now, just as a modern tourist can stand in Paris and meditate upon a Roman wall, and feel himself somehow linked to a past which is forever gone, so do places, buildings, and living things serve in science fiction to make a link between the traveler's owntime and the outtime to which he goes, or to aid him in his voyages between the two. We have seen, for example, how the Dakota enables Si Morley to travel into the New York past; the arm of the Statue of Liberty, standing all alone in Madison Square, enables him and Julia to return to his own time.

In his article "The Discovery of the Past," Poul Anderson notes that Alfred Korzybski described man as "a time-binding animal," and describes his own shelf full of time-binders: a stone spearhead made by a friend, an Egyptian scarab, and an oyster shell from a Viking site in York. Anderson is also notable for his use of one particular sort of animal as time-binder: birds. In the past, it would seem that any bird-watching tourist would find wonderful opportunities: "Beyond one or two hundred years back . . . the daytime sky is always full of wings." (This observation, from *There Will Be Time*, is made at the crucifixion.) In *The Guardians of Time*, when the travelers arrive in Saxon A.D. 464, not so far in time and place from the destination of the Yankee, there are so many birds at dawn that their racket is "unholy"; in California in 1280, "birds were home-bound in such flocks that they could darken the sun." In *The Corridors of Time*, in the Denmark of 1827 B.C., the marshes are "aswarm with ducks, geese, swans, storks, herons."

Winged things obviously have a special symbolic value to Anderson; he is, after all, the creator of two splendid races of winged sophonts, the Ythri of Stormgate (*The Earth Book of Stormgate*) and the Drak'honai of Diomedes (*War of the Wing-Men*). But he is not alone; in Silverberg's *Up the Line* we get this passage:

Mists rose in the south. Spanish moss clung to graceful trees. A flight of birds darkened the sky.
  "The year is 1382," said the guru. "Those are passenger pigeons overhead. Columbus' grandfather is still a virgin." (23)

Birds are, if we care to think about it, really quite remarkable symbolic embodiments of at least three ways out of the here-and-now. As the first two quotes from Anderson suggest, birds have all manner of associations with Great Time; they suggest the Holy Ghost, angels, "I'll fly away."

Birds embody the future inasmuch as to fly like the birds has been a dream of future technology since the myth of Icarus; the promise of human flight, fulfilled from the Montgolfiers to our day, has been the promise of a technology which now offers us mightier and mightier flights—to the planets, to the stars.

And birds are also of the past, if not in such an obvious way as the General Grant Tree or Notre-Dame. Family folk like us, musicians and architects like us, they are nevertheless tiny feathered dinosaurs and therefore, like the crocodiles and the turtles, somehow much older than we are. Birds are mysterious and magical, as anyone with good sense knows, and yet they are somehow very homely, very familiar. And the dream of flying is something like the dream of escaping the chains of time.

The mana, then, that the everyday tourist or birdwatcher finds in places or things or birds, is like the force that links past and present for the time traveler.

THE TOURIST ON SAFARI

Except for medieval aristocrats, the hunter-tourist is a creation of the nineteenth and twentieth centuries. Before our times, most people did not generally view hunting as a recreation; if one hunted, one did so to eat or to avoid being eaten or to complete a religious ritual. Hunting could become a sport only with the introduction of cheap and reliable firearms; nobody in his right mind would expend precious hand-made arrows for fun. And the very technology which made sport-shooting possible also, within a few decades, made it necessary to travel in order to shoot big game. The Blackfeet shot buffalo out of need, and on home ground; within a few decades, eastern sportsmen were traveling west on the railroad to "shoot the last buffalo."

In the late nineteenth and early twentieth centuries, big game was typically to be found in areas of the world which were sparsely populated and underdeveloped (the tiger of India being a notable exception)—Africa, Brazil, Tibet, the Canadian Rockies, Alaska. As we shall note in more detail when we consider the time traveler as imperialist, such areas, because of their "primitive" economies—hunting rather than herding, herding rather than sodbusting, sodbusting rather than industry—are easily viewed as "the past." It is not simply that it is *convenient* for Sir Arthur Conan Doyle to set his *Lost World* in the middle of the South American jungle—he could not, after all, very well situate it in an area which had been thoroughly explored; it is also that the jungle is somehow *primitive* and therefore *old* and therefore an appropriate place to find ape-men and iguanodons and pterodactyls.

The safari-goer, then, is a tourist in search of the past; and many a time traveler is a safari-goer, as anxious to pot a tyrannosaur as his mundane cousins were to shoot the last buffalo, and for reasons about as creditable. If, for Hemingway's Francis Macomber, the mundane safari is a way he may seek his manhood, then for the temporal Macomber, killing in the past takes on definite Oedipal overtones. Claude Ford, in Bryan Aldiss' "Poor Little Warrior," is fleeing his wife Maude (back in 2181) and seeking his manhood, in the Jurassic. ("Holy mom, is this a travelogue, nor are we out of it? . . . God, if adolescence did not exist it would be unnecessary to invent it!") Like Macomber he shoots his prey (a brontosaurus), and like Macomber he dies, not, however, at the hands of his wife but at the claws of the parasites on the body of the beast he has just slain. ("You're going to like it up there on top of the Rockies; you won't feel a thing.")

Ray Bradbury's hunter, in "A Sound of Thunder," is not so much in search of manhood as of youth: "Out of chars and ashes, out of dust and coals, like golden salamanders, the old years, the green years, might leap . . . white hair turn Irish-black, wrinkles vanish." He does *not* kill his tyrannosaurus, that "great evil god," but a butterfly, and with it the present that he had left; and in the return to his new and evil present he dies, as might a safari-goer returning from a primitive place to find a war going on in his civilized homeland.

August Holtzinger, in de Camp's story "A Gun for Dinosaur," is a figure we have come to recognize as a fairly typical time traveler:

I'm a completely undistinguished kind of guy. I'm not brilliant or big or strong or handsome. I'm just an ordinary Midwestern small businessman. You never even notice me at Rotary luncheons, I fit in so perfectly. But that doesn't say I'm satisfied.

The narrator of the story, a caricature white-hunter figure, takes Holtzinger back to get his trophy; unfortunately Holtzinger, though acquitting himself bravely, is too small not to be knocked over by a .600 dinosaur gun and is eaten by a tyrannosaur. (The other sahib on the party, no sportsman, has to be knocked down by the white hunter; in an attempt to return to the past and avenge himself, he is torn apart by temporal forces.)

Hunters on temporal safari generally come out badly: the past is not, it would appear, the place to search for manhood or for youth—at least not in any of the more obvious ways. A hunter in an Anderson story, "The Little Monster," comes off rather better. A 12-year-old Scout, he drops into the Pliocene by accident and confronts a band of his primitive ancestors (with a Scout knife) and a lion (with fire); rescuing his ancestors from the lion, he leaves them the legacy of fire. On his return to his present, he recognizes and appreciates his kinship with his ancestors; back in their time, they see him as "Old Father." His Oedipal conflicts thus symbolically worked out, his maturation process symbolically completed, the boy is a better god because he did not try to become one, a better hunter because he hunted out of need, and a better understander of the past because the past came on him by accident.

THE TOURIST AS CARICATURE AND DEBUNKER

In de Camp's "Gun for Dinosaur," as soon as Professor Prochaska of Washington University invents the time machine, he is inundated by scientists who want to study and businessmen who want to set up safaris. Similarly, the invention of a time machine in Finney's "Such Interesting Neighbors" results in a land-office transtemporal tourist business, just as it does in Simak's *Mastodonia*. And in *Up the Line* Robert Silverberg, in a zany and complicated book, gives his hero the job of tourist guide to the past.

Had we world enough and time, we might do a lengthy and detailed comparison between Silverberg's book and *Innocents Abroad*, but let us be satisfied with a few points. Like the *Quaker City* in Twain's *Innocents Abroad* (I), the advertising agency in *Up the Line* makes exaggerated claims:

An advert globe . . . hovered about four feet away from me at eye level, radiating a flickering green glow designed to compel my attention, and said, "Good afternoon. We hope you're enjoying your visit to twenty-first-century Athens. Now that you've seen the picturesque ruins, how would you like to see the Parthenon as it *really* looked? See the Greece of Socrates and Aristophanes? Your local Time Service office is on Aeolou Street, just opposite the Central Post Office. . . . (105)

The customers of the Time Service are echoes of those abroad the *Quaker City*: some are vulgar money-flashers; others are scholars of a sort in search of the past, collecting artifacts and trying to smuggle them through customs; some cluck condescendingly at the folkways and fashions of the natives and complain about the lack of homelike accommodations; and most look with condescending pity at the times and places they are visiting. Because Silverberg is not writing in Twain's century, he is free to allow his tourists a good deal of transtemporal fornication, rather after the manner of salesmen on the loose in Paris. Acts of violence—wars, assassinations, and executions—are the most popular destinations, combining the thrill of immediacy with the insulation of temporal distance. When a destination gets too popular—Byzantium is very big this season—there is always the danger of tourist pollution.

And some of the tourists in *Up the Line*, like many a tourist in *Innocents* or in the novels of Sinclair Lewis, are hilariously vulgar:

At the Augusteum [Conrad Saurabend] whistled and said "What a parking lot this would make!"
Inside Haghia Sophia he clapped a white-bearded priest on the back and said, "I just got to tell you what a swell church you got here, priesto."
During a visit to the icon-smashings . . . he interrupted an earnest iconoclastic fanatic and said, "Don't be such a dumb prick. You know that you're hurting this city's tourist trade?" (174)

Just as Mark Twain's tourists find that guidebooks often deceive, so do temporal tourists often find that History is the Bunk. At the completion of Haghia Sophia, Justinian does *not* say "O Solomon, I have surpassed thee," but his "first exclamation upon entering the architectural masterpiece of the age [is] . . . 'Look up there, you sodomitic simpleton! Find me the mother-humper who left that scaffold hanging in the dome! I want his balls in an alabaster vase before mass begins!' " (123–24)

We have seen some hints of this sort of history-bashing in the *Yankee*. La Cote Male Taille gets his name not, as in Malory, from the ragged coat left him by his father, but from the sandwich-board which Hank Morgan has got him to wear (XVI). Merlin is a silly old fraud—most of the time, anyway. Nobody in England is *supposed* to have dated from the Incarnation until the seventh century, but Clarence knows that the date is June 19, 528. And so on.

THE TOURIST AS STUDENT

In the literature of time travel, the tourist whose primary motive is learning comes off rather better than either hunter, casual visitor, or debunker. The narrator of A. Poleshchuk's "Homer's Secret" is a pleasant enough fellow, a classics professor and member of the Moscow Society of Lovers of Ancient Literature. At the behest of a friend, he takes on himself the job of teaching a group of 16- and 17-year-old technological students whose headmaster fears their understanding of the humanities is lacking.

Like many another teacher of prospective engineers, he is delighted at their intelligence and surprised at their interest and attention. The silent Spartan of the class, Artem, indeed takes such interest that he begins to learn ancient Greek.

If the narrator, who appears to be an inspiring teacher (or, at any rate, to be blessed with inspiring students), has a fault, it is that he relies too heavily on scholarly tradition. His students, rejecting the somewhat overdogmatic conclusions of received scholarship ("Homer never existed"), cobble together a time machine and go back to see.

All of us, but particularly those of us who teach the humanities in institutions primarily devoted to technology, or engineering in institutions primarily devoted to the humanities, are aware of the Two Cultures and the strains and hostilities which have developed between them. And those strains and hostilities are often accompanied, on either side, by a certain ruefulness: the scientist or engineer sometimes regretting the departure of poetry, and high aspiration, and magic from his discipline, and the humanist somehow wishing that history, and literature, and philosophy could stand on the pragmatic experimental base of science and engineering—a wish reflected in a good deal of recent study and criticism.

In Ward Moore's *Bring the Jubilee*, the attempt to unite the Two Cultures by using time travel comes to a tragic end. There are no shortcuts, we are warned repeatedly in that book; and that caution seems to mask a long-standing and deep-seated suspicion of technology and science on the part of humanists. There are no quick technological fix-ups for our deep human problems, they keep telling us—doubtless partly rightly and partly wrongly; the real solutions lie in the domain of the moral and spiritual—which is to say, in *my* territory.

But in "Homer's Secret," the wished-for shortcut works, with no ill effects. The professor and the boys travel into the past, finding Homer not in 850 B.C., but just after the Trojan War. He is indeed blind; in fact, he has been blinded. In an age of peace, not unlike our own 1920s and 1950s, nobody wants to hear his songs about the glories of war. "Are you gods?" he asks the travelers. (They are, of course, to an extent.) No, they say; we have come from the distant future (an assertion which Homer accepts with an odd lack of surprise and confusion). Your songs, they tell him, have been written down and remembered.

"Written?" says Homer, more baffled by this word than by time travel. Oh yes, he says when the process is explained, I have heard of the Phoenicians doing something like that. And the interrelationship between the arts and technology is established once again. Like good people, the boys give the starving old man a cheese sandwich; with the callousness of the scholar, the professor quizzes Homer about apparent contradictions in his poems.

What happened after the end of the *Odyssey*? he finally asks, quoting Homer's own words at him with a combination of reverence for the poem and desire to display his own learning. The fishermen, Homer replies, who carried the bodies of the slain home, returned with the families of the slain and attacked the house of Odysseus. The first to be killed was Telemachus; Eumaeus, "the loyal, courageous old man," was likewise killed. Odysseus, a bound prisoner, was spared his life by those who remembered his service; but they . . . blinded him.

The man of action then becomes the man of art; after all, the verbal skills of Odysseus, and his ability to fabulize, are throughout both Homeric epics part of the source of his skill in action. And the poet who memorializes the deeds of the soldier is better remembered, and more revered, than the soldier himself.

At the very end of the story, as the professor and the students are departing for twentieth-century Moscow, the professor still cannot bring himself to accept empirical evidence: "The old man considers Odysseus and Homer to be the same person. . . . I don't know what my colleagues will think of this. Some will unquestionably meet my information without enthusiasm." The professor, then, while intending to bear the truth which he has seen back to his own century, still only half believes it; he is unable to reconcile scholarly authority and tradition with empirical evidence. It is left to Artem, the student who developed the machine, to do the reconciliation:

It was only when Artem started back along the path toward the old man, who rose and came to meet him, and their images began to quiver and melt away, that I realized Artem was staying. And from somewhere, strangely distorted, came the old man's cry:
  "O Zeus, great father of us all! The gods still live on bright Olympus! Is this you, in truth, my son Telemachus?"

As in Anderson's story of the Boy Scout in the Pliocene, past and present have recognized their kinship, and in that recognition is the annihilation of the years which separate them.

In the *Connecticut Yankee*, be it noted, the time traveler is as thoroughly committed to the empirical arts as the professor is to his books; the humanist is conspicuously lacking in both the Yankee and the *Yankee*; and that lacuna is in itself significant. It is clear throughout the *Yankee* that Twain expects a familiarity with Malory from his reader; it is likewise clear that he delights in exploding the expectations of those readers who have a romantic-nostalgic view of the Middle Ages and of Arthuriana. His typical reader, then, might well be expected, in the place of the Yankee, to spend a good deal of time and energy checking out the historicity of Malory or of earlier writers about Arthur. The Yankee, totally committed to engineering, never gives the matter a thought; and the result is, early in the book, the wanton destruction of Merlin's tower and, later, the holocaust of the Sand-Belt. Only at the very end of the book, in his delirium, does he show a spark of that human concern which transcends time; and M. T. casts a shadow of doubt over the whole business by calling the Yankee's ravings "his last effect." One concludes that, of the technology-humanities, future-past pairs, the Yankee is strong where Poleshchuk's professor is weak, and weak where the professor is strong.

Now we close in on another possible hint as to the answers to the original questions we asked; particularly, why did travel to the past appear in the nineteenth century, and why does it have a place in science fiction, when its premises are manifestly fantastic?

It is a truism that literature arises very largely from the need to reconcile the irreconcilable, from the tension between equally truthful opposites: Sophoclean tragedy from the tension between destiny and choice, Dantean epic from the tension between man as temporal animal and man as immortal soul, and nearly all fiction from the tensions between the valid claims of the individual and the equally valid claims of the group.

If in his *Trillion Year Spree* Brian Aldiss is correct, and he seems to me to be, science fiction arose in the nineteenth century as a result of the tensions between the largely urban past and the industrialized future: none of the earlier utopias, travelers' tales, or moral allegories seem to have had a real sense that the future would be substantially different from the past, and that the present was involved in dynamic change, least of all that science and technology were to be centrally involved in that change.

In science fiction, from the beginnings of the nineteenth century on, it becomes apparent that both past values and future potential have valid claims on the intellect; both have their grubby and frightening sides, as well as their ennobling and enriching aspects.

The simplest responses to this tension are the least rewarding, intellectually and artistically: the nearly whole-hearted embracing of future technology, as in the work of Jules Verne; the equally enthusiastic rejection of an apparently sordid, depressing, and bourgeois future, as in the thought of C. S. Lewis, J. R. R. Tolkien, and the pre-Raphaelites; or the sideways avoidance of the whole business for a world of fantasy, as in much of the work of Poe or the later H. P. Lovecraft. It is when the past is seen as nasty, brutish, and servile *and* sacred, noble, and inspiring, and when the future is ominous, dehumanizing, and threatening *and* full of high aspiration and potential, that science fiction reaches that complexity which has the potential to engender true art. Thus Wells; thus Aldiss; thus Anderson, at his best; and thus the reason we find Finney better in *Time and Again* than in "The Third Level."

Now, if the central tension of science fiction may be described as past pulling against future (or rural against urban; agricultural against industrial; the village against the metropolis; Pope ["presume not God to scan"] against Faust/Frankenstein; handcrafts against mass production—any of these will do to state a part of this complex theme), then *the literature of time travel to the past has a place in science fiction, not because of any intrinsic plausibility, but because its central tensions are the same tensions—and more nakedly expressed—which generate the central energies of science fiction.* And Mark Twain, who began as a Hannibal Tom Sawyer and finished as a would-be Connecticut Yankee ("I was born in the country/But I have come to town'') carries a heavy load of values on both sides of the tension.

The themes of ''Homer's Secret'' appear again in ''April in Paris,'' the first story for which Ursula K. Le Guin was paid. As in ''Homer's Secret,'' the hero is a professor, Barry Pennywither, who is, like many another time traveler (and many a mundane tourist), a middle-aged male. Again typically, Pennywither is bored with his present, having achieved neither the power, nor the sexual happiness, nor the respect and love of his contemporaries and himself which might logically be expected in the prime of one's life.

At forty, impoverished and unloved, he is certainly prepared psychologically to depart from the present, even though his departure is unplanned and surprising. He has come back to Paris in an attempt to replay his student days there, and it is not working. All he cares about is Villon; and his theories about Villon's death, on the strength of which he vainly hopes to write a book that will get him tenure, turn out ultimately to be wrong. Professor Barry Pennywither is a wimp and a loser.

''At the same moment'' back down in 1482, however, Professor Jehan Lenoir, another frustrated loser, has turned to magic. A frustrated scientist looking in vain to the future, just as Pennywither is a frustrated humanist looking to the past, he turns to an old book of magic as a last desperate resort. Pennywither, who, in filling his cigarette lighter, has spilled fluid on his hands and—typically ineffectually—managed to set the fluid on fire, appears in Lenoir's room, not as a poor twentieth-century wimp, but as a flaming giant yelling ''Hell!'' As soon as his initial, and understandable, terror passes, Lenoir determines that his visitor is human: ''Mais vous êtes de Dieu,'' he says, correctly. A moment later he is wondering whether Pennywither is not ''a filthy Goddam.'' Right again. Later in the story, when the two of them conjure up a slave woman from Roman Gaul, Pennywither unwittingly puns as he identifies the author of *this* strange creation: ''Woman, by God,'' he says quite correctly. All mere humans, Le Guin implies (and likewise the works of mere humans—past or present, literary or scientific), can be diabolic in appearance, but they are of God—failed, damned, ineffectual, and yet somehow gloriously transcendent of their own limitations in time and place.

If Paradise does not lie before us, then perhaps Eden lies behind; still another time traveler in ''April in Paris,'' Kislk, a woman from the ninetieth century, reacts to her past very much as does Finney's Si Morley: past people are *realer* than people of her own time: ''Now I've seen an unhygienic room with insufficient heating. Now I've seen a cathedral not in ruins. Now I've met a living man who's shorter than me, with bad teeth and a short temper. Now I'm home.''

Notice the lack of hygiene and heat; Le Guin, like Finney in *Time and Again*, insists on the shortcomings of the past. Although in 1482 the chestnut blooms are in full glory, and in 1961 they are blighted by frost, still Le Guin insists on making a point of the lice that infest everyone's clothing. (The Connecticut Yankee, on the other hand, confronted with the shortcomings of the past—no tobacco, no chromos, no telephone operators, no newspapers—moves straight-away to invent whatever he sees lacking.)

None of the shortcomings of the past deter or discourage Pennywither; he is, after all, in search of Youth. His studies center on Villon, "the greatest juvenile delinquent of all time." It is not, however, Villon whom he finds. The poet has been dead for seventeen or eighteen years. It is himself.

Notice how his names change as the story progresses: he begins as "Professor Barry Pennywither" and stays that way for several pages. Then he becomes "Barry Pennywither," and finally just plain Barry. Jehan Lenoir, his fifteenth-century friend, calls him "Barrie," which suggests the eternal youth of Peter Pan.

He does not become young again, but in his midyears he returns to the past and renews his youth; then the process of his maturation is complete. Nature is in the past. Love is in the past. Our parents—Pater Noster and Notre-Dame—are in the past. True religion, "a cathedral not in ruins," is in the past. And in that past one finds the resources to face the future; because it is to the ninetieth-century Kislk that Jehan Lenoir, the man from the past, allies himself.

"You can't go home again," said Thomas Wolfe. "You *must* go home again," we might read Freud as saying, "go home *and then return*." Joseph Campbell sees the monomythic hero as having to venture underground—where the dead and the past live—and then return to the land of the living—the present. "Now I'm home," says Kislk. "I'm where I can be myself, I'm no longer alone." In our childhoods, we were not alone; we become so as we grow away from our parents. To become adults, we must capture and demythologize our own pasts and incorporate the children we were into the adults we would become.

Part of the reason for the psychic success of the three travelers in this story seems to be that their travel is not contaminated with commerce. Unlike Hank Morgan who, like many a mundane tourist, is never really on vacation, Pen-nywither never takes advantage of his privileged position. He is a smoker—indeed, on his second trip from 1961 he brings a stock of Gauloises Bleues—and he arrives in 1482, and Le Guin permits him and Lenoir to stare at each other "like wooden Indians"; and any twelve-year-old would jump at the date and the hint and dash off to anticipate Columbus by ten years, thereby assuring himself not only immortality and profit but a lifetime supply of Bleues. None of that ever enters Pennywither's mind. Nor does he attempt to use his twentieth-century knowledge to become The Boss, or the Isaac Newton of the fifteenth century, or even a tenured assistant professor. Both he and Lenoir are "perfectly happy. They knew they would do nothing with what they had learned from each other." They have discovered that value which transcends usefulness.

This business of getting one's middle-aged act together in the past is (like most of Le Guin's work) fraught with Taoistic contradiction. One stays oneself but becomes someone else; remaining one's own age, one symbolically becomes young by being joined to elder times. The past is different, but familiar: the Seine in "April in Paris"—itself an admirable time symbol—is still there and insisted upon, and so is Notre-Dame; and there are a windmill and good bars in the country town of Montmartre. And Jehan Lenoir, Le Guin makes clear, looks very much like Robert Oppenheimer.

The past is, indeed, a splendid and many-valued symbol for the contradictions of the Tao, so central to much of Le Guin's work. The contradictions are built into our language, and therefore into our conceptualizing: the past is old, we say, the Old Times; but the past is young because everything, including Notre-Dame, was younger then. "In the Old Days," we say, "when the world was young," and do not even notice the paradox. Perhaps a folk wisdom tells us that there is really no contradiction at all.

In the past, time travelers find themselves able to become merely human, if they dare, as in Le Guin's *Left Hand of Darkness*, in which, faced with sexual ambiguity, the hero learns to see "mere humans." They may begin, like Hank Morgan and King Arthur on their voyage incognito, by shedding names and honors. When Pennywither and Lenoir meet, it is very important to both of them that they are Doctors. But directly they become Jehan and Barrie, like the tourist who finds it easier to be genuinely and simply himself when he is away from those things which define him.

Because all the travelers remain in a medieval postcardish Paris, the story, in spite of its many insights, savors a bit of romantic escapism of the Finney sort. Pennywither is a bit like our own mundane native-goers, Eliot and James, who found sanity in removal to a European past; in this story, in spite of its qualifications about the past, the arrow essentially points backward toward Eden.

THE TOURIST AS ARTIST

I should say that "Homer's Secret" and "April in Paris" are two very splendid short stories, just considered in isolation; and that both of them are essential reading for one who would consider the traveler as tourist. I might get argument on this point from some readers; but I should expect no disagreement about my third choice of short story, "Vintage Season," by C. L. Moore and Henry Kuttner.

Of this story, Barry Malzberg in *The Engines of the Night*, naming it as one of the all-time top ten of the genre, justly observes, "It has been rewritten endlessly and has directly influenced hundreds of short stories and at least two dozen novels, but none of its descendants have improved upon the basic text" (137–38). The hero of the story, Oliver Wilson, is neither time traveler nor tourist, but the native who must endure the tourist incursion.

Living a short time in our future, he rents his house to a group of fascinatingly different folk who seem to spend a good deal of time collecting and observing and cherishing things which he either ignores or takes for granted. As "Vintage Season" works on, of course, the reader becomes aware, somewhat before Oliver does, that these people are tourists from our future.

But from the beginning, Oliver reacts to them, however unaware he is of their origin, as a poor native of an underdeveloped country might react to a horde of American tourists:

He didn't want them there. They were foreigners. . . . They had the curious name of Sancisco. . . . that peculiar arrogant assurance that comes from perfect confidence in every phase of one's being. . . . The first thing Oliver thought of when he looked at them was, Expensive! . . . There are degrees of wealth beyond which wealth itself ceases to have significance. . . . There was a curious air of condescension in the way they moved. . . .

Quite naturally, when another group of mysterious foreigners makes him a better offer, Oliver tries to break his previous arrangement with the first group; what are tourists for, after all, if not to make money from? Like the Innocent, the tourists are on a pilgrimage; indeed, *pilgrimage* is underlined by the fact that they have spent the earlier part of their trip in Chaucer's Canterbury and, after their stay in the twentieth century, will be off to Rome in the year 800 to see the coronation of Charlemagne. They are dilettantes in search of the perfect spring, summer, autumn, and winter, and are ranging the centuries on a tour which promises them. They have travel papers; there are rules of travel they must obey; they react to some native foods with relish and to others with disgust, and then they hole up in their rooms to munch on goodies they have brought with them; and one among them enjoys a brief sexual fling with Oliver, with a decadent air of amusing herself with a barbarian inferior, nearly an animal, certainly, from her point of view, a dead man, with whom an affair can have no possible real or lasting effects.

(In contrast, the outtime sexual affairs of Pennywither and Lenoir seem, rather than contemptible exploitation and decadent self-indulgence, to be pure acts of love, *actes gratuits*. Certainly, in fifteenth-century Paris, Pennywither cannot hope to profit from Kislk's family's money or status or use her to impress his colleagues or advance his tottering academic career. Out of our own time, as in it, sex can be many contradictory things.)

"They're typical tourists, all right," says Oliver. Just as a comfortable American visitor might go about snapping pictures of the quaint but suffering natives of some impoverished Central American republic, so Cenbe, a time tourist, turns the sights and sounds of his past into multimedia symphonies; and it turns out that the Blue Plague, which is to break out at the end of this most perfect of springs, is one of the attractions which has drawn him and his fellow-tourists to this time and place. Oliver, indeed, is to die of the plague; and it is his suffering eyes which will dominate the climax of one of Cenbe's greatest artistic triumphs.

Thus is demonstrated the gulf which separates not only tourist from native, time traveler from past person, but also artist from subject matter. You could change all this, cries the anguished Oliver; "All of that passed away long ago," replies the impassive Cenbe. People in the past and people in other places are fair game, whether for imperialist or for artist. Just as a certain inhuman distancing is necessary for the Connecticut Yankee to become an artist who takes sixth-century Camelot for his canvas, so a similar inhuman distancing is needed to make something beautiful out of other people's sufferings. Mark Rose (107–108) acutely observes that ''Vintage Season'' is ''built upon the analogy between temporal and aesthetic distance, . . . a suggestive exploration of the processes that transform the immediacy of human experience into material for contemplation.''

Another Taoistic contradiction, then: on the one hand, artistic creation deals with the deepest emotions and highest aspirations of humankind, and the artist in the act of creation becomes a sort of god; and, on the other hand, artistic creation requires a grim ruthlessness and imperviousness to suffering which is godlike in quite another sense. Another crucial point, then: *the figure of the time traveler appeals to the artist as a distorted reflection of himself, desperately needing the experience of the Other as material, just as desperately needing to distance himself psychologically from that same Other.* Artists are tourists in time and space. The wrestling of Twain with his every book, desperately needing as he did the material goods he could get with them, the approval of his wife and children, the adulation of the public, and the approval of the critics, at the same time as he needed his own self-approval and his own approval of his work, seems to have stalled him in book after book after book. And Hank Morgan, an artist in his own way, seems likewise to have been pulled between self-aggrandizement and self-approval, the love of money and power and the desire to do some permanent good in the world; and Morgan is, I suggest, a reflection of his artist-creator in ways I doubt Twain consciously understood.

The artist, then, is no friend to his subject matter; and one of the favorite notions of that fearful and paranoid century, the twentieth, has been that all of us are characters in somebody else's artistic creation. Johnny Bornish, for example, in Damon Knight's short story ''You're Another,'' is a chronic and clumsy loser given to falling into ponds, spilling paint all over himself, and knocking over fruit stands. He discovers the reason: he is an unwitting actor in a ''livie,'' a slapstick comedy, being made by a producer-director from the future, ''your calendar, uh, 4400-something.'' This future has, apparently, an appetite for sadism like unto that of Imperial Rome. Indeed, in this story, most of the world's present woes are inflicted upon it by the needs of the story lines of future livie script writers, a pleasantly paranoid notion reminding one of a citizen of a third-world country blaming the troubles of his nation, rightly or wrongly, on the manipulations of the richer and more technologically sophisticated nations.

In Harry Harrison's *The Time-Machined Saga*, similarly, a contemporary motion-picture company, in dire financial straits, makes a deal with an eccentric inventor to move a shooting troupe back to the 1003 Orkneys to film the discovery of America by the Vikings. Ascertaining that the said Vikings have not the faintest intention of discovering America, the travelers hire them to do so (once again, the traveler becoming part of his own past); a fight breaks out in Vinland between Vikings and Native Americans, and several are killed on each side while the cameras grind merrily on.

"It is nothing but a tragic waste," Jens said.....

"But it makes good film," Barney said. "And we're not here to interfere with the local customs...."

"Not interfere with the local customs, very humorous. You disrupt these people's lives completely for your cinematic drivel, then you avoid the consequences of your actions. ...."

Unlike "Vintage Season" and the *Yankee*, Harrison's story ends happily, for the protagonists if not for the dead Vikings and Skraelings, with the head of the now-prosperous studio planning yet another temporal filming expedition. Harrison does not fail to see the bitter irony in the actions of these artistic Hank Morgans; the new script will reduce Jesus of Nazareth to the status of actor. The whole past has already been summed up in the line "What a location!"

In "E for Effort," T. L. Sherred does not allow his filmmakers actually to travel in time, only to take pictures and motion pictures of past events; even this limited sort of travel, the narrator says, makes one "feel like a god"; and, godlike, the filmmakers (after the fashion of the Yankee trying to reform sixth-century Britain) try to use their device to ensure world peace. The results are, of course, catastrophic; as in Asimov's "The Dead Past," the ability to see the past means also the ability to see the past of ten seconds ago, and all privacy disappears. In the event, the would-be-godlike filmmakers precipitate the very war they are trying to prevent. Treating people like movies or pictures is not without its hazards.

SUMMARY

Remember now what we said at the beginning of our chapter: although all people seem to discuss time in spatial terms, the American is unusual, perhaps unique, in that he can locate the past or the future in a specific geographical direction or location; and when he goes to the old country as a tourist, he is in a sense a pilgrim to the past. Here, then, another piece of an answer to our original questions: *the nineteenth century is, because of the transcontinental steamship, the first great tourist century.* The apparent exceptions, the pilgrims of the Middle Ages, spring to mind: but they were motivated by quite different needs and probably represented a relatively small fraction of the population. In the nineteenth century, then, we have substantial numbers of literate people taking steamships to the part of the world which for them is the past, including that same Mark Twain who had made, and was to make, such extraordinary spatial-temporal moves in his own nation. He makes the point again and again in the *Innocents* (VI): "Everything [in the Azores] is staid and settled, for the country was one hundred years old when Columbus discovered America.'' (*There is an interesting temporal perception*: just how old was *America* when Columbus discovered America? In the American temporal sense, things tend to date A.D. *anno discovery* and B.C. *before Columbus*.) "The principal crop is corn, and they raise it and grind it just as their great-great-grandfathers did. . . . Oxen tread the wheat from the ear, after the fashion prevalent in the time of Methuselah.''

Here, then, is another piece of an answer to our questions about why time travel of the sort we are discussing should develop in the nineteenth century, and in America, and in the mind of Mark Twain.

All of our time-traveling tourists, the naïves, the debunkers, the gone-natives, the safari-hunters, the tour guides, the amateur historians, the seekers after mana and sex, the discoverers of love, and the artists, remind us again and again of the more mundane tourist as Twain presents him in *The Innocents Abroad*:

The gentle reader will never, never know what a consummate ass he can become until he goes abroad. I speak now, of course, in the supposition that the gentle reader has not been abroad, and therefore is not already a consummate ass. If the case be otherwise, I beg his pardon and extend to him the cordial hand of fellowship and call him brother. I shall always delight to meet an ass after my own heart when I shall have finished my travels. (XXIII)

In another context, that old Great-Time-tourist, Dante, might have said much the same thing.

Chapter 5

CHILDREN OF THE YANKEE: CECIL RHODES AND COMPANY

I admire [Rhodes], I frankly confess it; and when his time comes, I shall buy a piece of the rope for a keepsake.

—Mark Twain

Some tourists temporal and mundane settle like the Yankee more or less permanently into their new scenes, whether as beachcombers, immigrants, or White Gods. Some, however, dream even vaster dreams than those of White Gods: and they take steps to make those dreams come true, destroying whole races (''T,'' Brian Aldiss), looting the natural resources (''Wildcat,'' Poul Anderson), stopping the collapse of civilizations (*Lest Darkness Fall*, L. Sprague de Camp), or replacing one whole civilization with another (*Serving in Time*, Gordon Eklund). Outtime becomes a vast field for potential exploitation, not unlike the Americas of the seventeenth century or the Asia and Africa of the nineteenth.

Here the geographic symbolism becomes confusing, and the reason is precisely the mixed attitudes we have toward time and progress. As demonstrated in our discussion of the temporal tourist, for most Americans the symbolic equivalent of the past is the Old World, precisely because it is (from a Euroamerican perspective) *older* than our part of the world.

On the other hand, from a European perspective shared by many Americans, it is the technologically underdeveloped areas of the world which symbolize the past, because they seem *more primitive* than Europe. (Tempted and tried, I shall nevertheless not discuss the defects of this view of history; it is not with history, but with perceptions of history, that I am here dealing.)

The technology of the non-European nations during periods of colonizing was less advanced, particularly and crucially their weapons technology; from a European point of view, their governmental structures seemed primitive; and nineteenth-century European anthropologists, with misguided eagerness, delightedly studied technologically less sophisticated tribesmen in order to gain, as they thought, some insight into the behavior and mentality of their own Stone Age ancestors.

In the literature, then, as in real life, when the American confronts Europe, he is likely to see the past as superior—at least in some ways—to the present, whether artistically, spiritually, intellectually, or aesthetically. In such case, the traveler to the past, like the traveler to Europe, is likely to approach his destination as a tourist or as a student. On the other hand, when the European (or the American) confronts technologically less advanced countries, the past appears inferior in other important ways. And in such case, the traveler to the past, like the nineteenth-century British traveler to India, is likely to take on some of the characteristics of the imperialist. These conflicting visions of the past as superior and as inferior are not new; it is, I think, useful to see them as late echoes of the late-seventeenth- and early-eighteenth-century Battle of the Books. Sometimes, as in the *Yankee*, both visions of the past manage to coexist in uneasy truce.

In Anderson's "Gibraltar Falls," the hero is a time patrolman, a familiar figure in the literature of time travel: open up a frontier, and the first thing you know, you need a marshal. In spite of the ironclad rule against meddling with the past unless to undo the meddling of others—because "none less than God can be trusted with time"—he deliberately circles back in time to save a human life. So does the hero of another story in the same series, "Time Patrol."

Anderson well understands that because we are human, we need rules. Gods do not, and to the extent that humans have power, to that extent they take on the role of gods; and the time traveler has powers which only a god should have. Larry Niven says that the whole point of travel to the past is changing the past, and the whole danger of travel to the past is that someone will do it. A fine Catch 22: the time patrolman has power which he must and must not use.

A similar moral dilemma confronts the mundane colonizer. He knows full well that if he introduces alien concepts, alien technology, or alien values, he will very likely shatter a whole unique and irreplaceable culture. Nevertheless, possessed of the agricultural technology which would save a generation of starving children, or of the medicine which would save a woman's eyesight, or of the machines which would relieve humans of killing labor to maintain a starvation economy, has he the right *not* to introduce such technology, whatever the impact on the culture?

The published rule of Anderson's "Time Patrol" is an unequivocal and unqualified "No." Time may not be changed, however worthy the motive; the dangers are too great. We have heard this again and again in time travel literature from people like Bradbury ("A Sound of Thunder") and Moore (*Bring the Jubilee*), who show unexpected and horrid oaks growing from heedless past acorns, and like Asimov (*The End of Eternity*) and Bayley (*The Fall of Chron-*

opolis), whose time-altering imperialists at length see the folly of their ways and renounce all interference with the past.

Nevertheless the dilemma remains, and it is one of those unsolvable problems which fuel artistic creation: if one *has* the power of a god, is he not obliged to use it? And if one can *develop* the power of a god, is he not obliged to develop it? It is the problem of Victor Frankenstein, as it was the problem of Robert Oppenheimer, as it is the problem of the genetic engineer of our day. When more advanced technology impinges on less advanced—whether by geographic movement, by travel to the past, or by new technology moving into the present— whatever the holder of the technology does, he will be wrong.

If the imperialist, temporal or mundane, chooses one course, he will warp or destroy an irreplaceable culture; if the other, he will allow the suffering and death of irreplaceable human beings. We have posed the problem before: if I *can* prevent the rise of Hitler, or the killing of Dr. King, or the outbreak of the Thirty Years' War, must I not do so? And even if I profit thereby, doing well by doing good, does that alter the matter?

RUNNING THE MADHOUSE: MORGAN AND CRUSOE

In *Dreams of Adventure, Deeds of Empire* Martin Green has judiciously demonstrated the workings of imperialistic themes in both *Robinson Crusoe* and the *Connecticut Yankee*, and to him I am much obliged. Crusoe is, in truth, an ancestor of Hank Morgan, as Morgan himself perceives; indeed, all tales of temporal stranding are *robinsonades*:

I saw that I was just another Robinson Crusoe cast away on an uninhabited island, with no society but some more or less tame animals, and if I wanted to make life bearable I must do as he did—invent, contrive, create, reorganize things; set brain and hand to work, and keep them busy. Well, that was in my line. (VII)

There speaks the nineteenth-century work ethnic; there also speaks the Eurocentric chauvinism which counts Columbus or Erikson the "discoverer" of an America already loaded with "more or less tame animals." Twain makes that last phrase double-edged, not only satirizing a blind Eurocentrism but also expressing that pessimistic side of himself which could see all humanity as animals tamed rather less than more, reminding one rather not only of the end of *Gulliver's Travels* but also of that of H. G. Wells' *Island of Doctor Moreau*.

In the Yankee, we recognize the take-charge American entrepreneur: given lemons, one not only makes lemonade, one sets up a lemonade factory and uses it as a financial base with which to buy up the rest of the local culture.

Hank Morgan's first reaction, on landing in the sixth century, is to fancy himself in a madhouse; to the newly arrived traveler, spatial or temporal, the primitive natives of course seem mad, or at least feeble-minded, just as, to the natives, the foreigner is not playing with a full deck. Again the double-edged Twain sword: on the one hand, it is delightfully funny that one's own ethnocentrism always defines sanity; on the other, we are, when all is said and done, a race of fools and madmen.

In the western tradition up to the nineteenth century, wise men do not mess around with the gods; prudent men do not mess around with tradition; and sane men do not even think of messing around with time. Those are three different ways of saying the same thing. No wonder, then, that in much of time travel literature up to the 1950s, by which time the idea was well entrenched in the literature, time travelers are all the time doubting their own sanity, being seen as mad by the natives, or being buttoned up in asylums on their return from outtime. Just try to tell anybody about your time voyage, and you will be in the position of the philosopher returning to Plato's cave, or the square in Edwin Abbott's *Flatland* trying to explain three dimensions to a two-dimensional world.

Whether the madhouse is literal or figurative, Morgan will run it, proposing to the King of the Lunatics this very sane bargain:

You [Arthur] shall remain king . . . but you shall appoint me your perpetual minister and executive, and give me for my services one per cent. of such actual increase of revenue as I may succeed in creating for the state. If I can't live on that, I sha'n't ask anybody to give me a lift. (VI)

In effect: as one-eyed man in the country of the blind, or as sane man in the country of the foolish and insane, I deserve a return in both money and power for the use of my sight and my sanity. Similarly, Robinson Crusoe, *because he has the technology and for no other reason*, deserves—as he and Defoe both seem to think—to become monarch of all he surveys.

Just as Defoe created a whole new subspecies of fiction with *Robinson Crusoe*, a hymn to rugged individualism and the processes of technology, so among Twain's many accomplishments must be numbered the adaptation of that subspecies to the temporal sphere: that the Yankee, unlike Crusoe, ultimately comes to grief shadows but does not obscure his delight in technology. Defoe, to be sure, cheats a bit at the game he is inventing by conveniently leaving Crusoe a wreck laden with goodies to loot; but, as I say, he is inventing the game and one cannot fault him for not playing by the rules. Do give him credit for his meticulous documentation of the processes by which Crusoe struggles up from naked ape to monarch, a microcosmic version of humanity's supposed progress.

Twain, however, has nowhere near the understanding or appreciation of technology which Defoe does. Twain's love of machinery, as his infatuation with the Paige typesetter demonstrates, was always a romance rather than a marriage, based on dreamed-of possibilities and hoped-for quick returns rather than on reasonable profits and realizable realities. Like the Yankee, Twain always had his eye more on the potential gain than on the technique itself. All of the Yankee's new technology Twain dismisses with a wave of the hand, not even attempting, in Chapter IX, to explain the provenance of the crosscut saw which Morgan lends the surgeon. Morgan has said he is a jack-of-all-trades, and that must suffice.

What the Yankee clearly lacks, and what Twain does not trouble to give him, is a technological infrastructure. Defoe does so with Crusoe, after a fashion, by presenting him with a ship to loot; but looting is only a temporary measure in the history of a civilization. A technology, after all, is the product of many people working over many generations: and in a literature driven by technology, written in a land driven by technology, this fact makes difficult the position of the traditional SF hero, who singlehandedly is supposed to change the fate of a nation, of a planet, or of a galaxy.

Such heroes are a necessary source of tension, the affirmation of the worth of the individual in a mass society. John Henry affirms the strength of the human against the machine; in the movie serials, Flash Gordon again and again triumphs over menacing alien science with sheer force of character and body. His removal from the mass society of the nineteenth century gives the Yankee the opportunity to become such a hero, and clearly Twain intends him to be, up until he looses nemesis on him, but the details—like those of many a heroic space opera—are just not very well worked out. How, as a nineteenth-century machinist, can Morgan make copper wire in the sixth century? How, without benefit of his Hartford machine shop and the iron mills of Pittsburgh, can he make a pump? How does he get a generator, a typewriter, a steam engine, all from scratch?

And yet, in seven short years, Mark Twain has the Yankee getting the nineteenth century, complete with bicycles, telegraph, electricity, gunpowder, and printing presses, going full bore in the secluded alcoves of the sixth. The whole process is disposed of in three or four pages. No contemporary science fiction writer would dare do so; howls of reader outrage would be heard from sea to shining sea.

Why all the hurry? What it is about is *speed*, quick change, quick riches. It is the very dream that Twain pursued all his life: the big score, change and wealth, very nineteenth-century, very American: to walk into the jungle like Willy Loman's brother and walk out, by God, rich. Small wonder, given the fortunes being made all over the place in the post–Civil War North.

Hank Morgan is in pursuit of just such a quick fix, and Twain lets him have it with a godless and unjustifiable speed. Morgan is going to drag the sixth century, with its serfdom, superstition, ignorance, and torture, kicking and screaming into the nineteenth, taking a shortcut of some thirteen centuries. It is the dream of Horatio Alger applied to history. And, just as quickly, Twain takes it all away from him; as in Moore's *Bring the Jubilee*, there are no shortcuts in history.

Even so, that lack of credible technological process is troublesome. But just as we cannot, in all fairness, fault Defoe for cheating a bit against rules he has not yet invented, so we must not judged Twain too harshly. After all, Crusoe had predecessors of a sort in literature, all the way back to Odysseus on Kalypso's isle. It is only the technology which is new, and the drama of technological man confronting a non-technological environment. But the Connecticut Yankee, and Twain, had no such predecessors.

Twain's game, then, while it is an elaboration of Defoe's, is a new one: his Robinson is isolated in time as well as in space, isolated from the whole temporal technical structure which made the technology of his home time possible. A similar isolation of perception, be it noted, separates the SF reader of the 1980s from the *Yankee*: since the publication of that book, the rules of the game have been honed to a fine edge, and most SF readers are well aware of them.

The game, which many of us have played in fantasy, lands us in a given time—pick it—with nothing except what we have on our persons or in our minds, the latter including our understanding and misunderstanding of the technology of our own age and the history of the ages preceding. What we know of technology will give us the advantage of any Crusoe-brand imperialist; hindsight will give us the godlike ability to call the plays after we have seen the rerun. Note that, after his first inexplicable use of hindsight to predict an eclipse, Morgan's historical knowledge amounts to exactly zero in terms of what he can do with it; with his usual splendid irony, Twain establishes that any wandering faker is more likely to be believed than is Morgan.

THE MADHOUSE RUNNING: *LEST DARKNESS FALL*

The important novels in this particular tradition are three: *Robinson Crusoe*, which invented the *robinsonade*; the *Yankee*, which acknowledges its descent from Crusoe and extends the idea to time past; and *Lest Darkness Fall*, which, it is said, de Camp, a much more technically sophisticated man than Twain, wrote in reaction to the *Yankee* to show how the game *should* be played. In both books, the hero suffers a physical shock which sends him back to the sixth century, where he invents journalism and advertising, wrestles with the religious establishment, makes himself The Boss while leaving the local monarch his titles and dignity, inflicts much of the technology of his owntime on a hapless past, corrupts his own character both because of his environment and because of his own powertripping, and attempts to put finish to the world and to the history that otherwise would have been.

Furthermore, both travelers, Twain's Morgan and de Camp's Padway, find important resemblances between themselves and the local rulers (age in the *Yankee*, stature in *Darkness*). The cities of the past, Camelot and old Rome, are both explicitly compared to cities in the travelers' owntimes, Bridgeport and Philadelphia respectively. Artifacts already old in the sixth century—Merlin's castle and an ancient column—are misused to the travelers' advantages; Padway, a bit more sensitive to the values of the natives, shows some remorse over his action, as Morgan does not. Both heroes pretend to be magicians and take advantage of hindsight to pose as prophets, Padway with more practical results than Morgan. Padway, however, unlike that super-showman Morgan, insists that he is "just an ordinary man" with a special and limited gift: as indeed he is, with the special and limited gift of having been sent back in time. Both discover that old jokes, stories, and turns of phrase are new and impressive in the past; strangely enough, it is the usually canny Yankee who finds this fact annoying, Padway who takes advantage of it. Twain had, however, planned at one stage (California *Yankee* 640) to include a competition of bards in which the Yankee would win by "whirl[ing] in some . . . Tennyson, with a touch of Shak & Browning," not unlike the poetic hash created by the Duke in Chapter XXI of *Huckleberry Finn*. It would have been a noble irony for Morgan to inflict the Victorian sentimentalities of *Idylls of the King* upon the grubby and ignorant originals, but inappropriate for an "ignoramus" like the Yankee.

And both travelers are jailed relatively early on in their sojourns in the past, escaping captivity and possible death by the use of their wits.

Nor Iron Years a Cage: The Past as Prison

Indeed, the jailhouse scene, whether literal or figurative, inflicted on the traveler before his departure from owntime, during his stay in outtime, or upon his return (if return he does) to his owntime, is so prevalent as to deserve a long parenthesis here. To be sure, some of this near-ubiquity can be explained in terms of plot: if one is going to indulge oneself in *robinsonades*, after all, falling into the hands of hostile natives is the least one can expect.

Furthermore, imprisonment followed by release followed by success is a staple of the nineteenth-century romance, which is another of the ancestors of science fiction. Consider those two French Yankee entrepreneurs, Valjean and Monte-Cristo. Consider, also, that the freedom won so hard by these last two becomes, in its turn, a sort of imprisonment, as do those of Morgan and Padway: "Except for business errands [Padway] had hardly been out of his house for four months in his desperate anxiety to get his [printing] press going." (47) The Yankee himself is imprisoned, literally or figuratively, four times: he is tossed into a dungeon on his arrival, prefatory to his intended execution; he is enslaved along with Arthur during their voyage incognito; he ends his time in the sixth century in a concentration camp of his own making; and the rest of his life in the nineteenth century is as an exile like that of Hale's "The Man without a Country."

Let me give a few more examples of the motif as it appears in time travel fiction: Joe Bodenland, in Aldiss' *Frankenstein Unbound*, is imprisoned for the murder of Victor Frankenstein. In Farley's "Rescue into the Past," the traveler is imprisoned by American revolutionaries as a Tory spy; in the same author's "Man Who Met Himself," the traveler is jailed as a result of a dispute with the religious establishment. The traveler in Alison Uttley's *Traveler in Time* is imprisoned in a tunnel designed as an escape route for Mary Queen of Scots. In de Camp's "Aristotle and the Gun," the protagonist is arrested in ancient Greece as a Persian spy.

Extend the concept of imprisonment just a bit, and the examples multiply. In

Anderson's *There Will Be Time*, Havig is put in chains by the Sachem in his own future; the same author's "My Object All Sublime" gives us a criminal exiled to our time from the future who, when he sets down roots here, is exiled to a still more distant and disgusting past; the protagonist in Aldiss' "T" is sent to the past in the straitest of traveling dungeons; the hero of G. C. Edmondson's *Ship That Sailed the Time Stream* is enslaved by Romans; and in Howard Goldsmith's "Proust Syndrome" and Mort Weisinger's "Thompson's Time-Traveling Theory," the travelers, returned to owntime, are buttoned up as lunatics.

The examples might be multiplied many times if one cared to do so; they are so very many as to make the easy explanations of happenstance or need for melodrama quite inadequate. One may hypothesize thus: during the Renaissance, European perspective on geography—that is, Terran space—changed drastically as explorers and settlers opened up new horizons; quite naturally, whether they wished or no, the native victims of European expansion likewise had a new and expanded geography inflicted upon them.

If, as for many medieval people, there were not many places out there one knew about to go to, then the notion that staying in one place was a sort of imprisonment would occur to few people. If, on the other hand, there is a good deal of sparsely occupied territory about which one knows, then, for the ambitious or the malcontent, one's home turf may, if one cannot leave it, appear a sort of prison. *Freedom of movement*, that freedom so prized by most Americans, does not seem to have occurred to any people not in a nomadic stage as a basic human right before the Renaissance; even the Crusaders appear to have simply moved from one static location in the West to new static Latin states in the East.

But the centuries from the sixteenth to the nineteenth can be seen as a time in which ever-growing numbers of decently settled agriculturalists and tradesmen (no nomads, they) struggled in one way or another to burst the bonds that tied them to a given tract of territory. And part of the lingering appeal, I would suggest, of figures such as those of the cowboy, the frontiersman, and the pirate lies in the *sense of continual movement* associated with them.

Similarly, with the crumbling of the little 6000-year time frame, from Eden to the Last Judgment, with which Europe began the nineteenth century, and the widespread acceptance of a time stretching millions or billions of years into past and future, one's own time, I suggest, begins to look more and more like a strait cell, just as one's own place did after the Renaissance.

Here again, then, a suggestion why travel to the past first surfaces in the late nineteenth century: just as, from the sixteenth century to the present, the spatial traveler may begin as a prisoner and end up as a (literal or figurative) exile, so, with the expanded vision of temporality occasioned by the collapse of Biblical chronology, the rebel of the nineteenth century may find his own time a prison. If he is a chronic optimist, he will pine for the better future; if not, he may seek his liberation in the past (Edward Bellamy and Mack Reynolds in the first case, the pre-Raphaelites in the second). The skeptic, like Twain, may finish with the somewhat glum perception that all times have been, or would be, prisons of one sort or another. The hero of fiction is nearly always a freedom-seeker; and if the author's perception is that no freedom can be found in owntime, then the hero must seek outtime.

The development of this idea in non-time-travel SF is clear; once the possibility of leaving an overly regulated planet becomes the matter of SF rather than of fantasy, the individualistic hero may seek his freedom again in space. Verne's Nemo does so in the inaccessible depths of the sea; Burroughs' Tarzan does so in the temporarily inaccessible depths of Africa; and thousands of heroes of space opera have done so in extraTerran space.

Here, then, another suggestion about why fiction of travel to the past, in spite of its fantastic nature, finds a place in SF: *There is a direct line of thematic descent from pre-SF-SF like Defoe's* Crusoe, *early and late fiction of travel to the past like Twain's* Yankee, *and non-time-travel SF like "Doc" Smith's* First Lensman. *And it is the continuity of theme, that is, the desire to escape the prisons of space and time, which pulls them all into the same category, rather than any intrinsic credibility of the idea of travel to the past.*

Padway, the Ex-Prisoner as Colonizer

The colonizer, then, is one who longs for a freedom he does not have at home. Like his friend Tancredi, Padway finds in his own time "nothing big, nothing new." (Is it not passing ironic that one must go to the past to find something new?) The colonizer, typically, is a nobody in a technological and mass society who, armed with that same technology, can become a somebody in a less developed time or place. Padway in his own America is short; in sixth-century Italy, like Pennywither in fifteenth-century France, he is a giant.

If a figurative prison exists in owntime, the traveler often encounters another in the past, because as soon as he can ascertain that he is not mad, he must contrive to stay alive and make a living: under the pressure of a new and hostile environment, the would-be-empire-builder may find his movements are initially even more seriously limited than they were in his owntime.

If a person knows that he is going to a primitive environment, present or past, he can prepare for it and therefore is no Crusoe. But Padway, like Morgan and many another traveler, has no chance to prepare before the shipwreck. All he has is what he has in his pockets—and his wits.

What Padway does with those wits is much more carefully worked out than what Hank Morgan does. Needing capital, he heads for a bank, where he agrees to teach the banker the use of Arabic numerals in exchange for a loan. (As in Simak's "Big Front Yard," the best medium of exchange is ideas.) Then Padway goes into the distilling business, all the difficulties of building a still with sixth-century metalworking techniques being scrupulously documented by the author.

Both Morgan and Padway are quick to see the advantages they possess. Padway considers that, as poor a businessman as he was in his own century, he can "hold his own well enough in competition with these sixth-century yaps," while

Morgan sees his situation as an opportunity to Go West, Young Man: "Look at the opportunities here for a man of knowledge, brains, pluck and enterprise to sail in and grow up with the country" (VIII). Note that both Padway's term "yaps" and Morgan's half-quote from Horace Greeley reinforce what we have said about the identification of the past—and the future—with the frontier.

After a bit of time in the primitive locale, the imperialist's dreams are likely to get larger: he is no longer satisfied to earn a living, or even to get wealth and power. Like both Morgan and Padway, he is likely to conceive the idea of becoming a moving force of history.

The Yankee decides to shortcut thirteen centuries of history and bring the nineteenth century to the sixth, complete with technology, Presbyterian church, Gatling guns, and manhood suffrage; more modestly, and yet with greater vision, Padway decides that, like Seldon in Asimov's *Foundation*, he can perhaps prevent the Dark Ages and thereby give history a several-century shortcut.

Padway, like many a man of science, sees the whole medieval period as essentially "dark":

The Age of Faith, better known as the Dark Ages, was closing down. Europe would be in darkness, from a scientific and technological aspect, for nearly a thousand years. That aspect was, to Padway's naturally prejudiced mind, the most, if not the only, important aspect of a civilization. (39)

It is important to notice how in this passage de Camp distances himself from his hero, showing himself too sophisticated to buy the easy equation of "medieval" with "dark," and careful to lay this equation off on the natural prejudices of Martin Padway. Both Twain and de Camp tempt us, first to identify with their heroes, and second to accept the equation of their heroes with the authors; and both of them have inserted traps to warn us away from such courses.

As Padway considers his strategy, three elements remind us of the Yankee: first, the importance of communication; second, the standard SF theme of the hero changing a society against fearful odds; and third, the increasing arrogance of the budding imperialist, as the Cheevyian and Mittyian dreams of "Mouse" Padway begin to take on a past-possibility: "Could one man change the course of history to the extent of preventing this interregnum? . . . The web [of historical intertia] might be tough, but maybe it had never been attacked by a Martin Padway" (40).

Padway knows more about sixth-century Italian history than does the average man; and like an imperialist (or like an artist) he is able to see disaster not as the fearful suffering of human beings, but simply as a troublesome impediment to his own Grand Design: "If he lived long enough he might see the Lombard invasion and the near-extinction of Italian civilization. All this would interfere dreadfully with his plans" (51). The irony of sentences in *Lest Darkness Fall* like the last one has gone largely unremarked: like Twain's Yankee (and like Swift's Modest Proposer and Gulliver before him), Padway is allowed to say, or think, hideous things in a most matter-of-fact way. All these characters are, at least in one part of their beings, caricatures of the imperial mentality, as is Kurt Vonnegut's narrator in *Slaughterhouse Five*, who can respond to any and all human atrocities with the endlessly repeated and totally inadequate "So it goes."

All of de Camp's processes, unlike those of Twain, are clear and logical, all of his technology credible: Padway does not introduce the telegraph, but the semaphore tower; not the firearm, but the crossbow; not gunpowder, but the telescope. And at the end he is confident that he has, unlike the Yankee, achieved his ambitions: "Darkness would not fall."

Originally published in a shorter version in *Unknown* in 1939, *Darkness* was published in its present form in 1941 by Henry Holt and Company, unusual treatment indeed for pulp SF at that time. It is generally regarded as the most important work of an exceedingly talented and prolific SF Nebula Grand Master, and is a classic of the field, partly because its characters are more interesting and complex than those of most SF of the period, but more particularly because it is the first novel of travel to the past properly to play the game which Defoe invented and Twain extended into the past.

By 1962, *Darkness* was familiar enough to the SF reader that Frederik Pohl could parody it in "The Deadly Mission of Phineas Snodgrass," in which Pohl's protagonist returns quite deliberately to ancient Rome in a time machine: "He stole the idea from a science-fiction novel by L. Sprague de Camp, called *Lest Darkness Fall*."

A big-hearted do-gooder, Snodgrass introduces antibiotics and glasses and anesthesia and the germ theory of disease. He lives to be one hundred and dies confident that Darkness Will Not Fall. Under the pressure of population, technology develops apace: the Nile is dammed at Aswan in the year 55, and by A.D. 300 the world population is a quarter of a trillion and hydrogen fusion is producing energy and food from the sea. And by the sixth century there is no place to lie down on the Earth, which is full of healthy humans.

A time machine is constructed and a volunteer "(selected from the 900 trillion who applied)" goes back to the year 1 and shoots Snodgrass as he arrives in Rome. "To the great (if only potential) joy of some quintillions of never-to-be-born persons, Darkness blessedly fell."

A still more recent (1987) piece of science fiction, Kirk Mitchell's *Never the Twain*, gives the screw still another turn. The time traveler, one Howard Hart, has decided to use Twain's device of travel to the past against Twain himself. Had Twain only held onto his claim in Aurora, Hart's theory goes, he would have become rich by mining silver and never have become the literary giant of the late nineteenth century; that place would, Hart believes, certainly have been taken by Bret Harte, his ancestor, and thus Hart would have inherited the money made in our continuum by Twain, and subsequent copyrights to the value of some $75 million.

This novel deserves more careful attention than it has hitherto received. Like Finney's *Time and Again*, it is based on careful research into the destination time (1862) and place (Carson City). It lets its hero, like Si Morely in the Dakota, use old buildings as time-binders, and like Finney's book shows some nostalgia for a past which seems more simple, more genuine, and more pockmarked; as in *Time and Again*, the hero decides to remain in the past with the woman he has learned to love there; like many another traveler to the past, he becomes part of the past he already had in a snake-swallowing-tail operation; like the Yankee, he is both motivated by avarice and prone to spasms of do-gooding; and, again like the Yankee, he quite unwittingly makes small changes in history (in the Yankee's case, "paying the shot," in Hart's, the idea of right and left boots being different). Like Anderson's *Dancer from Atlantis*, the book makes clear the psychological needs filled by time travel ("It's far too easy for an orphan to become obsessed by the past"); like Martin Padway, Hart, a giant in the past, stumbles unawares into a fight which means nothing to him (various heresies being violently discussed in a sixth-century bar in Padway's case, Unionists versus Rebels in Hart's). Further, Hart gets involved in a process which may just win the Civil War for the South, recalling Moore's *Bring the Jubilee* (though it doesn't work out that way). Although Hart remains in the past, having discovered when his plot against Twain fails that true value lies elsewhere than he thought, his adopted brother and alter ego, in the present, achieves psychic integration as a result of the trip, recalling *The Dancer from Atlantis* again; and, most important for our present purposes, Hart prepares himself for his voyage of temporal imperialism by following a CIA manual called *A Logistical Matrix for the Insertion of Operatives into COMBLOCK or Potentially Hostile Destinations*.

A recent reprise of the *Lest Darkness Fall* motif, very competently done, is Leo Frankowski's Conrad Stargard quadrilogy (*The Cross-Time Engineer*, *The High-Tech Knight*, *The Radiant Warrior*, and *The Flying Warlord*). Frankowski, like de Camp, has an engineering background and this series, even though the Yankee figure is inhumanly efficient, works out the engineering details with a care worthy of de Camp. A Polish engineer stumbles accidentally into a Time Patrol (Historical Corps) transporter and is returned to 1231, well aware that the Mongols are due in ten years. Like Morgan, he manages to build up an industrial empire; and his slaughter of the invaders in the fourth book echoes the Battle of the Sand-Belt in spite of the author's apparent approval of the process. Though the hero thinks of himself as a socialist, he ends up as a Yankee-style capitalist; there are many echoes of de Camp and of the *Yankee* and even some mock-Twain prose: "There was certainly nothing halfway about his psychosis. Apparently he had studied hard to get there" (*The Cross-Time Engineer*, 18). Apparently the Crusoe-Morgan-Padway game is not played out yet.

CECIL RHODES, THE BOSS

At the very time Twain was writing the *Yankee*, a maker of history very like Hank Morgan was operating in Africa. At the age of 19, Cecil Rhodes had made enough of a personal fortune to satisfy almost anybody; at the age of 22, he made it his life's work to ensure British domination of Africa and, indeed, of the world.

In the year 1888, a year before the publication of the *Yankee*, Rhodes had negotiated a most Yankee-like deal with the native king of Mosilikatze, a treaty whereby his syndicate, in exchange for 100 pounds a month, 1,000 rifles, and 100,000 rounds of ammunition, gained effective sovereignty over a territory as large as France, Germany and Holland combined.

Very Yankee-like again, Rhodes within a year was involved in railway-building, mining, encouragement of immigration and trade, and the construction of a telegraph system. The Yankee established a "man-factory" in Camelot; Rhodes is best remembered for his concern for education dedicated to the accomplishment of his imperial ends. I do not mean to suggest that the Yankee was *modeled* on Cecil Rhodes: the times involved are a bit too squeezed together for that. We do know from his *Notebooks* (III, 383) that Twain, while he was writing the *Yankee*, was looking for an article in the *Nineteenth Century* about England's rule in India, which he intended as material for a *Forum* article rebutting Matthew Arnold's criticisms of the United States. He never wrote the article, but his notes show his interest in British imperialism.

What he thought of it is clear in Chapter XXI of *Following the Equator*, a book which followed the Yankee by some eight years, in which, after a long and bitter passage, he concludes: "There are many humorous things in the world; among them the white man's notion that he is less savage than the other savages." On the other hand, Twain has positive things to say about what he sees as the real accomplishments of British rule in India, among which he counts the abolition of suttee and the suppression of Thugee. Here is the same ambiguity of attitude we saw toward Hank Morgan in the *Yankee*, which means the same contradictory attitudes toward the introduction of technology.

Unlike the Yankee, Rhodes was no Crusoe; he went to Africa deliberately and could leave when he would. And the technological infrastructure which supported him was always within a long reach; at any time he could return to Europe and then come back to Africa armed and prepared. When the implications of Wells' time machine work their way into SF, many time travelers cease being Crusoes and become Rhodeses full-blown; the time machine is to the temporal imperialist as the steamship is to the nineteenth-century spatial imperialist.

For it was in the nineteenth-century that Yankee-style imperialism made its great appearance. The earlier burst of European adventurism during and after the Renaissance seems to have operated out of, and given rise to, quite a different sort of consciousness. Largely preceding, as it did, that Age of Reason when a certain appreciation of non-European cultures began to percolate in European consciousnesses, Renaissance imperialism was in a sense the last hurrah of the Crusader mentality. There were few writers in the time to protest the Christianizing and consequent ruin of native cultures: natives were Ariels at best, Calibans at worst, and in either case needed the direction of European Prosperos. But the

Yankee is fueled by a tension between approval of and disapproval of imperialism, just as a similar tension centered on technology fires all science fiction; and those tensions were just not there in the days of the earlier European imperialists— who, given the lack of steamships, were in a position a little closer to Crusoe anyhow.

Here, then, another suggestion as to why the traveler to the past, a figure strongly suggestive of the European imperialist, first appears in Twain's time: *Just as the steamship made the nineteenth century the first great tourist era, just so the steamship and European weaponry made the same century the great, and morally greatly ambiguous, era of imperialism; and the time traveler, caught in the moral crack between respect for native humanity and appreciation of technological progress, reflects the moral dilemmas of imperialism.*

TO DO THE WORK FOR WHICH GOD CREATED ME

Poul Anderson's *There Will Be Time* presents us with the most fully developed Cecil Rhodes figure since the Yankee, one Caleb Wallis, who has almost none of the Yankee's endearing characteristics and a good many of his more repellent ones. The hero of this novel, Havig, is recruited by Wallis, a nineteenth-century adventurer known as the Sachem who, like Havig, has the ability to travel in time, apparently a rare mutation accompanied by sterility. Born a bit later than Twain's Yankee in 1853 in upstate New York, he has by the age of 35 used his gift to make himself a fortune; and like Rhodes, having made his pile, he goes on "to the work for which God . . . created me."

From his Eyrie in twenty-second-century Wisconsin, the Sachem sends out his recruiters, concentrating on those moments in history that many time travelers would be likely to visit, such as the crucifixion. When Havig first meets the Sachem (67–68), he recognizes the photos on the wall of the Sachem's office: the youthful Napoleon, Bismark, and Cecil Rhodes. The music accompanying the meeting is the "Entry of the Gods" from *Das Rheingold*. Wallis is strange: a Victorian gentleman in a Franz Josef beard dressed in a uniform part SS, part Ruritanian.

Like Rhodes, the Sachem believes in European civilization above everything. What is happening in Havig's own time? he asks, and in the manner if not the matter of Josef Stalin and Big Brother he answers himself:

Civilized man turning against himself, first in war, later in moral sickness. The white man's empires crumbling faster than Rome's; the work of Clive, Bismark, Rhodes, McKinley, Lyautey, all Indian fighters and Boers, everything that'd been won, cast out in a single generation. . . . (69)

When Havig, disgusted with the Sachem's ideas and actions, goes AWOL and marries in thirteenth-century Constantinople, the Sachem's reaction upon Havig's recapture is predictably racist and sexist:

It is not fitting for a proper white man to bind himself to a female like that. She was Levantine, you know. Which means mongrel—Armenian, Asiatic, husky, spig, Jew, probably a touch of nigger. . . . Mind, I've nothing against you boys having your fun. . . . But you, Jack, you *married* this'n. (135)

What follows is almost verbatim out of any number of anti-Semitic texts purporting to explain why the Superior Nordic is so often Outwitted by His Inferiors:

Because [the white man] is more intelligent and sensitive, he opens himself to those who hate him. They divide him against himself, they feed him lies, they slide their slimy way into control of his own homelands, til he finds he's gotten allied with his natural enemy against his brother. . . . Two of the greatest geniuses the white race ever produced, its two possible saviors from the Slav and the Chinaman, were lured into war on different sides. Douglas MacArthur and Adolf Hitler. (136)

This Klannish racism is not typical of temporal imperialists, although, as we have said, they are prone to see people from the past (who are "already" dead) as less than completely human; it is, however, an undercurrent even in the overtly democratic and progressive Yankee. Morgan begins with the amused and patronizing tolerance of a Rhodes who loves and helps his native inferiors, to his own profit, of course, while recognizing that they are not to be trusted too far out of his sight; he continues by deciding that Arthur's knights are little better than Apaches, of whose culture his opinion is clear; his original dream of a future democracy fades in the reality of his dictatorship, which seems likely to go on until he dies; and he ends by masterminding the genocide of the Battle of the Sand-Belt.

Havig himself has some attitudes, not unreasonable ones, which make him less resistant to the Sachem than he would otherwise have been; like many a nostalgic—and we have seen how often nostalgia turns into a tool of reaction— he views the future of our present (54) as a threatening one. Nor does he believe much in progress: if the past was not better than the present, it was at least not much worse. And so any hope for improvement, even from such a source as the Sachem, is welcome. It is the story of many a German citizen in the 1920s.

In the end, of course, he rebels, gathers his own forces, and puts an end to the Sachem's plans; then, having the power, he has the same moral problems anyone in possession of superior technology must face. What will he do with the Sachem and his men? He chooses to brainwash them chemically, leaving the Sachem with the delusion that he is still in charge and that everything is working out just fine. And that action, of course, raises two questions: whether anyone in authority can ever know what is going on, and whether any planned progress can be more than an illusion. Havig's solution, the most humane possible in the circumstances, is still not without its horror. In the end, for the Sachem, as for the old, old Yankee, all of his story seems a dream, and he can no longer tell what is or was real; only at the moment of his death does he glimpse the truth, as perhaps we are meant to believe the Yankee did.

OUR LITTLE BROWN BROTHERS

Part of the motivation of the imperialist, as we have said, is to do well; the other part often is to do good. While American soldiers in the Philippines were singing "Underneath the starry flag, Civilize 'em with a Krag," other American imperialists, quite unconsciously racist, sincerely believing themselves Christian philanthropists, went on about our duty to "our little brown brothers." The first voice is obviously that of the Sachem, the second that of those who, for the world's own good, would impose a benevolent and rational order on it.

Asimov's 1955 novel, *The End of Eternity*, depicts just such a benevolent imperialism in temporal terms. The members of "Eternity" keep chasing up and down the centuries, adjusting the past so that the future may become that which holds the greatest good for the greatest number. In a way, it is the flip side of Anderson's Time Patrol. Of course, the result is a future boring in the extreme, with neither adventure nor heroism—a problem common to utopias.

Finally, a member of "Eternity" chooses to effect a change in the past which will prevent that group from coming to be; this action shunts history back to the Basic State, exchanging eternity for infinity, security for adventure, certain life for possible death. Here again we hear echoes of older stories, not only the Three Wishes—at the end of which we undo all we have done—but Aesop's fable of the dog and the wolf in which the wolf declines to pay for sure meals by donning a collar.

A similar drama is played out in *The Fall of Chronopolis*, by Barrington J. Bayley. An empire changes time to support itself; those who glimpse the underlying time-strata become "like gods" and must die; ultimately the empire is limited by other empires to its own 1000 years, but left alone like the surviving remnant of the Byzantine Empire of the fifteenth century, as a horrid example to other ages of the dire results of temporal imperialism.

The entry of a second imperial power into the plot gives us the *Legion of Time* scenario, in which two empires are quarreling over time like Germany and England in Africa in World War I. When two imperial nations fight, as often as not much of the fighting is done by native mercenaries. SF has used this theme again and again in works like *A Century of Progress*, by Fred Saberhagen, in which a man of our time is recruited by a group seeking to eliminate Hitler from as many Paratimes as possible; *No Brother, No Friend*, by Richard C. Meredith, in which the analogy with mundane imperialism is explicit ("Hidden Kriths waging war with hidden Paratimers . . . most of the dying being done by ignorant locals"); *Birds of Prey*, by David Drake, in which Roman mercenaries are hired by a future traveler to fight extraterrestrials—and in which the imperialist, first seeing her hirelings as tools, learns to see them as people; *Bridgehead*, by the same author, in which travelers from 300 generations in the future return to develop a time machine here so that the loop can be closed—or so they claim (in fact, matter-transmission is being disguised as time travel, but Earthfolk are pawns all the same); and Gordon Eklund's *Serving in Time*, an echo of Jack

Williamson, in which the mercenary is involved in a fight between a pastoral and a tyrannical future, the decision involving eleven Jonbar hinges.

Once in a great while, in what we might call the Dien Bien Phu theme, the natives know their own terrain so well that the imperialist, in spite of his technology, is frustrated and defeated. Anderson did this once in a non-time-travel novel, *The High Crusade*, in which medieval knights, facing advanced extraterrestrials, find that their enemies have become too sophisticated to fight them well: for example, their metal detectors cannot find wooden catapults in the woods. Anderson's short story "The Man Who Came Early" does very much the same thing in the temporal frame, allowing tenth-century Icelanders to carry the day against a twentieth-century would-be Yankee.

A variation on this theme is played by Dean McLaughlin in "Hawk Among the Sparrows." Tossed back into World War I in his contemporary jet, the traveler manages to join a French squadron and somehow get enough kerosine to run his aircraft. He cannot fly the planes of 1918; his jet flies too fast for him to be able to shoot the enemy; and his missiles cannot track the little enemy fighters, made as they are out of wood and canvas. Totally frustrated, finally he takes out an enemy squadron with a sonic boom. His plane, without which he feels "just an ordinary man," crashes; but on rethinking the matter he reacts like a true Yankee: "A man from the future ought to have *some* advantage over the natives!"

Chapter 6

CHILDREN OF THE YANKEE: DEAR OLD DAD AND HIS GIRL

The Past is such a curious Creature
  To look her in the Face
A Transport may reward us
  Or a Disgrace—

Unarmed if any meet her
  I charge him fly
Her rusty Ammunition
  Might yet reply.

—Emily Dickinson

ARTHUR, FRANKENSTEIN, AND TWAIN

It is interesting to note the ways in which Biblical and classical motifs keep showing up in Malory, as well as in his predecessors in Arthurian literature. The classical motif in which I am here most interested is the Oedipal: it is not my purpose to assert any direct line of influence, but merely to note that the tangled family chain, with incest both inter- and intragenerational, is as much a theme in the Arthurian legend as in those early stories of ancient Greece.

Arthur himself, you will remember, is the product of a liaison between the innocent Lady Igraine, wife of the Duke of Tintagil, and Uther Pendragon, who appears to her disguised as her husband. Arthur avoids bastardy by the narrowest of margins: first, because of the duke's death before his conception, and second, because before Arthur's birth Uther marries the lady. She brings to the marriage daughters Morgan le Fay (who is thus Arthur's half-sister), Elaine, and Margawse (who is in some sources Igraine's sister rather than daughter).

Turning out to be his father's own boy, the young King Arthur casts his eye upon King Lot's wife, who is his half-sister (or aunt) Margawse—a fact not known to him, according to Malory. The result is Mordred, who Merlin foretells will be the death of Arthur. Here, clearly, is another version of the tale of Laios and Oedipus, and of the older story of Kronos and Zeus; and what Arthur does about the matter combines the stories of Laios and Herod:

> Then King Arthur let send for all the children born on May-day, begotten of lords and born of ladies; for Merlin told King Arthur that he that should destroy him should be born in May-day, wherefore he sent for them all. . . . and all were put in a ship to the sea, and some were four weeks old, and some less. (I, 27)

(This does not make a whole lot of sense, first because Merlin has already told Arthur that he has lain with his sister and that the child of that union will be his killer; and second, because children born on May Day would all be the same age.)

> And so by fortune the ship drove unto a castle, and was all to-riven, and destroyed the most part, save that Mordred was cast up, and a good man found him, and nourished him till he was fourteen year old, and then he brought him to the court. . . . (I, 27)

The Herod story, be it noted, is about a king of the Jews who does not want his (unlawful) heir to be born. And the Pharaoh/Moses story is about a king who gets a grandson from the very place he least wants him, in spite of slaughter.

When King Arthur goes overseas to fight Sir Launcelot, lover of the queen, he leaves England and the queen in charge of Sir Mordred, "because Sir Mordred was King Arthur's son" (XX, 19), and it is not long before "[Mordred] was crowned at Canterbury. . . . and said plainly that he would wed her which was his uncle's wife and his father's wife" (XXI, 1). In the battle which results, Arthur kills his son/nephew and, at his hands, receives a wound which results in either his death or his (until now) everlasting coma.

Furthermore, it is useful to note that in the earlier versions of the story, the pseudo-chronicles, the *Historia* of Geoffrey of Monmouth, and the translations by Wace and Layamon, Launcelot does not appear at all: it is his fellow-nephew Mordred who is the queen's lover, and who is beloved of the queen.

What appears to have happened between Geoffrey and Malory, then, is this: the original story—in which Mordred, son and nephew of Arthur, is the lover of Guinevere and ultimately attempts to marry her and take Arthur's throne, only to be killed and to kill his father—has been softened. The nephew has been split into two nephews, and the nephew who is not a son is the one taken by the queen as lover. I take it that in the mythic original, Morgan le Fay and Margawse would be identical, the love-hate relationship thereby intensified, and the presence of Morgan le Fay at Arthur's departure for Avalon thereby explained.

Now, historically and mythologically, the tabu against incest is one which can be (and *must* be) broken only by gods. Hera is both sister and wife to Zeus; Osiris and Isis fell in love in the womb; their parents, Nut, goddess of the sky, and Geb, the earth-god, were siblings; their father, Shu, personification of the atmosphere, and their mother, Tefnut, the mist, were twin brother and sister; *their* father-mother Atum conceived them in masturbatory union with him/herself; the god-kings of Egypt became notorious for brother-sister incest in the second millennium B.C. and repeated the pattern in the days of the Ptolemies; Akhenaten (Amenophis IV) had as first wife his mother, as second his cousin, as fifth his daughter, and while he did not kill his father, he wiped out all traces of his rule; in Milton's epic, arrogating to themselves the privileges of deity, Sin is daughter and mistress to Satan; and there are, of course, pseudo-incestuous overtones even in the Christian myth: as Maureen Duffy notes, "Mary the intercessor like a spiritual Godiva, the sorrowing mother . . . [became] by the fourteenth century . . . 'mother of her father and her brother,' reflecting one of the Church's deep obsessions: incest" (13).

In this view, Oedipus is punished not so much for violating a societal tabu as for satanically intruding on privileges reserved for the gods; and the association of incest with the Faustian/Promethean themes of the nineteenth century is part of an attempt to be as gods. Further, as noted by Gilbert and Gubar, citing Helen Moglen,

The devouring ego of the Satanic-Byronic hero found the fantasy (or reality) of incest the best strategy for metaphorically annihilating the otherness—the autonomy—of the female. "In his union with [his half-sister] Augusta Leigh," Moglen points out, "Byron was in fact striving to achieve union with himself," just as Manfred [in Bryon's drama of that name] expresses his solipsistic self-absorption by indulging in his forbidden passion for his sister, Astarte. (208)

Much science fiction reflects a Promethean search for godhood, whether in the galaxy-busting Skylarks of Doc Smith or the universe-adjusting heroes of James Blish's *Cities in Flight* or Pohl's *Annals of the Heechee*; on the road of time travel toward godhood, the first stop is actual or symbolic incest, the second masturbatory solipcism.

Now, if much of the Faustian/Promethean literature of the nineteenth century savors of incest; and if much of that literature is fueled (as Judith Wilt would have it) by the desire to achieve, and to achieve godhood, in a world running down to heat-death; and if (as Terri Paul would have it) one of the motives for travel to the past is the attempted reversal of entropy; then the marriage of an already rich SF tradition and an Arthurian legend filled with incest and merely formal Christianity, in the hands of Mark Twain, leads naturally enough to the Yankee's travel to the past.

If his biographers do not belie him, Twain was himself fertile ground for such ideas. Second-hand psychoanalysis at a distance of a century is not something any cautious person would indulge in; but Twain's devotion to Mrs. Fairbanks as to a mother-figure, and his replacement of her by Livy; his mixed relationship with his older brother Orion, in which he gradually took over the role of father-figure; his exaggerated guilt over the death of baby Langdon ("I killed him"); his smothering affection for his daughters, who loved and feared him, particularly Susy; his calling Livy "my child" while she called him "Youth"; and his propensity, in age, to make a fool of himself over young women—all are suggestive of a psyche constantly engaged in that confusion of the generations which smells of intergenerational incest.

If, on the other hand, Twain seemed to be fated, again and again, to return to that past which was his own boyhood (and all travel to the past is, I think, symbolically travel to one's own past), he did it, Kaplan says, with a demythologizing honesty: he shared with Howells "a refusal to sentimentalize boyhood or to cleanse it of terrors and anguish" (218), and the demythologizing of his own past which he accomplished in *Huckleberry Finn*, he attempted for the farther past in the *Connecticut Yankee*.

Invading the past, then, and taking it on in its own time, as is done, for example, in the motion picture *Back to the Future*, is like confronting one's father at one's own age and measuring one's manhood or boyhood against his, as the Yankee does with Arthur; and Twain's insistence on the fact that the Yankee and the king are of an age is an indication that this part of the Oedipal theme was conscious or near-conscious. Of the other part—the notion of the mother as potential sexual partner—there is, of course, no textual hint, nor is Twain likely to have consciously entertained the idea. Later writers were to do so.

Now, as we have hinted before, the Oedipal strains of the nineteenth century were peculiarly fierce, what with the remnants of an old patriarchal system still in place but under constant attack from a point of view which combined scientific detachment and religious skepticism; and that strain must have been intense indeed in Mark Twain, who combined many a past illusion about male dominance (fueling his constant chasing after the big money) and female innocence (witness his writing his fiancee that *Don Quixote* was not for her chaste eyes) with an atheistic skepticism that saw all humans as clever animals, after all. Further, these Oedipal tensions were reinforced, as we have seen, by the ambiguous but never tepid relationships between America and Europe, West and East, South and North, city and country.

Intensify all that with a conflict between past (parents) and present (progress) which is in itself ambiguous: in 1877, Kaplan says (236), Twain feared that Bermuda, an "Eden," would be ruined in a few years by the "triple curse" of radio, telegraph, and newspapers; in 1889 the Yankee, with Twain's apparent approval, inflicts two out of the three on the sixth century.

Here, then, is another hint which may help us account for the appearance of travel to the past in America, in 1889, in the hands of Mark Twain: *the incestuous themes of the early nineteenth-century romantic would-be gods find fertile ground in the mind of Twain, who on one level satirizes them and on another level*

*accepts them; and these ambiguous attitudes find reinforcement in the Arthurian
legend into which Twain projects his would-be Faust.*

THE INVADERS AND THE INVADED

Travelers to the past are tourists, filling up the bars and raising the prices; or
they are students, popping up with notebooks at odd and awkward moments; or
they are profiteers, bringing in their damnable technology and throwing honest
folk out of work. In any case, they are invaders, and the Oedipal adventurer is
the biggest invader of all. Sometimes in the literature other ages retaliate. The
invasion of our time by the past, for example, sometimes comes in the form of
a benevolent father rescuing a son in too deep for his own competence, like
Arthur's knights on the western front, or Barbarossa or Karageorge coming to
the rescue of a nation in need; or it comes on our own terms, with the father-
figure showing up as one of us.

In *Knight Life*, a very funny book, Peter David supposes that Morgan le Fey
is immortal and has lived until now, becoming very old and fat and useless.
(David does not spell all the names as Malory did, or as Twain did, but he is
only carrying on a tradition that goes back to the beginnings of the legend.)
Merlin comes out of his cave and Arthur reappears, quickly to be dressed in
three-piece suit, as Arthur Penn, complete with AMEX card. He is impressed,
moderately so, with New York ("Now these buildings are the reality, and it is
I who have become the fantasy") and with people's height. Guinevere, Lancelot,
and Modred are all reincarnated; Arthur runs for mayor of New York and—
because of his courage and old-fashioned honesty—wins, and he is on his way
to the Presidency. Modred once again faces Arthur; but this time, with the help
of modern medicine and modern helpers, Arthur survives and the spirit of Modred
is exorcised from the body it inhabits. On two levels, then, father faces son on
his own grounds and in his own age, and father wins; the neo-Lancelot loses
the new Gwen to Arthur, of course, and as they snuggle on the beach Merlin
turns on the TV to watch the Bing Crosby movie of *A Connecticut Yankee in
King Arthur's Court.*

If the past invades the present so that father can confront son, in "The Long
Wet Purple Dream of Rip Van Winkle," a pornographic fantasy, Philip Jose
Farmer brings the father into the present to confront contemporary women. After
his awakening in the Catskills, Rip is transported to the 1940s, the 1970s, and
the 1980s in succession; he has sexual adventures with Margot Lane (the Shadow's companion), and his own many-times-great-granddaughter—and, in spite
of temporal disorientation, proves himself sexually superior to our contemporaries. Under protest, he is returned to his own time by time patrolmen. The
story is a crude sort of version of the Lazarus Long fantasy (which I'll get to
shortly), in which the Old Father manages to prove himself still the champion
sexual athlete.

Or—reversing direction again—we might be invaded from our own future.

In an extraordinary novel, *Transfer to Yesterday*, Isidore Haiblum allows us to be invaded from an alternate future in which the Hitler-Stalin axis won. Scenes from that future alternate with scenes from our 1935, the parallels between the two eras, as in the *Yankee*, being clearly drawn. Part of the invasion is motivated by a future incest cult. And the invader from the future averts that horrid future by a murder in 1935 which is symbolically equivalent to killing the ancestor.

It is interesting that the literature always talks about the "killing-one's-grand-father" paradox, nicely camouflaging the desire to kill the father. And the paradox embodies real wisdom: if one succeeds in killing one's father, back in time, one kills oneself as well. Furthermore, the dream of childhood innocence is often fatal: in Philip K. Dick's *Martian Time-Slip* Manfred, a child, experiences his terrible old age and retreats into the womb, the last place he was happy; in Alfred Bester's "Hobson's Choice" the hero, in a terrible near-future, dreams of the past only to find that his own age is full of time-bums running from a future in which his time is viewed as a golden age: "Through the vistas of the years every age but our own seems . . . golden. . . . today, bitter or sweet, anxious or calm, is the only day for us. The dream of time is the traitor, and we are all accomplices to the betrayal of ourselves" (147–48).

THE LONG WET DREAM OF LAZARUS LONG

We have noted that, while incestuous themes seem especially evident in fiction of travel to the past, these themes also appear in non-time-travel SF. The most blatantly Oedipal of travelers to the past is, of course, Heinlein's Lazarus Long, and one might expect that Heinlein's other work would also show evidence of such preoccupations.

The most positive attitude, I think, that we can take toward Heinlein's later books, reflecting, I believe, Heinlein's later psychic life, is that the closer the guru in eastern systems approaches to perfect spiritual insight, the more his utterances sound to the uninitiate like the babblings of the village idiot. Indeed, I am more than half-serious about this line of thought: after Lazarus Long's ultimate connection with the mother-principle, there is hardly anywhere to go but into the solipsistic systems of *The Number of the Beast*, *Job*, and *The Cat Who Walks through Walls*—all books in which fiction is as true as truth, all possible things are true somewhere or another, and Heinlein circles warily around the ultimate insight of the sage: Merrily, merrily, merrily, merrily, life is but a dream. (One can understand this line of thought: if one senses oneself near to the end of life, then the recognition that living is not all-important may ease the whole process. The value of this quasi-Buddhist perception has been defended by many; it is not, however, I think, a state of mind which makes for very good fiction, which depends, as we have said before, on the importance and irrevocability of one's actions.)

Since *Time Enough for Love*, indeed, the only exception to this sort of book has been the very strange *Friday*, in which Heinlein tries to see the world and sex through the eyes of a very competent and independent woman. Here, I think overwhelmed by the task, he staggers backward, not only to an early Heinlein view which sees ultimate fulfillment and happiness for women in family, reproduction, and the PTA, but further still, into a John Norman sort of reaction in which the heroine falls in love with her rapist. Unlike most of Heinlein's later books, however, *Friday* is not primarily about sex or solipsism, but about racism. With this exception, however, the last significant action before Heinlein's Brahma begins snorting all the alternate possible worlds up his nostrils is that of Lazarus Long's sexual affair with his mother.

In *Time Enough for Love*, Lazarus Long is the oldest man in the universe, and hence almost everybody's ancestor; in spite of his venerable age, he has, by virtue of rejuvenative treatments, the sexual prowess of a young man. He is wiser, more cynical, more garrulous, more macho, and more of a sexual hero than anyone else in sight.

After several thousand years of life, however, he is becoming bored. The most interesting thing that has happened to him recently is a sojourn on a primitive world, where he rescued a girl, married her when she grew up, raised children with her in a frontier environment, and nursed her through old age to her death. The pseudo-incestuous themes of sex with the daughter-surrogate and sex with the mother-figure, and of lusty male action in a low-tech society, make this episode as close to travel in time as one can get without the actual travel. But now Lazarus Long is bored, and his descendants, for reasons that are not overly clear to the reader, do not wish him to die. Fulfilling a promise to find something new for him to do, they send him back to his own childhood, where, as an apparently young adult male, he meets his unknowing grandfather, makes love to his mother and tells her who he is, and finds his six-year-old self an appealing if irritating little brat.

Those actions are clearly therapeutic for Long, who rediscovers his youthful warriorhood and loses the fatigue which has made him wish for death; and it is the far-future result of other sorts of incest which rescues him from death in World War I and tells him that he cannot die. Long, then, can be Old Father and sex hero at the same time, drinking from the source and the delta of the Nile at the same moment; and in his life-giving descent into his own mother's womb, he is obviously supposed to take on godlike mythic stature, however much he may appear simply an irritating old fart.

It would be pushing things too far, I think to attempt to penetrate the author's psyche and assert that the fantasy was good for him as well as for Long; I do think, however, that the essential psychic identity of Long and Heinlein has been at least tentatively well established by H. Bruce Franklin. But it would also be neglecting an important part of Heinlein's fiction, and of the Oedipal syndrome in general, to ignore the other part of the matter—the confrontation with the father or the father-figure.

For a moment, remember that the title of Hank Morgan, the Connecticut Yankee in King Arthur's court, is the Boss, and then see how many of Heinlein's fathers or father-figures are either so addressed or have that position. In *Friday*, Kettle Belly Baldwin is, for most of the book, unknown to the heroine except as "Boss"; and only after his death is it made known to her that he is, in some sense of the word, her father. In *I Will Fear No Evil*, Johann Sebastian Bach Smith is the "beloved Boss" of Eunice, his secretary, whose body he inherits, and the father of his/their child. In *The Puppet Masters*, a much earlier novel, the boss is called "the Old Man," and it turns out at the end of the book that he is, in very truth, the father of the hero. In *Citizen of the Galaxy*, Thorby finds a "Pop" in an apparent beggar who is in reality a spy, acquires a mother in the society of the "Free Traders," and eventually, in true romantic tradition, discovers that he is the heir to a tremendous financial empire; rejecting his quasi-maternal heritage as over-repressive, he embarks on a crusade against the slavery which killed his biological parents. In *Double Star*, The Boss is ex-Supreme Minister of the Empire, "the most loved (and hated) man in the solar system": and the hero, Lorenzo Smythe, born Lawrence Smith, *becomes* The Boss, the Honorable Joseph Bonforte. In so doing, he redeems himself not only in his own eyes, and presumably in the eyes of the dead Boss, but also in the eyes of his now-dead biological father, also an actor, who beat Smythe's profession into him with a strap: "I think my father would rate it as a 'good performance.' " He also marries the woman whose fierce and daughterly devotion to Bonforte has earlier been outraged by the son's feeble attempts to imitate the father.

In *Farnham's Freehold* the son, overdevoted to his mother, does not heed the hardnosed survivalist advice of his father, and the reward, significantly, is castration; the father, on the other hand, ends up as The Boss, happily wed to a woman more suited in age to his son than to himself. And in *Time Enough for Love*, Lazarus Long is the Old Man of half a galaxy full of humans; his confrontation with the Old Man, however, is not with his father, but with his grandfather, who goads him into playing the man with an absurd and heroic enlistment in the World War I U.S. Army.

Looking at all these examples, we might have a go at constructing a paradigmatic scenario for the Heinlein Oedipal hero:

1. His/her father, The Boss, is an irritating, often enigmatic, tyrant who is almost always right.

2. The Boss knows how to survive to beget offspring; and a successful son (or daughter) will pay attention to his almost interminable epigrams on the subject.

3. The son or son-figure will make early attempts to break free of the father or father-figure—indeed, such attempts are almost indispensable if the son is to prove a true son—but the greater experience of the father will carry the day.

4. The Boss is often the object of the affection, sexual or otherwise, of a young and beautiful woman, whose first reaction to the son is likely to be rejection; as the son becomes The Boss, and the Old Boss dies, her affection is transferred to the Young Boss.

5. The Boss will often provide the younger person with life-saving help or advice; conversely, typically, the young hero will save the life, or the Cause, of The Boss in a fashion which validates him/her as True Child and Heir to The Boss.

This is a slightly more friendly scenario than that of the original Oedipus story, in which the father attempts to do in the son before the latter has a fair chance, and in which the only way the son can become the father is by doing *him* in. In Heinlein, at least, there is the opportunity for mutual recognition and respect, even time enough for love. The Old Man can die or retire with confidence that his child or child-surrogate will carry on his work and vindicate his life.

This father-and-son scenario which Heinlein has maintained over three decades has been significantly changed only recently: first with the introduction of the mother-figure not as a source of weakness but as a source of psychic nourishment (in *Time Enough for Love*); and second with the tentative admission (in *Friday*) that a daughter-figure might go through many of the same processes as a son-figure. The psychic danger for Heinlein, obviously, of this identification of the father with the son, the mother with the beloved, is that the whole business can end in solipsistic narcissism, as it does not only in Heinlein's three late novels but also earlier in "All You Zombies"—in which the action begins in a bar called "Pop's Place."

We have noted, then, that the Oedipal scenario which surfaces spectacularly in Lazarus Long's affair with his mother in *Time Enough for Love* is there in another shape through much of his earlier work—the confrontation of, rebellion against, reconciliation with, and transformation into The Boss, the father.

This sort of thing happens again and again in the literature of travel to the past. Jack Finney's *Time and Again*, while nowhere near as sexually explicit as *Time Enough for Love*, does give us a good approximation of the scenario: the hero travels back in time, confronts a man whose physical power, age, ability in his own time, and potential income and power are much greater than his; learns that this man is a rival for the hand of the lady in the case; wins the lady and saves the career of his rival, admiring in spite of himself the accomplished villainy of a man of his grandfather's generation. In Ward Moore's *Bring the Jubilee*, the hero, in order to gain status, first, with a woman who treats him like a silly child and, second, with a historian who, fatherlike, has dismissed his theories as the promising early efforts of a talented younger competitor, travels into the past only to discover that attempts at shortcuts can be fatal. In *Up the Line*, Robert Silverberg documents a good bit of transtemporal fornication, of which intercourse with one's female ancestors seems to be the preferred form, but no striking example of confrontation with the father takes place; the result of such action, however, proves fatal to the narrator, who manages godlike status only briefly.

If Heinlein and Finney seem to be saying that acting out the Oedipal drama is psychologically redemptive, Moore and Silverberg emphasize its dangers; typically, Twain manages both. As we have seen, Morgan learns to love the good father, Arthur, and conquers the evil father, Merlin, only to be conquered by that same Merlin at the moment of Merlin's death; and he becomes the king, sleeping the ages away in that fashion reserved for the greatest of culture heroes, all of whom are super-father-figures like Lazarus Long who, we are told by Heinlein, can never really die. But in the mouth of the Yankee it is ashes; making love to an ancestress and defeating the father-figure has left him—unlike Lazarus Long, SuperDaddy—loveless and childless in the age which should have been his home.

BACKWARD, TURN BACKWARD, O TIME

Had Mark Twain been a man of one mind, the *Connecticut Yankee* had been a simpler and more easily understandable book. Travel to the past would have been either simply a positive adventure—redemptive for the traveler, or beneficial to the past treated to an extratemporal spurt of progress; or, on the other hand, it would have been simply futile and destructive—feeding the traveler's ambitions to the point of power-mad monomania, or feeding the sixth century with technology which warps or destroys it, or resulting in catastrophe either for the traveler or for his own time. And the vision of the past—that is, Camelot, that is, childhood and Hannibal—and of Arthur—that is, the adult, the father—would likewise have been simple, either nostalgic and positive and admiring or satiric and base and brutal.

That is, the *Yankee* would have, on the one hand, been a book more like *A Christmas Carol* or *Lest Darkness Fall* or *Back to the Future* or Finney's *Time and Again*; or, on the other, it would have been more like Anderson's "Man Who Came Early" or Asimov's "Dead Past" or his "Winds of Change" or Bester's "The Men Who Murdered Mohammed."

Sight unseen, one would have expected the very first book of its kind to incorporate one of these simpler, more unified visions: either travel to the past as infantile wish fulfillment or travel to the past as Frankenstein's monster, monkey's paw, Three Wishes. But the *Yankee* was no such animal. Technological progress is both desirable and fearful; nineteenth-century democracy is both essential to human happiness and a futile attempt by talking animals to govern themselves; the past is inferior to, equal to, and superior to the present; and Arthur is both a monotonous nincompoop and a man of beauty and heroism.

For Twain was not a man of single mind; nor was he, as some would have it, a happy humorist in his youth who, having passed by marriage, financial ruin, and the death of children, became in his age a grim skeptic. Reread the *Innocents*, and you will find there all the skepticism, all the inhumanity of human to human, all the rage at economic inequality of Twain's later life, albeit more youthfully and more lightly expressed; reread "Letters from the Earth," and find there the slapstick, the burlesque, and the irony of Twain's youth.

Rather, this double-mindedness seems to have existed throughout Twain's life: a convivial, friendly, optimistic, loving, and happy man by nature, he was a pessimist and skeptic by intellectual conviction, and it is this dual vision which complicates and renders confusing his greatest works to those of us who are more single-minded. We are prone to see *The Prince and the Pauper* as a genteel romance—which it is, in part—and ignore its darker side: which darker side, I remember, gave me nightmares for many nights after I first read the book at the age of nine; we may love Tom Sawyer's wide-eyed romanticism or Huck Finn's skeptical practicality, but find it hard to swallow them both in one book; we may see *Personal Recollections of Joan of Arc* as a sincere and wondering tribute to The Maid and never notice the limitations and shortcomings of the narrator. Most of all, we are likely to see the *Yankee* as a hymn to nineteenth-century technology and political systems which went sour at about the same rate as the Paige typesetter, splitting itself in two as many are prone to see *Huckleberry Finn* breaking apart at the entrance of Tom Sawyer.

Great Time, you will remember, is that state where time and space are abolished and everything "happens at once"; but Dante, writing in our space and time, must perforce record his travels sequentially. Just so, a man of multiple mind will find himself recording one facet at a time, one attitude, one emotion at a time, it being impossible to record them all at once. If we observe that skepticism about technology runs from the beginning of the book, where the Yankee characterizes guns, revolvers, and cannon as "labor-saving machinery," all the way to the Battle of the Sand-Belt; and that love of the past runs from the first sight of Camelot to the Yankee's last delirium; and that belief in progress runs similarly throughout the book; then one may see the book as multiple, and therefore complex and confusing, throughout, rather than as broken in the middle.

This extraordinary complexity of vision which Twain brings to all his work is especially rich and appropriate when, as in the *Yankee*, he deals with childhood and age, past and present, human progress and human depravity, America and Europe. And it is the reason, I believe, that the *Connecticut Yankee*, the very first novel of its kind, anticipates so very much of what is to be done later with travel to the past by more single-minded writers.

A hundred years after the *Yankee*, and operating with the double benefits of a century of scientific thinking about time and a century of increasing sophistication both in the writing and in the reading of science fiction, Brian W. Aldiss is a man of double mind in his own way; Richard Mathews put it like this:

Brian W. Aldiss has a least two faces; two mythic personalities meet and merge in his writing. One conceals a sly grin, cracks jokes (just over the reader's head, like a whip), changes expression and appearance so rapidly that it's difficult to pin down this enigmatic character. The other face bears a noble and long-suffering gaze, full of daring knowledge, peering unflinchingly into secret and forbidden matters. Beyond the suffering one sees courage in these deep eyes, reflecting a personality of unchanging integrity set irrevocably against the forces of entrenched tyranny. (3)

Given the natural differences between an exceedingly civilized Britisher and a rowdy product of frontier America, the description might as well be applied to Mark Twain.

Aldiss is always surprising; a convivial man, fond of a party, a drink, a foolish joke, he is always probing the things we take for granted or those we would rather not think about. Like Dr. Johnson a man of massive common sense, like Johnson he is never quite free from the specter of madness; like Wells, although his vision of the future of the human race is a grim one, he never stops agitating for civility and justice between humans; like Twain, he manages to be both nostalgic and cynical about his own youth and about the past in general. On the one hand, his *Trillion Year Spree* is a thoughtful and audacious probing of the literary and scholarly values of science fiction; on the other, his *Science Fiction Art* is a celebration of the pulpiest of the pulp.

His earliest short stories of travel to the past, like "T," are fairly conventional visions ("What is written is written") of such travel, done with craft and skill. Later, as in *Cryptozoic!*, he takes large artistic risks to carry his reader through dark and complex channels of thought indeed.

To make very simple a very complex book: time "really" flows backward. Incest is the underlying motive for travel to the "past."

We have already noted that, according to Plutarch, Kronos, god of time, sleeps and dreams what Zeus actually brings to pass. A startling fragment from Macrobius (cited by de Santillana and von Dechend, 134–35) connects the ultimate power of Saturn/Kronos over the creation and the "division of beings" to a primal Oedipal attack:

They say, that Saturn cut off the private parts of his father Caelus [Ouranos], threw them into the sea, and out of them Venus was born. . . . From this they conclude that, when there was chaos, no time existed, insofar as time is a fixed measure derived from the revolution of the sky. Time begins there; and of this is believed to have been born Kronos who is Chronos, as was said before.

In Aldiss' *Cryptozoic!* incest may also be the original sin which gave us our mistaken perception of the flow of time; this mistake gave us power over our environment, our supremacy over the earth: but this Frankenstein monster was bought at a terrible price. Time travel is done by the mind, aided by drugs; and the protagonist, an artist, comes to these conclusions after penetrating to the Devonian and wandering through past and future. His time is repugnant to him, and people are leaving it as refugees, turning increasingly to the past. There is the distinct possibility that this sense of impending doom is behind the desire to perceive time as running backward; both the protagonist and the inventor of time travel end up in a madhouse, and it is not clear whether what is breaking down is the fabric of time or the mind of the narrator, or both.

The arrow of time, we are told by Sir Arthur Eddington (Fraser, *Time, the Familiar Stranger*, 505), always points in the direction of increasing entropy in the system as a whole. While the idea is a contribution of modern physics, it has its ancestors: "Chronos," says Marie Bonaparte (Fraser, 58), "begets his children before eating them, thus uniting in his person two functions, the creative and the destructive, which we attribute to time. But his cannibalism is more impressive than his procreative activities.'' In Pieter Brueghel's *Triumph of Time*, the figure of time, riding in a chariot pulled by sun and moon and surrounded by the signs of the zodiac, is eating a baby while his car rolls over tools, books, musical instruments, and other symbols of human effort; behind him rides death, behind him a city is burning.

If entropy increases with the expansion of the universe, and with the passage of time, then, as we have noted before, the world will either end in big smoosh or heat-death: bang or whimper. The ultimate end of the universe, some billions of years hence, can concern us but little, although some may manage a philosophic melancholy across the ages; more important is the fact that the increasing entropy of the arrow of time becomes symbolic of the possible horrors of the near future: the big smoosh as the analog of atomic war and heat-death as analog of famine, energy depletion, or faceless and static mass-society.

Now, all human effort to build, to organize, to understand, is a local and temporary reversal of the process of entropy, as is made most explicit in the non-time-travel novel *Seventh Son* by Orson Scott Card, in which the talents of the young warlock seem a divine gift in the service of the struggle against the Unmaker (who seems not only entropic but Satanic). In the Christian view of history, in spite of temporary mundane setbacks in this struggle, ultimately (after the temporary loosing of Antichrist, which I take to be Entropy's Last Stand) the New Earth, in which there is no more moth, rust, corruption, death, or entropy, will be instituted. In the more optimistic moments of the Age of Reason, and in the belief of many Marxists/Leninists/Maoists, a similar last Revolution will precede an orderly and structured human state which, whatever the ultimate destiny of the universe, will be maintained throughout the life of the human species.

When neither of these views of progress holds center stage, and when the works of reason (whether in technology or in science proper) seem to be tending toward an unreasonable end, then movement in the opposite direction seems one of the few psychic alternatives. Simple fleeing to the past (as in, for example, Finney's *Time and Again*), however, is a temporary escape, rather reminding one of the constant and pathetic movement of Daniel Boone toward the frontier in a futile attempt to escape the civilization which dogged his heels; at its extreme, as in Finney's ''Such Interesting Neighbors,'' the attempt to flee depopulates the world, leaving the future free to grind its way toward ultimate entropy unhampered and uncomplicated by human effort or aspiration. That scenario, of course, is a reflection of our fears that we will destroy ourselves.

Whichever of these grim scenarios one chooses, they result from the vision of death and disintegration, not only for the individual but also for the species, a vision which comes to Aldiss again and again; in ''The Sterile Millennia,'' for instance, he says, ''Time unrolled itself like a long carpet, down which man ambled toward extinction'' (24).

Now, the solution to the individual's problem of aging and death—entropy as experienced by the individual—is the return to childhood, which many aged people tend to do, in memory; but that return inevitably involves one in all the Oedipal difficulties of childhood once again, unless, as in H. Beam Piper's "Time and Time Again," the father has the good sense to abdicate in favor of his child. Similarly, the escape from entropy on the large scale involves return to the childhood of the race.

An even more amiable solution for the individual would be to fantasize that time was running backward, so that every day one felt oneself leaving death and decrepitude a day farther behind, every day becoming younger and stronger. To be sure, as Harold MacKaye points out very early (1904) in *The Panchronicon*, once one passed the bloom of one's adulthood, reverting to childhood would have its inconveniences, not the least being spanked by figures of authority. (Similarly, of course, on a cosmic scale, reversing the flow of time would result in a temporary loss of entropy, but would bring us back to the Cosmic Egg more quickly than the normal flow of time would get us either there or to heat-death.)

In a short-short-short story, "The End," Fredric Brown has fun with the notion that such a process would result in its own kind of entropic gibberish: by reversing the field of time, making it run backward, Professor Jones reverses the story itself, which ends "years many for theory time on working been had Jones Professor."(Which reminds me that Dante does a very similar thing in the *Paradiso*, II, 23–24: "faster than an arrow can hit the target, fly through the air, and leave the bow." It would seem that Dante's mundane senses, perceiving from the perspective of Great Time, sometimes see actions in reverse. Also see *Paradiso*, XXII, 109.)

In the short hundred years since the appearance of the *Yankee*, SF writers have worked travel to the past over so thoroughly that it is difficult to find a new idea to play with; in *Collision Course* Barrington J. Bayley finds two. First, life and consciousness exist only at the moment of the "now-ripple"; while there are people in the past, they are unconscious zombies. And although our artifacts persist into the future, there is nobody there to take care of them, so that the farther one goes into the future, the more beat-up the works of man look. A nice depiction of the arrow of time, there: the past, because conscious-nessless and predictable, is orderly, much as in Pirandello's *Henry IV*; the future, just a second in front of us, is lifeless and crumbling.

The second interesting notion is that 400 years out in front of us there is a time-wave, a "now-ripple," going in the opposite direction, toward us. The first inkling of this fact is the discovery of the ruins of *that* time's artifacts, which seem to get newer and newer as our time goes by. When the waves collide, some 200 years in each future, cataclysm will result, both for the backwards-moving time and for ours, in which society has turned into a fascist dystopia which probably deserves no better.

However, another entity, near-godlike, going in still another direction, oblique to these two, manages to divert "our" time flow onto many alternate Earths on many alternate time lines, so that, first, the grim and heat-death-like homogeneity of a fascist future is isolated on its own Earth, leaving all the others to develop and prosper; and so that, second, the big-smoosh-like temporal cataclysm is averted.

In John Brunner's *Tides of Time*, while time does not flow backward, the travelers travel ever further backward in time, in the process becoming progressively more alienated from their own presents, ultimately forgetting their origins; as they go, rather like children swapping Three Wishes stories, they tell each other stories the moral of which is that getting what one wishes for is not always a good idea. The effect is very much like becoming younger and younger, losing more and more of one's adult memories in the process; or like time flowing backward from civilization to prehuman history.

BEAM ME BACK, PIPER

H. Beam Piper's future history space operas and the related Fuzzy stories range widely through space and time, but the stories dealing with time travel and with Paratime travel are constantly touching base in his home turf of Pennsylvania. And the first and last of these stories (which, handily enough, are the first and last of the Piper canon) are positively *anchored* in Pennsylvania.

His first published short story, the 1947 "Time and Time Again," just misses being our third work by the same title. It is a very early example of travel to the past in which the consciousness of the traveler ends up in his/her earlier body (as Phoebe feared nearly fifty years earlier in MacKaye's *Panchronicon*). Allan Hartley, 43, is killed in World War III during the battle of Buffalo in 1975. At the moment of his death, some strange combination of factors moves his consciousness back into the body of his 13-year-old self in 1945 in Williamsport, PA, almost exactly at the end of World War II. He has all the memories of a 43-year-old born in 1932, but he is stuck in the prepubescent body of a big child.

You will recognize this scenario as a variant of the game invented by Mark Twain and refined by Sprague de Camp with the additional complication *you are a kid: how do you get anyone to take you seriously*? (And yet the scenario is a familiar infantile-and-escapist one: it is rooted in the thousands of sighs of middle age—"Oh, to be 18 again, and know what I know now!")

Allan Hartley finds his job a bit easier than it might have been because he is so much like his father. Well, not exactly: it is more that both of them are very much like H. Beam Piper. Allan Hartley is 43 when he is killed outside Buffalo, just the age of the author in 1947, when the story was published. Allan returns to age 13 at the end of a major war; when Piper was 13, his country was getting ready to enter a major war. Allan is born in Williamsport, where Piper lived as an adult, rather than in Piper's birthplace of Altoona. Like Piper, who wrote a mystery, *Murder in the Gunroom*, featuring an alternate-worlds SF writer, Allan wrote—or will write—mysteries as an adult; but the titles of his novels—*Children of the Mist*, *Rose of Death*, and *Conqueror's Road*—hint that they may also be science fiction or heroic fantasy. Like Piper, Allan is a free thinker in matters religious. He "dies" from a nuclear blast; and, in his later years, Piper was much preoccupied with the threat of nuclear war.

Allan's father, Blake Hartley, is also very much like Piper: single, agnostic, a gun collector, 48. Unlike Piper's minister father, Blake is a lawyer; unlike Piper, Allan attended Penn State. Thus Blake is both Piper and the father Piper perhaps wished he could have had; and Allan is partly Piper, partly what Piper could have been, and partly the son Piper never had.

Once Allan has oriented himself, he proves that he can change past events by foiling a murder which he remembers as having happened; and then, taking his father into his confidence, he plans his new future, one in which the world war which killed him will not occur. Too conveniently—just as the Connecticut Yankee too-conveniently remembers the date of an eclipse—Allen remembers the winners of the Derby, Preakness, and Belmont races from 1945 to 1970, which should give the pair plenty of operating capital. Just as conveniently, like the Yankee (who "could make anything"), Allan has a hobby of chemistry which will enable him to make I. G. Farben look like pikers. And then his father will be elected President, and so on, and the death of the first Allan Hartley, and the war in which it happened, will be prevented.

Most of us who have had to work for a living have indulged ourselves in the fantasy *if my father had only been rich* and daydreamed about how much easier and more colorful our lives would have been; but most of us have then gone on to recognize that we would thereby have been deprived of the pleasure of making it on our own, and of the possibility of excelling, besting our fathers at their own games, becoming The Boss by worth and not by birth. Allan Hartley conveniently has the best of both worlds: his father will be rich and powerful, but it will be all Allan's doing. Piper has nicely managed to eliminate the sexual-conflict aspects of the Oedipal drama: Allan's mother has been dead for some years, and the only woman in the house is a dumpy German housekeeper; further, the body the 43-year-old consciousness inhabits is a prepubescent 13-year-old one. The Oedipal conflict then is a purely mental one; and not only because of hindsight, but because Allan is mentally a better man than his father (who is partly the cause of that excellence), his father, no fool, caves in quickly: "All right, son; I'll do just what you tell me, and when you grow up, I'll be president." *I and the Father are one.*

There is also more than a hint of Finney in the story: as in *Time and Again*, this is a bad world to live in. The generation or generations before us have messed it all up. The landscape is polluted and scarred; the heroic virtues are on the wane; people try to kill you; *and none of it is my fault.* Thus the Oedipal hero and the existential isolate become one. In Piper's heroic vision, the hero, having returned to the past, does in fact do things better than his forefathers and thus bring about a "present" which is a fit place in which to live.

In the last story of a too-short writing career, *Lord Kalvan of Otherwhen*, Piper once again played at changing the history of his beloved Pennsylvania.

Very much as Tom Sawyer peoples the landscape of St. Petersburg/Hannibal (and aren't those ironic names for the muddy little river town, the one with overtones of czarist luxury, the other with memories of Carthaginian campaigns?) with bandits and pirates, Piper, by sending his hero into an alternate, and more primitive, present, turns his native terrain into a medieval society. And very much as Twain allows the Connecticut Yankee to alter the court of King Arthur, Piper allows Kalvan to inject twentieth-century elements into a medieval landscape. And all of this is done against the imaginative background of Piper's tremendous Paratime Scheme, a scheme which allows the writer and the reader to look at our Pennsylvania and see thousands of Pennsylvanias, some wasted by atomic war, others still pristine forest, still others in the grip of Nazi tyranny, others utopian—and yet all still very much our own Pennsylvania. The banner of Hos-Hostigos is a red keystone on a dark green field.

In his use of the Pennsylvania of his childhood, then, H. Beam Piper managed to infuse a prosaic landscape with potential and with wonder. Unlike Twain, who wandered far from Hannibal in the body, but found himself returning in spirit all his life, Piper stayed mostly in the terrain of his youth, wandering far in his fancy: but again and again he made that fancy touch base in the Altoona-Williamsport area, much as Simak always keeps one foot in Wisconsin. Tom Sawyer, in his vision of a St. Petersburg infested with pirates and bandits, brought the past into his present; in his constructing of his own funeral, he brought nonevent into the world of events. Calvin Morrison and Allan Hartley do very much the same for Piper's Pennsylvania, which becomes a magic land filled with visions of things as they might be, had only we been in charge instead of our ancestors.

DEMYTHOLOGIZING AND PSYCHOANALYSIS

It was Brian Aldiss' *Cryptozoic!*, which in 1967 theorized that incest was the motive for travel to the past; it was Heinlein's *Time Enough for Love* which, in 1973, made return to the past and intercourse with the hero's mother the source of renewed youth and life. It was Poul Anderson's *Dancer from Atlantis*, however, which in 1972 most completely and sanely made clear the links between travel to the past and psychoanalysis, which is, after all, a confronting of the patient's own past and a demythologizing of that past. As if to acknowledge the debt all subsequent tales of travel to the past owe to *Lest Darkness Fall*, the book is dedicated to Sprague and Catherine de Camp.

Anderson is a fictioneer whose work has received less critical attention and appreciation than it deserves, perhaps because he is often perceived as a conservative by liberal critics, perhaps because his language, at crucial moments, is often inadequate to the weight of the ideas it bears. The very end of *The Dancer from Atlantis*, for example, where the goal for which the Yankee and all his children have been seeking is finally made clear, collapses in Hollywood banality. Nevertheless, Anderson has contributed, in Van Rijn and Flandry, two fully developed SF characters in a field where such characters are rare; he has given us a rich, if sometimes confused, future history; and he has played more changes on the subject of travel to the past—from imperialist to exile to student to Oedipal hero—than anyone else in the field.

In *The Dancer from Atlantis*, a time machine from the future quite by accident picks up an American architect, Duncan Reid, 40, from a ship in the Pacific in 1970; a trader from Novgorod, Oleg Vladimirovitch, from the banks of the Dnieper in 1050; a Hunnish horseman, Uldin, from the southern Ukraine in the fourth century A.D.; and a 40-year old ex-bull-dancer from Rhodes in about 1400 B.C. It then crashes in Libya, some twenty-four years before the date the last captive was inadvertently shanghaied; one anthropologist is dead and the other just alive enough to instruct Reid in the use of a translating machine and tell him what has happened. Just as Piper's Allan Hartley is landed in the past on the day before Hiroshima, so these folk are conveniently landed several months before Thera and its fellow-islands of the Santorini group blow up in a super-Krakatoa volcanic eruption which Plato will later memorialize as the death of Atlantis.

All of this is, as you will have noted, a highly contrived and improbable scenario even for time travel fiction, itself a pretty improbable subset of science fiction, not the most mimetic of literature itself. It has some of the feeling of old jokes which begin "There were once an Irishman, a German, and a Chinese . . . "or of Aesopian tales which involve dialogues between animals composing highly improbable communities of discourse.

We are not surprised, therefore, to find that the book is rather more *intellectual demonstration* than it is fiction. Furthermore, in this scenario, no change can take place in the past unless it is already a part of that past: what is written is written. Therefore any question about what the travelers can accomplish becomes irrelevant. What *is* relevant is what is learned by the castaways and by the reader in the process.

The major protagonist of this book, and the character most often used as point of view, is the American architect, the first to be shanghaied; but the title focuses our attention on the last victim, Erissa, who, like Duncan, is going through a midlife crisis. They are about of an age; both have beloved spouses whom they underappreciate, not without guilt; and both are on a quest after revitalization. Reid, the father of a daughter and two sons significantly named Mark and Tom, bears more than a passing resemblance to Mark Twain himself:

. . . lanky, rawboned, wide-shouldered six-footer, a long craggy head, jutting nose and chin, heavy black brows over gray eyes, sandy hair. . . . (12) [He had] shaken off the Presbyterian theology of his boyhood [but had] to carry around the associated conscience. . . . (13)

Like Livy, his wife is a semi-invalid whose interests are not totally his. Reid is no hero; indeed, he reminds us of the early Martin Padway in *Lest Darkness Fall* and of Barry Pennywither in "April in Paris."

Unlike Hank Morgan, Reid does not claim to be more than he is; the Hun says (53), "You did not say you are a shaman, Duncan, nor do I believe you are. But you may have more wisdom that I thought." He does, however, yield to the temptation (54) to amaze the natives with his pipe lighter. His professional life has been lagging; and in an attempt to revitalize it, he is on a trip to Japan, where he will look for "inspiration at the source. In provincial villages especially." His feeling is that his own age, in which "human beings were maiming and killing human beings whose names they would never know," is tragic, but then, "had every year always been tragic, would every year always be?" In the midst of such musing, "the vortex seized him" in a pseudodeath—not unlike that of Piper's Allan Hartley—in which "he was snatched from the world" (14– 15).

The second victim, Oleg, is a trader; and in many ways, both in owntime and, in the past, he is a Russian Yankee, much as Anderson's great Nicholas Van Rijn is a Malay-Dutch Yankee: "Yes," Oleg says (17), "peace and brotherly love, those are good for trade, as Our Lord preached when he walked this earth." In the past, he goes quickly into the shipbuilding business. In his own age, he has been an Innocent Abroad: " 'I was on pilgrimage,' he reminded the saints. 'The Saracens made endless fuss and inconvenience. I brought back a flask of Jordan water and gave it to the Sophia Cathedral that *Knyaz* Yaroslav the Wise built in Kiev' " (52).

The Hun, Uldin, is a master of horses and horsemanship. Landed in the Thassalocracy of the Cretan Minos, he is momentarily at a loss. But just as Poseidon is god both of the sea and of horses, so history is working to bring together the seafarers of Crete and the landlubbers of Achaea, and the Hun will become a part of that process.

The bull-dancer, Erissa, is the only person in the group who is not taken totally out of her own time. Twenty-four years in her own past, she recognizes Duncan Reid as a god: baffled, he reacts nevertheless to her as a woman and as a wise one. Later, of course, he meets the 17-year-old Erissa and likewise reacts to her. *This* Erissa's misapprehensions about what is going on will leave the older Erissa with the delusion that she has, in the past, been impregnated by a god. Only when the older Erissa can confront the problem of her younger self without illusion, can she understand herself in the present and rid herself of her delusions; only as she can react with compassion and understanding to that younger self can she learn to love her older self and be able to truly become that older self and return to her husband and children complete and fulfilled.

Similarly, Duncan Reid, returned to his own time by rescuers from the future, is completed and ready to reembark on career and marriage with confidence and love. For both Reid and Erissa, travel to the past and the demythologization of that past has been the ultimate therapy: for what is psychoanalysis, after all, but a confronting of the past, of the younger self, and a seeing of that past and that self in demythologized terms?

As we have said, both Reid and Erissa are the double hero/heroine of the novel; and throughout the novel there is a challenging of traditional sexual distinctions. ''I have never,'' says Uldin (94), ''awaited meeting a she-shaman.'' Later, in a crisis, he demands of her

Blood brotherhood sworn between us. Faithfulness to death, you for me and I for you, by all our gods, demons, ancestors, hope of descendants, and blood of our veins that we mingle. . . . I never heard of its being done between man and woman, but you're different. (153)

Then, reverting to traditional roles, he moves in on her sexually.

The Achaeans are god-worshippers; the Minoans worship the Great Goddess, whose shrine is on Atlantis. But the name of Atlantis in Cretan is *Kharia-ti-yeh*, Land of the Pillar, for the smoke rising from the volcano: and the pillar of smoke is the symbol of the paternal god Yaweh. And in Atlantis Asterion, as well as Britomarte, is worshipped in terms which seem (136–37) to make a direct appeal to the monomyth, worship which is intended to assure that the god claims the ''Bride Who was also his Mother and Grandmother.'' All this appeal to the Campbell monomyth; all this divine incest as source of human joy, fits well with the whole idea of travel to the past. Just as the Campbellian myth-hero travels to the underworld to find the sources of new life, so the Oedipal Yankee travels to the past to find the present self.

The Minoan Thassalocracy, Reid reflects, has been a good civilization, however it will be later remembered:

Reid wondered how the Keftiu, preservers of law and peace, carriers of a trade that brought prosperity to every realm it touched, clean, friendly, mannerly, learned, gifted, totally human, would come to be remembered for a man-devouring monster in horrible corridors. (110)

The answer, of course, is that even the best of human civilizations, like the best of human beings, is Yang and Yin, dark and light, angel and animal, lifegiving and deathdealing, Bronze Age and Atomic Age, horse and seafoam, female and male. In the past, as in Campbell's underworld, is the reconciliation of contradictions.

From the year 1400 B.C. Reid can think of Plato as a thousand years in the future, misreading history so as to put Atlantis in the wrong ocean and the wrong era. (Throughout the book, as in many novels of travel to the past, the author has an opportunity to float theories of history without the apparatus necessary to an historian.) Plato also, we remember, had the notion of the original bisexual animal being split in two: and in this novel, not only the truly understood past but the original androgyny is there in the past to be discovered. Reid and Erissa, as well as the older and younger Erissa, are one; and in the discovery of that oneness lies sanity and reconciliation with one's own present.

Reid has not neglected to see the parallels between the Minoan civilization living under the shadow of volcanic destruction and tsunami (here the Japan Reid was seeking shows up in the Bronze Age Mediterranean) and our civilization living under the shadow of atomic destruction; he has seen Greece before classical deforestation denuded it, and he anticipates further environmental destruction in our own future. But in the destruction of Atlantis, with the advantage of historical perspective, he and Erissa see, through the cataclysm, a future:

"It was a victory, that we and those in our care outlived the end of a world and even saved much of it for the world which is to follow. If we had only a single road to walk, that twisted back on itself, still, we walked it...." "A thousand years hence, Athens shines in a glory that will gladden the rest of mankind's time on earth. And its secret seed is that heritage it got from your people." "There is comfort to live by: that my country was, that theirs will be...." (190–91)

In addition, then, to mending their private psychic circles, and mending their Yang and Yin into an androgynous whole, Reid and Erissa have somehow mended the circle of history and given themselves faith that out of suffering can come survival and even triumph.

This is the victorious vision that was denied to the Yankee; Twain, however, may have achieved just such a synthesis in his annotations of his dead daughter Susy's biography of him. Fascinated by himself, by her, by her vision of him, and by his vision of her, he sees her both as a charming child and as a grown woman, both as a physical presence and as a powerful intellect. There is more than a hint that Susy was a lesbian, and that her parents had some inkling of that fact; in Neider's edition of Susy's biography and Twain's annotations there are charming photographs of Susy as the Prince and of Mark Twain in a woman's dress, amply bosomed, in "a charade" with Susy. In the notes written in Susy's last delirium, over which "last things that would flow from that subtle brain" Twain lovingly pored, one strong motif is, as Neider puts it, that of "the queen of God's light against the queen of his darkness; spiritually versus earthiness." Yang and Yin.

In the burning heat of those final days in Hartford she would walk to the window or lie on the couch in her fever and delirium, and when the cars went by would say: "Up go the trolley cars for Mark Twain's daughter. Down go the trolley cars for Mark Twain's daughter." This was no more than a day or two before the end.

(Thus Paine in *Mark Twain's Notebook*, Neider, 51.) It is comforting to hope that out of these oppositions, and those with which he had lived all his life, Twain may have won through in his late years to the integration Anderson dramatizes in *The Dancer from Atlantis*.

Chapter 7

CHILDREN OF THE YANKEE: THESE CURIOUS STRANGERS

I shall never see my friends again—never, never again. They will not be born for more than thirteen hundred years yet.

—Hank Morgan

AND NEVER THE TWAINS...

The *Yankee* is a Chinese box of a book: it begins with a preface by "Mark Twain," who may or may not be the Mark Twain who was the alter ego of Samuel L. Clemens. Likely enough he is, since what he says agrees well enough with what we know of Mark Twain from Clemens' other works. He writes from Hartford, July 21, 1889, chatting pleasantly about the laws of England in a way very like his remarks in *The Prince and the Pauper*, making innocent-sounding comments which hide a most profoundly ambiguous attitude toward history and human progress:

The ungentle laws and customs touched upon in this tale are historical. . . . Inasmuch as they existed in the English and other civilizations of far later times, it is safe to consider that it is no libel upon the sixth century to suppose them to have been in practice in that day also.

Things do not change, then; the nineteenth century, as becomes plain throughout the book, is very like the sixth. However, " . . . whenever one of these laws or customs was lacking in that remote time, its place was competently filled by a worse one." So progress of a sort may take place, after all, if only from worse to bad. (Twain seems to have worked hard on this part of the preface while he was writing the final portion of the *Yankee*: three earlier versions [California *Yankee*, 516–18] survive.)

"Mark Twain" then introduces the subject of the divine right of kings, in a paragraph omitted from the English edition, which gives him an opportunity to mention such "executive heads" of state as Madame Pompadour and Lady Castlemaine; this is a slyly implied obscenity, since we are obviously invited to read "executive tails" and to chuckle when Twain says he will defer consideration of this matter until next winter, when "I am not going to have anything particular to do." (In the original copy-text, as documented in the notes to the California *Yankee* [679–80], Twain had considered this matter in Chapter XXXV, allowing himself a still more graphic joke: monuments, Morgan said, should be erected for all "those honored and lamented ladies who in past centuries have wielded the sceptre of England. . . . ")

The preface is followed by the second container, "A Word of Explanation," obviously attributed to the same persona, "M. T.," who writes the "Final P.S. by M. T." at the end of the book. Now, this "M. T.," while he has certain points of resemblance to "Mark Twain," to Mark Twain, and to Samuel Clemens, gives us some reason to believe that he may be a different person altogether. For one, he is a much more credulous and placid tourist than was the Innocent Abroad; for two, he settles in with the foolishness of Malory in a way that the cynical "Mark Twain" would be unlikely to have done; and for three, when the antique Hank Morgan introduces himself, he does so not as a fellow-American, as would be normal, but simply as an American.

"I am an American," Morgan's narrative begins. So is travel to the past, of the sort we are considering, and for the reasons we are considering. Ireland invented the traveler as observer, and England invented the time machine; but Twain invented Yankeeing in the past.

"This curious stranger," M. T. has already called Morgan, and one of the meanings of *curious* is *strange*: this strange stranger. *Strange* can equal *foreign* and *stranger* can mean *alien*, and Hank Morgan, having returned some years back from the sixth century (where he had become naturalized), is the most foreign of foreigners. But it is also possible that M. T., who has found Malory so charming, is not an American. "We fell together," says M. T., "as modest people will." The Yankee in the sixth century was anything but modest, as was Mark Twain in the nineteenth; one might suspect an easy irony here, except that, returned to the nineteenth and much aged, the Yankee *has* become modest. At the very end of the book, M. T. refers to him as his "Yankee historian," much as an Englishman might refer to any American writer.

When the Yankee and M. T. fall in together in Warwick Castle, they do so because of common temperament rather than common nationality. Indeed, if M. T. and Hank Morgan share residence—or have at any rate both lived—in Hartford, we would expect them to recognize that fact. Maybe, we think, we are simply to read *stranger* and *one with whom one is unacquainted*; if so, it is a bit odd if M. T., like Mark Twain, is a convivial American westerner, he can nevertheless, after four whiskies, still refer to Morgan as *my stranger*. There seems to be nothing in the wording of M. T.'s writing to indicate either England or America, though "Midnight being come at length" seems not very American—or perhaps the reading of Malory is having its influence on M. T..

Though one cannot make out a hard case either way, then, there is plenty of reason for doubting a solid identification of M. T. with Mark Twain. After all this front matter, we are introduced to the spoken narrative of Hank Morgan, followed by his manuscript, followed by Clarence's postscript, followed by the final postscript by "M. T."

The reader is thus quite nicely isolated from the major narrative, the credibility of which is thus compromised in quite Jamesian fashion. Here is a novel with the preface like that of *Huckleberry Finn*, which emphasizes (as do Huck's opening words) the fictitious quality of what the reader is about to encounter; we then encounter an outside narrator who is credulous and devoted to medieval (read *Scotian*) romance and is perhaps English and not to be identified with the prefacer; finally, we have an inside narrator who is presented to us as ancient, flaky, and full of whiskey, who tells us a story of a vision he had after being rapped on the head.

This wheels-within-wheels process throws Hank Morgan's whole narrative into a mist-world of something between realistic fiction and dream-vision, where it would stay, were it not for the fact that Morgan cannot dream of a Camelot of which he has never heard. Twain, operating at the beginning of the time travel convention, needs to give himself permission to deal realistically with matter so patently fantastic; remember that in his notes the whole idea began as a dream.

As in *The Turn of the Screw*, the reader is seduced into granting credibility to the unbelievable because the narrative has been hedged about with so many possible ambiguities. Once one is well launched on Morgan's narrative, one discovers all manner of realistic detail intruding on the Malory matter, and thus belief becomes easy; it is only at the end, when Twain returns to his frame, that we have leave again to doubt the "reality" of Morgan's adventures.

In fact, the distancing has an effect not unlike that of epic theater. What began in Twain's notes as a joke, a piece of foolery, a dream, turns into a piece of grim didacticism. The ideas overburden the narrative; and thus the occasional lapses, in which the voice of Morgan gives way to the voice of Twain, may be aesthetically justified in the same fashion that the more deliberately contrived breaks in credibility in the theater of Brecht are justified.

This isolation of the narrative is also echoed in the isolation of the hero. When "M. T." first encounters Hank Morgan, he calls him "this curious stranger." Now, *curious* is a word rich, rare, and full of overtones. In context, its primary meaning would seem to be *strange*, and thus we get *this strange stranger*. (It also can mean, of course, *inquisitive, careful, attentive, skillful, rare*, and *surprising*, and all of these we may apply, well enough, to the Yankee at one point or another of the narrative.)

But *curious* in the sense of *strange* is used by the Yankee again and again in the course of his narrative; more often than not, he uses it in a cool and understated fashion when contemplating some particularly hideous example of human cruelty or some extraordinarily agonizing result of slavery or poverty.

But only at first: before his tale is done, it has become plain to Morgan that all the human depravity he sees as *curious* in the sixth century is very much of a piece with similar phenomena which he had taken for granted in his own.

Such playing with strangeness and familiarity is, of course, basic to all literature, and indeed to most of the arts. M. T. begins, for example, in a perfectly ordinary tourist situation only to discover that one of his companions is more curious than anyone in history or fiction up to that moment. Similarly, Hank Morgan, beginning in a prosaic Hartford environment, is suddenly shifted into a completely strange terrain. His first impulse is to wonder whether or not Camelot is Bridgeport, and the shining towers of Arthur's court those of P. T. Barnum's mansion. He instinctively attempts, that is, to see the strange in terms of the familiar and to explain away what he sees as not so strange at all. He is, after all, as commonsensical as Chaucer's Pertelote, who insists that the strange and frightening visions of her consort are due simply to constipation.

And if he is in Barnum's world, then he is all right. Like Barnum, he is a showman who counts on a sucker's being born every minute. When the Duke in *Huckleberry Finn* (XXVI) worries about the opinion of the doctor—who, like Pudd'nhead Wilson, is a skeptic and therefore dangerous—the King reassures him in Barnumesque terms: "Hain't we got all the fools in town on our side? and ain't that a big enough majority in any town?" Huck would agree: his lies, and those of the King and the Duke, and those of Pap Finn and Tom Sawyer, all go down the throats of most folk with a most amazing ease. So do the phony prophecies of the "Asian" magician in *Yankee* XXIV, whom we recognize at once as the spiritual ancestor of the King and the Duke.

But Barnum's world is not only the world of the con man and the showman; it is also the world of the circus. And the circus, we remember from *Huckleberry Finn* (XXII), is a world of illusion, a world in which a drunk, after shedding seventeen disguises, turns out to be a circus acrobat after all; and what is most appealing about Huck's recounting of the business is that Huck never penetrates to the last reality: that the ringmaster's having been fooled, and his subsequent chagrin, are likewise part of the illusion.

Remember, if you will, that Morgan's first reaction on being confronted with Sir Kay in "A Word of Explanation," is to say, "Get along back to your circus, or I'll report you."

The suspicion that the people one meets are disguised, that they are playing parts, is a profoundly alienating thought that runs through much recent literature, as is the familiar and related notion that we are all unwitting performers in a drama being organized by somebody else. The individual is helpless in the face of forces which he does not understand and cannot identify; he is unable to penetrate the motives of the director of the performance; he has no hope of finding any rationale for what is going on; like Kafka's K, he cannot even find out where to go to surrender. And because he has no faith that the director, however obscure the scenario may be at the moment, is wise and nobly motivated, he cannot even rise to the dignity of the suffering Job.

Much of a piece with that terrible thought is the one which next occurs to the Yankee: not seeing any sign of a circus, he concludes that he has come to in a lunatic asylum. In a sense, of course, he is quite right: the British sixth century, like Morgan's own nineteenth, is loaded with lunatics from one end to the other. But for the Yankee, at the outset, the terror which might afflict a more imaginative, less commonsensical individual is totally absent. Pertelote-like, he ignores the bad-dream quality of his situation; after just a moment's shudder at the possibility that he may really be in Camelot on June 19, 528, he settles back to business, much as does Padway, ''a hardened empiricist'' (9), in *Lest Darkness Fall*, determined either to run the madhouse or take over the sixth century—or both.

Like Padway, the Yankee shortly discovers that underneath all the strangeness of the sixth century is the same familiar human nature making the same familiar human mistakes; furthermore, both the Yankee and Padway immediately begin taking steps to make the surface of the sixth century more like the surfaces of their home centuries. The strange does not disorient them or alienate them: it is a challenge. They are, after all, imperialists, made more on the model of Cecil Rhodes than of Mistah Kurtz.

Like Huck Finn, who says (XXXIII), ''Human beings *can* be awful cruel to one another,'' Hank Morgan gradually discovers in the sixth what he had observed but not comprehended in his own century: that humans are not only as stupid in one century as in another, but cruel and vicious to boot, given half a chance. Nevertheless, he blithely continues to build his Brave New World, never suspecting that life may be a dream, or that *he* may be a clown or a lunatic, stupid or cruel, or that there may be no way to win this game, regardless of the cards one holds. The reader is more and more aware of the nightmare quality of the circus of which Hank is ringmaster; but Hank is not even aware that it *is* a circus. Only on his return to his home century does he appear to become aware that the world is a very strange place, after all, and that he is a stranger in it.

THE TRAVELER AS EXILE

Consider *stranger* as Camus' *étranger*: I mean the alone, the alienated, the unconnected, the person disjointed from humanity and human relations and the world of humanity. Consider how well a person marooned out of his own time might serve as such a figure.

In H. Beam Piper's *Lord Kalvan of Otherwhen*, after the hero has been marooned in a parallel Pennsylvania, he is asked where he comes from; despairing of explaining Paratime to the natives, he claims to be an involuntary exile from the future, getting this reaction from Xentos, the local priest: ''How terrible! Why, you have been banished as no man ever was!'' (34). It is a nice line, one that might apply, one might think, to any involuntary time traveler, whether to past, to future, or to Paratime. (Except for great mystics, shamans, saints, and suicides, people go, I suppose, into Great Time involuntarily; but believers in Great Time would, I think, assert that they are being released from an earlier banishment.)

To be exiled from one's own time would appear to be even worse than being exiled from one's own place—unless, of course, one is out of place or time to begin with. Some folk hanker for the future; more seem to suffer from the Miniver Cheevy syndrome, feeling that they would have done better in the past. Even though it seems to the reader that Miniver Cheevy would have been as much of a drunken loser in the tenth century as in his own, one may believe that the graveyards are full of inglorious Miltons who, in another time or at another place, would have found their talents both developed and valued. The converse is likewise true: heroes like Joshua or Basil the Bulgar-Slayer or Richard the Lion-Hearted would almost certainly find themselves cordially hated by most contemporary law-abiders, while likely Li Po and Gotama and Jeremiah would get themselves locked up in the nearest mental hospital.

Of all people, Americans should understand the stranger. None of us, even the displaced Native Americans, are very far from being foreigners; we live in a century of technology-driven alienation; and change moves at such a pace that in adulthood, as often as not, we find ourselves, like Twain, strangers in our own lifetimes. Still, we understand the opposite figure and encounter him every day, and sometimes, if we are lucky, feel him even in ourselves: the person comfortable with the world, with his time, with his work, fulfilled in his family, his thought, his travail, well connected with all that surrounds him. *Un bon bourgeois*, we may call him disparagingly; or, approvingly, we might use the *honnête homme* of the Age of Reason. As opposed to the stranger, the alien, *l'étranger*, he is the *engagé*, the *citoyen*, the citizen.

Now, if a time traveler begins in one time, proceeds to one or more outtimes or otherwhens, and either returns to his own time or does not, he will touch all those bases as either citizen or stranger. For instance, if he begins alienated in the present and finds himself in the past and then (if he returns to his owntime) finds himself alienated again, the pattern would be Stranger-Citizen-[Stranger], those brackets at the end taking care of those heroes who do not return, but whose attitude may be reasonably presumed from the text.

Let us inspect several such patterns: their analogs, of course, may be seen in mainstream literature by substituting mundane equivalents for "owntime," "outtime," and "return." One of the extraordinary things which we will note is how many of these patterns, *in esse* or *in posse*, are to be found in Twain's *Connecticut Yankee*.

The Conquering Hero: Citizen-Citizen-[Citizen]

This is the chronopera track, the temporal equivalent of the space opera track which was by far the most common in the SF of the 1920s, 1930s, and 1940s.

The result is adventure pure if not simple and a hero who rarely doubts either himself or the worth of what he does, nor ever frets much about the workings of his psyche or his place in the ultimate scheme of things. *Citizen* is often an awkward term for him, because he is often a loner, but he is never alienated in the way the very prosaic citizen Leopold Bloom is.

At its worst, as I say, this pattern gives us space opera or chronopera pure and simple. Just as the Galaxy gave E. E. "Doc" Smith a huge western plain, high-tech horses, and planet-busting six-shooters as a backdrop for his interstellar cowboys, so outtime can afford the heroes of a Robert Adams novel all manner of adventure opportunities. In juvenile time travel fiction, it must be said, such a pattern seems to invite the young reader into the past and may generate an interest in history which might otherwise not come to be and, to the extent that the history is creatively and accurately done, may serve a useful pedagogical function.

At its best, this pattern may result in a study of the way technology and societies work and the way in which individuals can use or oppose the resources of such technologies and societies. There being little or no existential isolation, the interest is in the actions performed, and the tension arises, not out of any consideration of the worth of those actions, but over whether or no the hero can successfully perform them.

In Robert A. Heinlein's *Door into Summer*, the hero, Dan Davis, an inventor, has been swindled by his partner and his fiancee out of his greatest invention; he has a moment of despair in which he momentarily considers the quasi-suicide and escape of The Long Sleep, a Van Winkling device which would get him some decades into the future. But he rejects that solution and decides to fight things out in his own time. He is shanghaied into The Long Sleep anyhow by the bad guys, lands on his feet some thirty years in the future, and makes another bundle there-then. Never at a loss, he manages to flimflam an eccentric scientist into sending him back into 1970, where (now a traveler to the past) he can enjoy Yankeelike advantages. He arrives a bit before his departure, pulls everything together almost without breathing hard, and then returns to 2000 to settle in comfortably. His attitude is pure citizen:

"There's a divinity that shapes our ends, rough-hew them how we will." Free will and predestination in one sentence and both true. There is only *one* real world, with one past and one future. . . . Just *one* . . . but big enough and complicated enough to include free will and time travel and everything else in its linkages and feedbacks and guard circuits. You're allowed to do anything inside the rules . . . but you come back to your own door. (157)

He does wonder for a moment whether a previous traveler, Leonard Vincent, might have ended up as Leonardo da Vinci, marooned and impotent and frustrated in the fifteenth century; but straightaway he regains his optimism:

I don't worry about philosophy any more than Pete [his cat] does. Whatever the truth about this world, I like it. . . . "Back" is for emergencies; the future is better than the past. Despite the crapehangers, romanticists, and anti-intellectuals, the world steadily grows better because the human mind, applying itself to environment, *makes* it better. With hands . . . with tools . . . with horse sense and science and engineering.

Most of these long-haired belittlers can't drive a nail . . . I'd like to . . . ship them back to the twelfth century—then let them enjoy it.

But I am not mad at anybody and I like now. (158)

Notice how closely this quote echoes the sentiments of Hank Morgan, up until his return from the sixth century. Had he won his battle, had he remained in the sixth century, Morgan would have fit the pattern to perfection. Before his departure, to be sure, he is unattached save for a romance with a telephone voice: Puss Flanagan, to whom he is "almost engaged to be married," does not even enter his mind until Chapter XI, and then only as an excuse not to go questing with Sandy. And his alienation at the end of the book is one of the things that is most to his credit, grounded as it is in his love for his wife and child.

Asimov's "Winds of Change" follows this pattern, though the ending is less fatuously optimistic than that of Heinlein's novel, because the traveler, Dinsmore, is a Bad Guy, a Yankee without scruples. He is content with himself and with his occupation, which is physics professor; all that rankles is that a colleague is becoming university president instead of him.

"I do not wish to cease to be me. Even if in my place I would create someone who was more intelligent, more sensible, more successful, it would still not be *me*. Nor would I want to change you, Muller, or you, Adams. . . . I would not want to triumph over a Muller who is less ingenious and spectacularly bright, or over an Adams who has been less politic and deft at putting together an imposing structure of respect. I would want to triumph over you as you are, and not over lesser beings."

Concerned only with his own narrow world of physics and university politics, Dinsmore does not scruple to travel in time and alter history so as to leave Muller and Adams the same people, while changing the society. (You will remember that in "Vintage Season," the isolation/involvement of the artist found a metaphor in that of the temporal tourist; here Asimov finds a similar parallel between the time traveler and the scientist and academician.)

Dinsmore has found his niche in owntime; he enjoys himself while playing with the past; and on his return he finds himself the triumphant president. He has changed the present into one run by the Moral Majority, and his enemies are nailed for liberal positions they have taken in the past. Whatever Asimov and his readers think of Dinsmore, from his own point of view he is citizen-citizen-citizen straight down the line; and, obviously, it is Asimov's ironic commentary on our own time to create an amoral reprobate like Dinsmore who is perfectly happy in it. As Twain's *Yankee* develops, one sees the same thing happening in that novel.

Once in a while, the snake-swallowing-its-tail paradox can fit the conquering-hero pattern, but only if the universe is a conspiracy organized for the benefit of humanity: in Lester del Rey's "And It Comes Out Here," such a scenario founds a whole future civilization:

You pick up an atomic generator in the future and bring it back to . . . your present so that it can be put in the museum with you as the inventor so you can steal it to be the inventor. And you do it in a time machine which you bring back to yourself to take yourself into the future to return to take back to yourself. (46)

The question of alienation really does not arise, even though the paradox resembles that of Heinlein's "All You Zombies"; but while the latter's paranoia is negative and isolating, del Rey's is positive and reassuring.

The Alienated Hero: Stranger-Stranger-[Stranger]

Here is the opposite track. The hero is isolated from beginning to end: alone in owntime, alone in outtime, and, should he return, alone at the end. Moving about in time does not one little thing to change his relationship to himself and to the universe. How could it, time and space and human nature being what they are?

In the literature of time travel this pattern appears most obviously in the solipsistic story. The word *solipsism, solus* and *ipse*, self alone, perfectly describes the scenario; as it is worked out by SF writers, time travel becomes a perfect setting for an isolation Kafka might well have envied. Unfortunately, perhaps, the despair is somewhat attenuated by the mathematical puzzle aspect of many of the stories: time travel leads into a series of paradoxes which leave the hero totally isolated from any connection in time or space, looping back onto himself like some sort of human Möbius strip. The best-known example, oddly enough, comes from the same Heinlein who wrote *Door into Summer*, a short story called "All You Zombies." Summarizing it is an exercise in confusion:

In 1945 a baby girl is left in an orphanage; she grows up and in 1963 is seduced and impregnated by a man whom she never sees again. She delivers a baby girl, who is kidnapped straightaway; she then discovers that she has been a true hermaphrodite and that her female organs have been ruined by the delivery. Henceforth she will be male. In 1970 he tells his sad tale to a barman; the barman, a colonel in the Temporal Bureau, recruits him and takes him uptime to 1963 and finds him a girl. After impregnating his earlier self, the hero ends up in a 1985 barracks. After considerable undescribed service, he becomes a recruiting officer and opens a bar, recruits himself in 1970, pimps for himself in 1963, kidnaps himself in 1964, and delivers his baby girl self to Cleveland in 1945. He retires, a good day's work done, in 1993; the story ends thus:

Then I glanced at the ring on my finger.

The Snake That Eats Its Own Tail, Forever and Ever. . . . I *know* where *I* come from, but *where did all you zombies come from?*

I felt a headache coming on, but a headache powder is one thing I do not take. I did it once—and you all went away. . . .

You aren't really there at all. There isn't anybody but me—Jane—here alone in the dark.

I miss you dreadfully!

The snake that eats its own tail, in this story, keeps on eating until it swallows its own head and disappears, because all reality is only a pain in the head. The only way any author can go any further along that line is to make it still more complex and still more determinedly narcissistic, as David Gerrold does in *The Man Who Folded Himself*, an exercise which defies summarization: suffice it to say that self-seduction becomes multiple narcissistic orgy, the ultimate lonely masturbatory compulsion. The hero is nobody's baby, nobody's parent, nobody's friend: a stranger all the way down the line.

But the solipsistic scenario is not necessary for the alienated SF hero: we see him in the protagonists of Aldiss' "Judas Danced" and "Not for an Age." In the former, the hero, quite mad, is involved in a truly Kafka-like circle in which he constantly returns to the past to murder his twin brother—his other self, of course—only to be constantly frustrated and reprieved from execution, carrying all the memories of all the deaths with him. In the latter, a bubble from the past—our present—is taken to the future for the amusement of the public; the protagonist is caught in the nightmarish replaying and replaying of an ordinary day. It is quite clear that the ordinary day is a mini-nightmare in itself.

The ordinarily modestly optimistic Frederik Pohl has a story which fits this grim pattern: "Let the Ants Try," 1949. An atomic war in 1960 leaves the hero bereft of his family; the silly fellow does not even think of using his time machine to go back and stop the war or get his family out of his nuked Detroit. Instead he drops mutated ants 40 million years back, determined to give some other species a chance at hegemony over the Earth. "I feel like God," the hero's companion says, a sure sign that Nemesis is about to clobber Hubris. On their return to an ant-present, they find an ant civilization even less civilized and more cruel than ours. The survivor of the encounter tries to return to the past to prevent his earlier action and bring things back to normal, but is foiled by ant time travelers.

The same de Camp who gave us the neo-Yankee triumphant in *Lest Darkness Fall* gives us a no-win time travel story in "Balsamo's Mirror." The writer *says* that his character, Newbury, is not modeled on himself, but the reader has some room for doubt; the "friend in Providence," he allows, was modeled on H. P. Lovecraft. Enamored of the eighteenth century, the two travel there to find that each is entrapped inside a native. The Lovecraft figure quickly becomes disenchanted by the dirt, the narrow-mindedness, the brutality, and the superstition of the eighteenth century; but, at the end of the tale, asked if he will return to and be reconciled to the twentieth, he demurs: "The real world, anywhere or in any age, is no place for a gentleman of sensitivity. So I shall spend more time in the world of dreams.''

The alienated hero seems a long way from the bluff and vulgar Connecticut Yankee; as we have said, from Hank Morgan's own point of view he is nearly a conquering hero, up until his almost accidental wounding in the Battle of the Sand-Belt. However—and this is a fascinating complication of the *Yankee*—from the point of view of the author and the reader, he turns out to have strange resemblances to the Existential Loner. In owntime, in Hartford, he is a clever man: but his energies go toward making ''guns, revolvers . . . all sorts of labor-saving devices.'' In the sixth century, he does likewise, with great resulting slaughter. When he is jerked away from owntime, his regret for his lost friends is momentary and melodramatic; his sorrow for his lost almost-fiancee is shallow and late; and in the sixth century he marries a woman for whose intelligence he has the utmost contempt. (In a rejected passage, indeed [California *Yankee*, 515], Twain flirted with the idea of giving Sandy scarlet fever and thereby rendering her deaf and dumb; ''the only obstacle to their union being thus removed, [Morgan] resolves to marry her.'') Clarence is the Yankee's protégé rather than his friend, and Morgan's friendship with Lancelot comes late and is disposed of in three paragraphs.

But, one might object, just such detachment is what makes the Conquering Hero's activities and triumphs possible. True. But the moralizing about history and human affairs which broods over the *Yankee* makes it impossible that we should regard the Yankee as a Skylark of time: we are invited to see that his vision of himself is ill-considered and that, indeed, he is a loner without really recognizing it.

Folk like the hero of *High Noon* are alienated from their societies because of the shortcomings of those societies; we can likewise say of Morgan that his *lack* of alienation from the sixth century, as from the nineteenth, is likewise rooted in the shortcomings of those societies, those shortcomings being shared by the hero and made explicit for the reader by the author. To be adjusted to a malad-justed society is to be maladjusted; and in spite of Hank's momentary spasms of revolutionary virtue, it is clear that he means to remain dictator of his nine-teenth-century sixth-century nation as long as he can, and that he will maintain that position by any means necessary.

From his own point of view, then (up until his return), and from what he *says*, Hank is a Conquering Hero; from what seems to be Twain's point of view—that of a *sans-culotte*, he says—and from what Hank *does* and the quality of his relationships with his fellow-humans, he looks to us more like an Isolate.

''I was just as much at home in that century as I could have been in any other,'' he says (VIII). Probably true: he is certainly not *made* an Isolate by being jerked into the sixth century; he is not ''banished as no man ever was'' until he is returned to his own time. In another sense, he has always been banished; he can never be a citizen of the universe in any century.

The Romancer: Stranger-Citizen-[Stranger]

I suppose that almost everyone we know has entertained the notion, at one time or another, that he or she was born in the wrong year. If I had only been born in 1900, I could have heard Buddy Bolden and the young Louis Armstrong; if my birth had only been postponed to 2000, I might reasonably expect to experience space travel as a passenger. Outtime, past or future, has appeals the present can never know. *Death of a Salesman*'s Willy Loman is happy only when he is dreaming of a past in which he was still a young middle-aged man and his sons were boys, and he gives up what future is left to him in the hope that his sons can recapture that past and assure their own futures.

Part of this pattern, of course, overlaps with the nostalgia-monger we have dealt with earlier, the person for whom the past is already and always overpowering the future; not much wonder, when you consider the number of well-intentioned adults who hovered over our childhoods and adolescences yelling "Enjoy! Enjoy! these are the best years of your life." Given all the pains of childhood, all the difficulties of adolescence, it is no wonder that many of us become suicidal, overtly or otherwise, before reaching adulthood; those who do arrive at adulthood are often those who have bought the idea and decided that a long downhill run is better than no run at all.

I take it that the rational part of our minds knows that the past was, on balance, less pleasant and more sordid than our present; that, in spite of clichés, most of our ancestors were more crowded and hurried than we are; that day followed day like pebbles dropping into a pond; that many features of existence which for us would be major crises (headlice in my children's hair!) were daily facts of life; and that the men and women whom we have made into demigods were very like us: plodding, persevering, enduring, often whining and impatient folk, winning through upon occasion to beautiful memories or solid accomplishment or elevating daydreams or transcendent ecstasy.

And yet, in our nostalgic moods, we find the heroes of the past bigger than those of today; and in our trufan moods, we seek the great heroes out in the future. Steak yesterday, steak tomorrow, hamburg today.

You will remember Barry Pennywither from Le Guin's "April in Paris" and Si Morley from Finney's *Time and Again*. You may even remember Si saying, "We're a people who pollute the very air we breathe. And our rivers. . . . In Asia we burned people alive, we really did. . . . it becomes harder and harder to continue telling yourself that we're really good people." This is the excellent foppery of the nostalgic: to tell yourself that the problems of your own age, or of your own self, are new and unique. The ancient Greeks stripped the forest from off the whole countryside, leaving a rocky terrain on which, in Periclean times, nothing but the olive and the grape could grow; nineteenth-century London turned the Thames into an open sewer and the air overhead into perpetual smog; and in the European Middle Ages they burned people alive, they really did.

If the strident self-confidence and facile optimism of Heinlein's Davis in *The*

Door into Summer offend us, as well they should, how much more should we be offended by the neo-pre-Raphaelites who would stop time and reverse it, playing, like Victorian ladies and gentlemen, at being knights and ladies of the Table Round? Even Booth Tarkington's Penrod, with the common sense of a Huck Finn, knew better than that.

Twain, in his disdain of Scotian romance, knows better too; but the Yankee doesn't always. Remember his delight (VIII) as he realizes that, however competent he was in his own age, he is a giant in the sixth century; remember also, that in spite of his becoming The Boss (which translates to Il Duce or Der Fuehrer), he is itched by the fact (VIII) that he can never be accepted as True Nobility. It is a strange intrusion of romantic nostalgia in a character so devoted to nineteenth-century engineering values.

In spite of these harsh words about this scenario, however, one must hasten to point out that it is the basis not only for Le Guin's excellent "April in Paris" but also for Asimov's splendid story "The Ugly Little Boy." Patrouch points out that this story and "The Dead Past," two time travel stories, are rare examples of hostility toward science in the fiction of Asimov; and that Asimov's first story was about time travel, and that Asimov's favorites among his fiction are "The Ugly Little Boy" and "The Last Question." The latter, while not involving time travel, involves itself with the struggle against entropy by the much changed collective intelligence of the universe, and the establishment of a circular time line.

"The Ugly Little Boy" has as heroine a misfit—a single, unloved, but competent nurse who is hired to take care of a three- or four-year-old Neanderthal child who has been snatched from the past. (As in "The Cosmic Corkscrew," Asimov's first story, one can reach only specific points in the past.) "Orphaned as no child has ever been orphaned before" (203), Timmie, like many a time traveler, is imprisoned, not by anyone's fiat, but by physical laws, in a Stasis bubble not quite part of our space-time. The heroine, caring for him, comes to love him and, when, after four years in our time, Timmie has to be sent back to his own time, chooses to go with him rather than to lose the boy whom she regards as her son. In this story, as in "April in Paris" and many another story of travel to the past, it is love—sexual, friendly, or parental—which triumphs over time, just as in the solipsistic time travel story it is self-love which traps the protagonist in a meaningless circle.

In Richard Meredith's *Run, Come See Jerusalem!* a saboteur leaves a theocratic dystopia in the twenty-first century to attempt its abortion in the twentieth; in a stay in 1871, a time which, like Si Morley, he finds agreeable in spite of its problems, his pursuers cause the Chicago fire. Infected before he left his present, he pollutes the gene pool in 1871 so that on his return to his owntime he finds the human race all but doomed. Here we find the romantic scenario, of course, merging with that of the meddler and with the myth of the Three Wishes.

Alfred Bester and L. Sprague de Camp use this pattern to similar effect in "The Men Who Murdered Mohammed" and "The Best-Laid Scheme," respectively. In the former, those who would change the past in order to affect the present find themselves being affected instead; the more changes they make in the past, the more wraithlike they become in the present, since their owntime being is dependent on all past history. In the latter, two travelers to the past, a blackmailer and a pursuing policeman, come back to the 1960s and discover that, by making changes, they have changed themselves; the cop settles down to be a poet and the blackmailer to raise flowers, and both live happily ever after in the 1960s.

It is impossible easily to categorize Michael Moorcock's fiction, all of it being lush and outrageously imagined; but his *Alien Heat* fits the romantic pattern of time travel by burlesquing it. In a future decadence rife with incest, the occasional traveler from the past shows up. One of them, Li Pao, asked if he would go back to the twenty-eighth century, asks why he should think of such a thing: "What would I tell my people? That all their work, their self-sacrifice, their idealism, finally led to the creation of your putrid world?" (53). Rather, he will attach himself to the future and play Jeremiah to a population which (56), having never really been able to be young, cannot really grow up.

A traveler from the late nineteenth century tries to teach the hero Christian morality with some success, doing it (85) in terms of Arthurian virtue; when she is sent back to 1896, he follows. Like the Yankee (112), he shows powers of prognostication that work better at long distance; sentenced to die because of his ignorance of the nineteenth century (on which, in his own age, he is rated "an expert"), he is snapped back into his own age, where he spends his time recreating the nineteenth century and pining for his lost love.

Moorcock is quite obviously viewing his own age through the distorting glass of the future, holding the twentieth century up to supposedly Arthurian standards of the past and finding it wanting; he is also having a jolly burlesque romp through the conventions of time travel we have come to know well over the last century. We hear through all the filters the echoes of the *Yankee*.

The Exile: Citizen-Stranger-[Citizen]

We have noted that early and for a moment, at the beginning of his stay in the sixth century, the Yankee has a moment where he feels himself exiled and reflects that his friends will not be born for 1300 years; we have likewise noted that, having put down roots and acquired wife and child in the sixth century, he becomes, at the end of the book, a terrible exile in his own time.

The ordinary citizen, well rooted in his own era, well adjusted to being himself, without dreams of glory in some past history, would likely find the past a prison or an exile; and if regret for the vanished past—his own youth or the past beyond his life—intervened, the thought of the price he would have to pay would quickly wipe such an idea from his mind.

In his introduction to *Future Perfect* (x), H. Bruce Franklin says that "Oliver Wendell Holmes, insofar as he was a writer of fiction, was a writer of science fiction''; and it is Holmes who puts the time travel wish into personal perspective in his 1854 Class of '29 poem, ''The Old Man Dreams'':

> Oh for one hour of youthful joy!
>   Give me back my twentieth spring!
> I'd rather laugh, a bright-haired boy,
>   Than reign, a gray-beard king.
>
> Off with the spoils of wrinkled age!
>   Away with learning's crown!
> Tear out life's Wisdom-written page,
>   And dash its trophies down!
>
> One moment let my life-blood stream
>   From boyhood's fount of flame!
> Give me one giddy, reeling dream
>   Of life all love and fame!

(Notice that what the poet seeks in the past is the *illusion* of a brighter future—that is to say, the now-present. *Make me ignorant again*, he is ironically saying. What follows, then, comes as no surprise.)

> My listening angel heard the prayer,
>   And, calmly smiling, said,
> ''If I but touch thy silvered hair,
>   Thy hasty wish hath sped.
>
> ''But is there nothing in thy track,
>   To bid thee fondly stay,
> While the swift seasons hurry back
>   To find the wished-for day?''
>
> ''Ah, truest soul of womankind!
>   Without thee what were life?
> One bliss I cannot leave behind:
>   I'll take—my—precious—wife!''
>
> The angel took a sapphire pen
>   And wrote in rainbow dew,
> *The man would be a boy again,*
>   *And be a husband too!*
>
> ''And is there nothing yet unsaid,
>   Before the change appears?
> Remember, all their gifts have fled
>   With those dissolving years.''
>
> ''Why, yes;'' for memory would recall
>   My fond paternal joys;
> ''I could not bear to leave them all—
>   I'll take—my—girl—and—boys.''

The smiling angel dropped his pen,—
  "Why, this will never do;
The man would be a boy again,'
  And be a father too."

And so I laughed,—my laughter woke
  The household with its noise,—
And wrote my dream, when morning broke,
  To please the gray-haired boys.

Holmes always referred to his classmates as "the boys," but here it comes especially appropriately: the graybeard may contain the boy, but the boy cannot contain the husband and father out in the future. Holmes' husband and father, then, returned to his youth, would not be a youthful imperialist ("18 and knowing what I know now"), but a man bereft of all that makes the life of his older consciousness worth living: an exile. Thus the last line: we may be twenty-five years older than when we graduated, but there are compensations. The angel's words, which we recognize as the words of our own common sense, make us laugh at our own foolish and infantile dreams of youth.

In Anderson's poignant tale of temporal exile, "My Object All Sublime," the narrator meets a man named Thad Michaels with an odd accent who is introducing new ideas into housing: "Like it or not, he said, this was the middle twentieth century and mass production was here to stay" (69). He is, he says, a displaced person who has changed his name from Tadeusz Michalowski because he wants no part of old-country sentimentalism: "I'm a zealous assimilationist." He has settled in well in his new country, introducing new ideas and acquiring a wife and sons. "Nonetheless," says the narrator (70), "he was a lonely man."

After a Thanksgiving dinner, everyone in Michaels' family in bed, he and the narrator sit up late drinking and, in an echo of the *Yankee*, when Michaels has become a bit unsteady, he begins to tell what he says is a fantasy. It is, he says (71), "a cold story," echoing the narrator's thoughts of a moment before about the stars: "I had not often seen so big and frosty a view" (70). From time to time, as he speaks, Michaels looks at "a picture on the wall, a somber, unintelligible thing which no one else liked [but from which] he seemed to get strength" (71). The picture, of course, is not from the future, but is one of those products of our time, now neglected, which will be prized by the future: an echo of "Vintage Season." One may also think of the Yankee's resentment at the lack of his owntime art—chromos, ironically—in the court of King Arthur.

In Michaels' "fantasy," which of course turns out to be his own story, he comes from thousands of years in the future. Anderson quickly steps on a couple of reader expectations: outtime would not fear changing the present by changing the past, because, as in Anderson's *Dancer from Atlantis* and *Corridors of Time*, what is written is written. Nor is the future interested in exploiting or robbing the present, as Piper's Paratimers exploit more primitive time levels. No, the past is being used as a temporal Devil's Island, a place to maroon future criminals.

Anderson does not allow the reader the familiar paranoid scenario, either (the reason things are so terrible now is that we are either a jail or an insane asylum for another place or another time); he has Michaels point out, in a speech which underlines the terrible quality of temporal exile, that

the worst crime in the world depends on the particular year of the world's history. Murder, brigandage, treason, heresy, narcotics peddling, slaving, patriotism, the whole catalogue, all have rated capital punishment in some epochs, and been lightly regarded in others, and positively commended in still others. (73)

And, as in "The Man Who Came Early," Anderson steps on the notion that a temporal exile could become a competent imperialist: "Imagine yourself left naked and alone in Babylon. How much Babylonian language or history do you know? . . . What are the laws and customs you must obey? . . . You'd be lucky if you ended up scrubbing floors" (74). But modest success *is* possible, as Michaels' own example shows. He talks about homesickness very passionately, and loneliness; nevertheless he has Gone Native and put down roots here, and says he would not go back. Drawing once again the parallel between spatial and temporal displacement, he says, "But, voluntarily or forced, people have always been emigrating. We're descended from those who could stand the shock. I adapted" (77). Therefore (the reader is led to think) Michaels is no longer truly an exile; his new place has become home. Whereupon Anderson snaps his trap: the narrator is also from the future, an agent of the civilization which has banished Michaels, and Michaels' whole "fantasy" is something the narrator has known before Michaels told him. In spite of Michaels' pleading to stay with his wife and children, "I left him in Damascus the year before Tamerlane sacked it" (78).

In other works, Anderson has given us travel to the past as opportunity for high adventure, or for a meaningful attack on entropy, or for psychic reintegration; but in this Kafkaesque vision, Michaels is in the position of the truly alienated. Like K, he has committed a crime which is never named; his guilt is made the more guiltless by the fact that whatever he has done is only a crime because he happened to be in the wrong place at the wrong time; and the powers that be in his universe will never let him settle down to being a citizen, however intelligent, selfless, and worthy his efforts. To make bad matters unnecessarily worse, those whom he thinks to be his friends may turn out to be in on the conspiracy against him.

It is interesting, and extraordinary, that both Heinlein and Anderson, both ordinarily hearty yea-sayers to the value of human intelligence, common sense, judicious craft, and heroic action, should have produced such paranoid visions as "All You Zombies" and "They"—both Heinlein's—and this story by Anderson.

Dmitri Bilenkin of the USSR adds a dimension to the idea of exile in "The Uncertainty Principle," the title of which refers to an extension of quantum physics into the temporal dimension: "In traveling to the past, you can either appear in a predetermined point in space or a predetermined point in time. In principle, it is impossible to do both simultaneously" (1).

Time shifting in this story is used very carefully out of fear of disturbing history; only automatic cameras are sent back to study the past. One is lost, however, and Berg, chosen not because he is a specialist or a genius but because he is lucky, is sent back to extract it. "The first, and, let's hope, the last" traveler to the past, he is uniquely isolated. Bilenkin makes the point that the future, which has not yet happened, is even stranger than the past: "Berg would be a visitor from somewhere that did not exist for anyone he met" (2).

He is even strange to himself; he has "normal, strong, callused hands," but the calluses are the result of long study in the future on how to duplicate this strange archaism. In the past, Berg runs on a cross with his own name on it; coming presumably from an atheistic society, he finds this not only ominous but ominous in truly alien fashion.

Berg continues into town, which he finds gloomy, depressing, and murky, although he does admit to himself that the church serves some necessary function; though the society is different and anxiety-ridden, the church does offer comfort that is understandable but, to Berg, repellent. He wants only to do his job and return to his owntime, in which he will not be faced with such ugly facts as beer-drinking and meat-eating. In a familiar motif, he is imprisoned (on charges of witchcraft) and gets out with a Yankee-like superiority, but this time because of superior powers of mental-muscular coordination.

Very like Duncan Reid in *The Dancer from Atlantis*, he runs up on a lady who claims to have loved him in her past, and is faced with the problem of whether to aid her in her escape (and thereby risk contaminating his own past). He understands that the girl, pregnant somehow with his child, is potentially "a happy . . . child of the twenty-first century" and sends her there, ending up himself totally lost to that century, some years before discovering his own grave. Now, he knows, he will meet the girl, get himself executed, and somehow return Christlike after several days in the ground. He is exiled in a past earlier than the one in which he partially went native—very like Anderson's Michaels—and yet out of his exile he draws triumph:

. . . his life would be a worthwhile one. He would enter battle and win. He would have time to love and be loved. Have time to give happiness to someone who had never dreamed of it. Have time to become a father. And perhaps that was a worthy accomplishment for a man of any era. (22)

The Student: Stranger-Citizen-[Citizen]

"The Student" is the best name I can come up with for this paradigm, but I'm not over-happy with it. It would fit a student, right enough: a person troubled and unhappy in the present who finds knowledge and understanding in the past and returns completed to his own time. But it also fits heroes like that of Michael Bishop's *No Enemy but Time*. Joshua has an extraordinary talent for dreaming, wherefore—rather like the hero of Finney's *Time and Again*—he is able, with the help of a machine, to travel to the Pleistocene, where he meets *homo habilis*. More than most, this novel plugs into the rest of the literature: Poe, Proust, Swift, Le Guin, Alex Haley, and the Arthurian legends are all explicitly evoked. The first book read to the baby Joshua (then inexplicably called John-John) is *The Hobbit*; later he is to see his remote ancestors as hobbits.

Joshua's flashbacks, however, are not stimulated by Proustian madeleines but (invoking much of Anderson) by birds. Unlike the stupid Gulliver, Joshua understands the humanity of the Yahoos and can even love them: and at this point we remember that Yehushua is the Hebrew equivalent of the Greek Jesus. A biracial Spanish/American, Joshua returns from the past with his daughter, thus becoming a link between America and Africa, his foster and his biological parents, and the past and the present. Partly we may see him as a student; partly he anticipates what we will say about the pattern of the demythologizer, who finds healing for the present in the past.

Similarly, in Philip Jose Farmer's *Time's Last Gift*, a group of scientists go back 14,000 years on a four-year trip to study the natives. Among them, unbeknownst to the rest, is an immortal, born in 1872, who appears to be Tarzan of the Apes (in spite of the fact that in *Tarzan Alive*, Farmer has Tarzan born in 1888 and refutes (305) Peter Ogden's claim that he was born in 1872). By 2070, at any rate, having disguised himself as his own son and grandson, he has become John Gribardsun, M.D., anthropologist, botanist, and linguist. He leads the group of four.

As one might expect, he finds it very easy to go native and does, staying behind when the expedition leaves. He does, however, live through the next 14,000 years, becoming Hercules, Quetzelcoatl, and Terah the father of Abraham (and his own ancestor). Returned through longevity to 2070, he seems fulfilled and happy, ready to depart on a cold-sleep voyage to the stars.

As is so often true of Farmer's novels, the novel is scattered and unfocused, the prose clunky, and the ideas fascinating if distracting from one another. Clearly, this Tarzan scenario, while fitting out "Student" pattern, has some resemblances to the "Romancer" pattern in that the hero finds in the past a satisfaction denied him in the present and that he elects to stay there; his return to a more satisfactory present by a circuitous and lengthy route, however, leads me to deal with it here.

This pattern will not really jell for me, however, since it also adequately fits the successful meddler. Take Richard Cowper's *Time Out of Mind*, for example. A Laurie Linton from 2005, in which a dictator reigns, visits his 1987 self, a child with a fishing rod, and tells him, "Kill Magrobian." The child grows up and becomes a narc; he hears of a drug which will enable a person to contact his earlier self, and his reactions are predictably Yankeeish: "Say he . . . knows that a certain obscure company is going to become fantastically successful. So he tells his earlier self to buy a packet of shares in it. The moment he does it, *presto!*—his adult self's worth a fortune" (109–10). The adult self kills Magrobian, who would have become dictator, and the ugly and inhuman future from which he came back to his childhood does not have to happen.

Similarly, in Leo P. Kelley's *Time Rogue*, an historian from a dystopic future sends his spirit back to inhabit the bodies of seven of our contemporaries; given visions of the future effects of their actions, they are able to prevent that future in spite of the destruction of the historian. Note that all of these treatments of this pattern tend to involve the respectful treatment of the past which is characteristic of the student—the anthropologist who respects his subjects rather than the Yankee who would exploit them.

The Tragic Hero: Citizen-Stranger-[Stranger]

The tragic hero typically begins in his own time very well—if not on top of the world, then at least well adjusted and content. When the past rolls over him, he discovers himself to be alienated in ways he has not hitherto suspected; and whether in past or present, he ends his life in that alienation. If we consider the Yankee in Hartford, the Yankee toward the end of his stay in the sixth century, and the Yankee on his return to the nineteenth century, he fits the pattern.

In mainstream literature, of course, the tragic hero does not return to the past in a physical sense; instead, the past (or sometimes some other force outside the here-and-now) impinges on the balance he is maintaining in the present: Hamlet's father's ghost from the past, prophecies from the future for Macbeth.

Oedipus is the most obvious example. In spite of the importunings of Iocaste, who is older and has better sense, he insists on continuing to rediscover the past, to open it up, with the result that his secure present is totally wrecked. As soon as he "gets to" his own past, he finds there a terrible alienation, and that alienation transfers itself into his own present. (All tragic heroes do not, of course, suffer this impingement of the past on the present—it would be difficult to make this pattern fit Othello or Caesar or Antony—but the pattern is still tragic, and Oedipus is the archetype, as he was of the transtemporal fornicator.)

Oedipus Tyrannos is not only a tragedy; it is the first true detective story. And the pattern appears in many modern detective stories. In the novels of Ross MacDonald, for example, typically a relatively minor question in a generally placid present opens up barrels of worms in the past and reveals the apparent coherence of the present to be built on very flimsy foundations indeed.

Furthermore, as we have noted hitherto, movement in space is often analogous to movement in time; and in *Gulliver's Travels*, for example, the hero's movements in space have the same alienating effect. Lemuel Gulliver, a placid, progressive, confident man of his own time and place, moves through three books of voyages and experiences which would totally alienate a more intelligent or sensitive man, without ever losing confidence in his values or his position in the scheme of things; but confronted with the Yahoos—who may reasonably be seen as representative of the race's subhuman past, among other things—Gulliver becomes so estranged from himself and from his species that, upon his return to England (which would serve as the return to the "present," in the SF versions of this pattern), he is a more total stranger than almost anyone else in our literature. Ironically enough, in this pattern, it is upon returning to his home place or time that the curious stranger is *exiled as no man has ever been.*

In time travel SF, a good example of this pattern is to be found in Ward Moore's *Bring the Jubilee*, an important and complex book which we have had occasion to mention in several earlier contexts. The hero, Hodgins McCormick (which implies "the reaper") Backmaker (which, of course, can mean "past-changer"), an historian from a 1952 in which the South won the Civil War, returns to the Battle of Gettysburg and finds himself in big trouble there; and that trouble assures the North of its victory in that battle and in that war.

The result is the destruction of the world in which Backmaker has studied, published, loved, and achieved a certain measure of happiness. Certainly, in spite of the fact that he is a citizen of the beaten, impoverished, and depressed United States, Backmaker has not the slightest idea of changing the past. Although he has, and has had, his own troubles in his own era, he is a sensible man who has achieved a more-than-modest and -satisfying success as an historian; and he has found a shelter from the harshness of his world in the Ivory Tower of Haggershaven. (A *lot* of post-Padway travelers to the past are academics of one sort or another.)

Backmaker has just published a massive Civil War history on which he has spent years of research; there being no publisher in the United States competent to handle the work, it has been published by the great Confederate house of Ticknor, Harcourt & Knopf. The last thing he would want to do, even supposing he did not have a devoted wife and dear friends in his own 1952, would be to invalidate all of his own scholarship. When first he arrives in the past, he experiences an academic apotheosis: "If there is a paradise for historians I had achieved it without the annoyance of dying first" (175). (Note the Twainish quality of that last phrase; and note also that Backmaker is totally wrong.)

Secure in his knowledge of what he thinks is going to happen, Backmaker approaches Gettysburg, pitying the soldiers who do not have his understanding of what it is that they are doing and how it will all work out. Later, he will find such knowledge a burden, as time travelers so often do. Finally and ironically, his presence changes history so that his knowledge turns out not to be true. Here, I think, we have the Uncertainty Principle of twentieth-century physics drizzling down into popular art: *there are no privileged observers; it is impossible to know what is happening when no one is looking; and it is impossible to observe a happening without changing that happening.* How do the natives act when there are no anthropologists taking notes?

Returning to the appointed spot at the appointed time to be plucked back into

1952, Backmaker is not so plucked, and finds himself stranded in the past. The only possible conclusion is that the future in which the time machine was invented has been wiped out:

Are they really gone . . . lost in a future which never existed, which couldn't exist, once the chain of causation was broken? Or do they exist after all, in a [parallel] universe in which the South won . . . ? Could another [inventor] devise a means to reach this universe? I would give so much to believe this, but I cannot. . . . (192)

Children, the narrator goes on to say, ask "Please God, make it didn't happen"— that seems to be where Larry Niven got the line. Adults, Backmaker says, think that the past cannot be changed; children know that it can—which is to say, as we have said before, that the desire to go back and change the past is fundamentally infantile.

Backmaker concludes that the easy solace of the idea of parallel universes is not a real one: "Once lost, [a] particular past can never be regained. Another and another perhaps, but never the same one. There are no parallel universes— though this one may be sinuous and inconstant" (192). In the reality in which you and I live, we cannot travel backward and make changes in time; we are stuck with the consequences of our actions, and we must live with the changes we have brought about. Hodge Backmaker is able to go into the past and change it; he has achieved the dream of the child who would escape the cause-and-effect scenario. And the result? He is forced to recognize, at that point, that he has done the irreversible and is stuck with the consequences of his actions. In short, he has been made to grow up. But he has grown up too late: he is not a child, but a man with a wife and friends and a home and possessions and a profession, all of which have been made never-wases because of his childish wish for shortcuts in the writing of history.

The wisdom of the traditional Three Wishes story lies in the adult knowledge that, however much we would like to have unlimited power over our universe and our destiny, we are better off without it. The Three Wishes story often ends happily, with the wisher back where he started, only wiser: a stranger-stranger-citizen or citizen-stranger-citizen scenario. But this version—the monkey's paw story—ends with the wiser stuck with his wishes and the horrid results thereof.

Bring the Jubilee is a SF novel extraordinary in its complexity of character, understanding of psychological and philosophical implications, use of folkish archetypes, and consequent approach to the tragic. The hero, like many a Campbell archetype, meets an older and alien man, in this case the Haitian ambassador to the United States, M. Enfandin. His name has overtones of *enfant*, and his wisdom is the childlike wisdom of the truly wise. The young Hodge Backmaker questions the value of fiction:

"What value has the invention of happenings that never happened, or characters who never existed?"

"Who is to say what never happened? It is a matter of definition. . . . "

"You can't learn anything from fairy tales," I persisted stubbornly.

He smiled. "Maybe you haven't read the right fairy tales." (53)

Just as Hank Morgan has a Good Father (Arthur) and a Bad Father (Merlin), so Hodge has several fathers; a mostly Bad Father is his boss, Roger Tyss, who is a materialist and a believer in determinism. For him, as for the hero of Heinlein's "All You Zombies," time is "the serpent with its tail in its mouth" (39). Of Tyss' view, Enfandin, the Good Father and a believing Catholic, says,

He has liberated himself from the superstitions of religion in order to fall into superstition so abject no Christian can conceive it. Imagine to yourself . . . time is circular, man is automaton, we are doomed to repeat the same gestures over and over, forever. . . . This is monstrous. (60)

Later in the book, Enfandin is replaced as Hodge's Good Father by Thomas Haggerswells, proprietor of Haggershaven, a Pennsylvania cooperative retreat for intellectuals; Haggerswells, descendant of a Southern officer who went north after the war—a sort of carpetbagger in reverse—has more than a passing physical resemblance to Thomas Jefferson. His daughter, Barbara, is a physicist, unhappy, moody, beautiful, brilliant, tormented, and tormenting; she is an echo of the siren who so often tempts the folk hero to his doom, the inventor of a time machine.

Hodge is attracted to Barbara, even a bit in love with her, but though she may give herself to him physically, ultimately she is unattainable. She is bewitched by her own intelligence and her own science; further, she sees herself as better than Hodge in intelligence, in morals, and in family.

Early on, Hodge does not believe her time machine will work: it offends his sense of order and logic. He sees it as a delusion growing out of her studies and rooted in her own psychopathology, as "the rationalization of a daydream, the daydream of discovering a process for reaching back through time to injure her dead mother and so steal all of her father's affections . . . " (123). An acute point, this, echoing much of what we have said in our discussions of the traveler to the past as Oedipally motivated. The dream of going to the past is surely rooted in infantile desires and motives; and many a tale of travel to the past, like many a Three Wishes tale, is at base cautionary: infantile desires and wishes are all very well, such tales say, but now, let us just suppose for a moment that such wishes were granted. What then? And, in time travel literature, for every Lazarus Long who, Sinbad-like, finds himself able to use the genie to bring life, there are a hundred Backmakers who find that the granting of wishes is the worst thing that could happen.

In this tale, though the motives behind the development of Barbara's time machine may well be infantile, unrealistic, and pathological, the machine is developed anyway. A thing does not have to be *grounded* in reality to *become* reality; the totally unscientific racism of Nazi Germany is perhaps the most striking example from recent history.

Even though, following the pattern of the monomyth, his love for Barbara will eventually result in his own catastrophe, Hodge does not stay in love with her forever; a woman whom he rescues after a brutal murder has gone mute with shock from the experience and seems quite idiotic. Haggershaven takes her in and cures her, over the petulant objections of Barbara, and she grows into the Ugly Duckling, Cinderella, Frog Princess heroine, a minor heiress of a great Spanish family.

There are echoes here, as elsewhere, from the *Yankee*. You will remember that originally Twain had planned to have Sandy go mute before her marriage to Morgan; here the lady regains her speech before her marriage to Hodge Backmaker. And just as the Demoiselle Alisande la Carteloise becomes Sandy in the *Yankee*, so the Señorita Catalina Garcia becomes Catty. And, of course, both husbands, victims in different ways of time travel in different directions, are left lorn and alone and apart from their wives at the ends of the books. The Yankee leaves Sandy and their child in France to hustle back to England and the Battle of the Sand-Belt and his Van Winkling by Merlin; Backmaker has listened to his wife urge him to remember that there are no shortcuts in the writing (and, one unconsciously supplies, in the making) of history. Still the temptation is too great; telling her that he is off to tour the battlefield of Gettysburg, but not telling her when, he gets a protest from her:

She pretended to believe me and begged me to take her along. . . . "But Catty, with you there I'd be thinking of you instead of the problem."

"Ah, Hodge, have we already been married so long you must get away from me to think?"

"No matter how long, that time will never come." (171)

The book is most carefully crafted (in spite of some apparent confusion of presidential terms in Hodge's continuum [43, 49]), with many mythic overtones and many echoes of the monomyth. One of the most suggestive and tantalizing comes at the very end, after Hodge has been stranded in an alien continuum, alien—ironically—because it was his side that won. Haggershaven, in that time line (which is *ours*), is a farm owned by a family with the unusual name of *Thammis*.

All my attempts to account for this name seem to me a bit far-fetched, but one cannot ignore a proper name so unusual. It suggests *Thamus*, the pilot who, during the reign of Tiberius, sailing near Paxi, heard, according to Plutarch, the cry which signaled the end of an era: "Great Pan is dead!" It further suggests *Tammuz*, god of the sun (and therefore of time) who was slain by his wife Ishtar, goddess of procreation and life. And it suggests the *Thamis*, as the name was set down in Saxon times, now *Thames*, a river whose name near Oxford used to be *Isis: Thame-Isis* is its name in folk etymology. Isis, worshipped as far from her native Egypt as Britain, was the mother of Horus, the sister-wife and ressurrector of Osiris. Choose which of these associations you will, you are appropriately involved with death, rebirth, time, the end of a time, and that old time symbol, the river.

One final point: Moore has gone out of his way to include a light tip of the hat to Mark Twain. He makes the apparently irrelevant point (79) that in Hodge's native continuum, in 1952, nobody has yet been able to develop a typesetting machine.

Operating very much in this same pattern, the traveler in G. C. Edmondson's "Misfit," departing from a world in which Belisarius became emperor and civilized and united the world under a Christian New Rome, wishing only to observe, takes plague back to the time of Belisarius and brings about our history.

In Damon Knight's "Time Enough," going back again and again into the past in order to get things just perfect ends up with the traveler a catatonic; this story fits the pattern we are discussing, of course, as does another fine story by the same author, "Beachcomber." In a not-too-far future resembling ours but with faster-than-light travel to the stars, a traveler from three million years in the future arrives. It is a wonderful future in which humans have achieved all their dreams; but it is being invaded from another dimension. At the moment when the enemy's weapon will destroy the whole universe, the traveler is sent back with—in his pocket—the whole universe, looking rather like a pebble.

The plan is for him then to return three million years to the future, which will be different, since changing the past changes the future. This is why, during his stay here, he is profligate with technical and scientific aid which will help make that change. As he tells his tale, however, it is revealed that when he landed in the water on a planet, he lost the pebble; and since then, for five years, he has hopelessly walked the beach looking for the pebble which is his whole universe.

A short story which we have mentioned before, Poul Anderson's "Man Who Came Early," deserves more detailed treatment here; like *Bring the Jubilee*, it is a crucial document in the history of literature of travel to the past, and it is a similarly tragic end-of-an-era story.

Gerald Roberts of the U.S. Army base on Iceland is out in Reykjavik in a thunderstorm (like Martin Padway) and gets tossed back in time to 993. Ospak Ulfsson, the farmer and Viking who discovers him wandering disoriented on the beach, says that he has been knocked from his own place to there by Thor's hammer.

As soon as Roberts orients himself—he speaks Icelandic, and that language has changed less than most in a thousand years—he discovers that he has been thrown back from near the close of the second millennium to near the close of the first, and that apprehensions about the end of time are as common then as now. In later days, telling the story, Ospak tells his Christian friends that he has hard evidence that, no matter what they think, the world is not about to end in the year 1000.

"I fear," says Roberts, "I was never a very good Christian," and so he falls easily into the pagan sacrifice of a horse by his host; Yankee-like, he invites himself to be a part of the killing, doing the job with his sidearm. At this point, we get the first indication that things are not going to work out well for this Yankee: Ospak notes with some irritation that Gerald has blown the horse's brains out, and that those are among the parts most toothsome to eat. A shameful waste, he thinks it.

Gerald likewise tries the familiar fire-fireworks business which we see so many times in the literature; he lights a cigarette with a match and slyly observes his hosts, hoping to terrify or at least amaze them. Not a bit of it. Ospak has heard of Greek fire and also of the expense and difficulty of making it, and is impressed neither with firesticks nor with firearms. Matches would be useful things for trade, he admits, but the Icelanders are a sober and practical folk with kin who have seen the wonders of Byzantium, and hence are not easily impressed or cowed.

The writer obviously assumes previous familiarity on the part of the reader with the *Yankee-Darkness* tradition. Gerald, like the reader, has the natural expectation that a visitor from the future, with hindsight and technology, can, with a bit of ingenuity and common sense, become The Boss. Notice how similar Gerald's qualifications are to those of the Yankee, and how similar his ambitions:

I was an . . . engineer . . . that is, I was learning how to be one. That's a man who builds things, bridges and roads and tools . . . more than just an artisan. So I think my knowledge could be of great value here. . . . Yes, give me time and I'll be a king! (98)

Ospak is not impressed. We have no king in Iceland, he says; we came here precisely to get away from kings.

As time passes, it turns out that Gerald lacks the skill to forge a spear or shoe a horse, has no understanding of the manners of honorable dealing among free people, and owns no land and therefore is *nithing*. Hank Morgan, you remember, no matter how great his power, could never become noble; but in Twain's scenario, that does not prevent his gaining power. In Anderson's, his lack of land causes Gerald to be despised, though—like the Yankee—he does take up with a woman for whom that is not an impediment. Finally, though Gerald does tell wonderful and incredible tales of New Jorvik, he has to tell them not in verse, but in prose, like a man of no culture. He finally realizes (103) that he can't get "the tools to make the tools to make the tools," and that he cannot "run through a thousand years of history all by [himself]." Hard-pressed, he uses his gun in a duel—another echo of the *Yankee*—and is forthwith outlawed as a coward who has to kill at a distance. Ultimately he dies bravely in a blood-duel. "They are an eldritch race in the United States," Ospak the narrator muses, "but they do not lack manhood."

Here there is, of course, no return to the narrator's present: but one may reasonably infer that such return would result in alienation, given the visions of kingship with which Gerald had indulged himself, and his memories of that kingship denied.

Now, Anderson is a lover of the past, and particularly of the Viking past and, in imagination, has spent a good deal of his artistic life there. That, we would say, is romantic. But the concluding words of "The Man Who Came Early" are anything but romantic. No man, Ospak says, may ripen a field before harvest time: and that makes the whole time-travel dream futile. There is here an echo from Samuel Johnson's *Rasselas*: no man, Johnson says, can enjoy the pleasures of youth and the wisdom of age at the same time; no man can dip his cup at the same moment into the source and into the mouth of the Nile. (I call your attention, once again, to the river image.)

In the very last lines of the story, the narrator looks into the future and shows us the difficulty of any age ever really understanding another. He sees his own age as less wonderful, but more free, than that of Gerald. That is an interesting and complex observation. Other ages are strange and wonderful, and that is the observation of Anderson the romancer; but Anderson the student of history knows that the Yankeeish illusions of increased freedom in some age where one might play the imperialist are bogus dreams. In a real sense, just as we individuals can cope with our own physical and mental distresses and shortcomings, while wondering all the while how other people can possibly manage with theirs, just so we are always freest in our own times, where we understand the rules and are at home with the technology and the manners. What looks like freedom to the native becomes a terrible prison for the outlander: "I think of this Iceland [a thousand years hence] and of the young United States men there to help defend us in a year when the end of the world hovers close."

(That's a deft touch: the end of the world always does, and does not, hover close. Since we became human, we have always had the capacity to wipe out whole civilizations and do incredible damage to whole ecologies, and at various moments we have done just that. Furthermore, for each person the world ends with his or her death; and not only are our lives at risk at every moment, but our very coming into being—as time travel literature constantly reminds us—is the result of an unbelievably improbable concatenation of circumstances: and thus it is easy to imagine scenarios in which we never were, in which for us the world not only ends but never had a beginning.)

"Perhaps some of [these young United States men], walking about the heaths, will see [Gerald's] barrow and wonder what ancient warrior lies buried there, and they may even wish they had lived long ago in his time when men were free" (113). Though the warrior of the twentieth century can never really understand the warrior of the tenth, and though either of them, transported to the other's time, would end up *nithing*, there is still community and identity between them. In these lines Anderson nicely combines the part of him which is romantic nostalgic and the part which is hard-headed SF historian.

In the history of our continuum, people like Cortez and Pizarro act out a Yankeeish sort of scenario, people with very limited resources but much in the way of bluff, understanding of technology, and management skills, who manage to flummox the natives out of their empires. The story of Gerald Roberts is told more as it might have been wished by Aguinaldo, Crazy Horse, the Mahdi Mohammed Ahmed ibn Seyyid Abdulla, or Nana Sahib: the triumph of indigenous culture against the technology of the invader.

To be sure, the Filipino Rebellion, the Indian Wars, the War of the Mahdi, and the Indian Rebellion all ended with Euroamerica triumphant, at least for the moment; but in all these cases the warriors of the victors were supported by the resources of their homelands. The traveler to the past is most often a Robinson Crusoe, depending on his own skills to change the course of history and make himself monarch of all he surveys. If he could import men and machinery from his own time, his victory would be that much easier; and, as we have said, if he could move about in time at will, he might even make himself into some sort of Satanic Deity. But in this story "no man may ripen a field before harvest season."

The point is underlined in the story, when the discovery of North America by Leif Eiriksson is mentioned. Nobody is much impressed; after all, who needs a cold land across the North Atlantic populated by Skraelings who shoot arrows at you, in which there is nothing worth looting? Both invention and discovery, made before they are needed and before their usefulness is apparent, die on the vine and are forgotten. Nothing was made of Hero of Alexandria's steam engine: slaves were a cheaper source of labor. Furthermore, in many a non-time-travel SF novel and story, races with advanced technology are forbidden to introduce such technology to groups in an earlier stage of development, lest the psychic development of their culture be aborted like those of the Native American, the Hawaiian, and the Briton.

For such a view to appear in popular fiction requires an anthropological sophistication on the part of the reader which is more typical of the twentieth century than of the nineteenth: it is, after all, only relatively recently that anybody much has cared what might happen to the culture of the natives of the Amazon basin or of the uplands of New Guinea. In the nineteenth century, most would assume, like the Yankee early on in Camelot, that the intrusion of Euroamerican technology could do nothing but good for such folk, however strenuously they might resist in their barbarous ignorance. With a bit of luck, they might not resist at all, or only briefly, being properly overawed by the White Man's technology.

In our own time and our own continuum, however, some so-called underdeveloped countries have recently shown a good deal of selectivity in their acceptance of Western technology and ideas and customs; indeed, some countries—like Iran, for example—while being willing to accept oil-related Western technology, have shown themselves actively hostile to a lot of values we would export along with it. The People's Republic of China seems reluctant to bolt Western Marxism whole; and though it failed in its attempt to replace the Pittsburgh steel pattern with a more folkish system of backyard smelting, it does seem to have wiped out the housefly, not with insecticides, but with the more traditional flyswatter.

If the time-traveling student wipes out the world which constitutes his body of knowledge; if the time-traveling would-be imperialist finds his plans aborting, either because of the nature of the temporal fabric or because of the resistance of the natives; if the time-traveling Oedipal hero finds that he cannot find true love and security in the maternal past, nor truly overcome the paternal past— then we have the tragic pattern. But this is the way the *Yankee* ends. Outside knowledge aborts when confronted with native skills and values; in the sixth century, Merlin's magic and the magic of the church ultimately win, and a book which starts out like *Lest Darkness Fall* ends with the conclusion of "Man Who Came Early": one may not ripen a field before harvest time.

The Meddler: Citizen-Citizen-[Stranger]

In this familiar pattern, which more directly than any other derives from the monkey's-paw pattern, the hero begins in an owntime with which he is not totally happy. That does not make him, like the romancer, alienated there: he is, on the contrary, so much of a citizen that he wants to improve his owntime. He does not wish, like Miniver Cheevy or Barry Pennywither or Si Morley, to escape to an earlier time. He just wants to improve things by monkeying with the past; or alternatively, he is sufficiently arrogant to think that he can fool with the past without adversely affecting the present. Whether he plays with the past deliberately or accidentally, whether he goes to the past or simply sends something there, the results are bad in his owntime, and he finds himself a stranger in a world he has constructed.

This is the folk wisdom of *it could be worse*. Wish for a lot of money, and you may get it at the expense of your son's life. Wish that in the past you had not done thus-and-such, and, if the wish comes true, you may find yourself with throat cancer or without your beloved daughter.

This scenario has obvious resemblances to both the Alienated Hero schema (Stranger-stranger-stranger) and the Tragic Hero pattern (Citizen-stranger-stranger), first, in that all of them end badly, and second, in that the catastrophic ending carries with it a Sophoclean warning about what happens to folk who have the *hubris* (or the *chutzpah*) to monkey with the past. Like the tragic hero, the meddler is in pretty good shape in his own time; the difference between them is the relatively minor one of the point at which the citizen-hero becomes stranger-hero. The tragic hero finds the past a prison whose walls get straiter and straiter as they approach owntime; the meddler gets along fine in the past, returning to an owntime which is worse than the reasonably good one he started from.

In his introduction to William Tenn's "Brooklyn Project" in *The Road to Science Fiction #3*, Jim Gunn says of time travel stories,

Usually all such [time travel] enterprises come to bad ends; in fact, there wouldn't be a story if they didn't. The time traveler gets trapped in the future or the past, or he commits some blunder, often ignoring instructions, that destroys him, or alters the present, or destroys life altogether. Or he finds himself helplessly acting out the inexorable past, as in Michael Moorcock's "Behold the Man." (154)

In Asimov's "Fair Exchange?" a good example of this scenario, a traveler who (like Asimov) is a Gilbert and Sullivan fan returns to 1871 to inhabit the mind of a person living then-and-there and to see a performance of *Thespis*. In his continuum, which seems to be ours, most of the score has been lost. While in the past, his will motivates his host to try to steal the score; as a result, Sullivan, who in our history was disgusted at the reception of the play and refused to publish it, decides that if the score is good enough to steal, it is good enough to publish. On his return to his own body and his own time, the traveler finds that the score was never lost, and is in fact well known; that in his new 1983, the experiment in which he tried to go back failed, and that the trip now exists only in his memory; that Bella Abzug was elected U.S. Senator in 1976; that he is strongly suspected of being insane; and that, worst of all, his wife has been killed and that he is in the hospital as a result of having attempted suicide.

"I had changed history. I could never go back. I had gained *Thespis*. I had lost Mary" (61).

In Ballard's "Gentle Assassin," in an Appointment-in-Samarra version of this plot, a scientist returns to the past to prevent the death of his fiancée and ends up causing it; this plot, in which the attempt of the time traveler to prevent something or to take advantage of it causes the event in question, is so popular and so ubiquitous that it seems to be about worn out.

The Demythologizer: Stranger-Stranger-[Citizen]

We have already discussed heroes who, like Lazarus Long, act out infantile fantasies in the past and find them somehow life-giving, improbable as that may seem. In *Dancer from Atlantis*, however, travel to the past is redemptive in a more believable fashion, in that it allows the traveler to confront that past without illusion: to demythologize it. In this pattern, then, travel to the past becomes a paradigm for psychoanalysis. Take this pattern and extend it further, and we have Twain demythologizing a Middle Ages which had been mythologized by Scott and, in the process, doing the same for his own nineteenth century (as he did for dreams of childhood in *Tom Sawyer* and *Huckleberry Finn*).

When the person alienated in her own time returns to the past, confronts her earlier self there in a past different from the one she remembers—in which, that is, she is still a stranger—and returns to her own time with her head together, as the dancer from Atlantis does, we have the Stranger-Stranger-[Citizen] heroine whom we might call the Demythologizer.

Like Anderson, Philip K. Dick used travel to the past again and again in many varied ways. Like the fiction of the later Heinlein, Dick's work seems reflective of the author's own psychological state; with a great deal more artistry than Heinlein, Dick almost always seems to be skirting the edge of madness.

Sometimes, however, he writes a straightforward story of a Yankee sort of profiteer: in "Captive Market," an avaricious 1965 shopkeeper travels into the future to a post-atomic-war world to sell goods at high prices; in order to keep her customers under her control, she sabotages their escape rocket. At other times, as in *Ubik* or *The Three Stigmata of Palmer Eldritch*, travel in time is hideously isolating and maddening. In *Martian Time-Slip*, the hero, a child, experiences his terrible old-age-to-come and, rejecting it, retreats into the experiences of the womb, the last place he was really happy.

In *Now Wait for Last Year*, however, the demythologizer pattern appears. In apparent anticipation of travel to the past, rich folk build "babylands"—simulacra of their childhoods in which they can be less unhappy. Then a drug is developed which can send folk either into the future or into the past; those who go to the past "get bogged down in manufacturing alternate universes . . . playing God until at last the nerve destruction is too great and they degenerate into random twitches" (143). So far, the pattern seems typical Dick: existential isolate all the way. But at the end of this book Eric, the protagonist, after meeting a later Himself, comes out of the experience with a determination to "endure reality," which, if not the upbeat cure of the Atlantis dancer, is at least something—rather more than one generally gets from a Dick hero.

In Michael Moorcock's *Breakfast in the Ruins*, Karl Glogauer spends a good deal of his time in a roof garden:

In the whole of London this was the only place where he could find the peace he identified with, the peace of his early childhood, the peace of ignorance (or "innocence" as he preferred to call it). . . . he knew all too well that the urge which took him so frequently to the roof garden was both infantile and escapist . . . of all his other [*sic*] infantile and escapist pursuits—his collection of children's books, his model soldiers—this was the cheapest. (14)

Through the extraordinary means of an affair with a mysterious black man, Karl is transported into past consciousnesses, occupying the bodies of other people named Karl Glogauer and having access to their memories. Always such trips are to crucial nexi of history; always we are given graphic demonstrations of human inhumanity. At first, Karl appears as a child; as the transportations come on down through history, he ages. Sometimes he is torturer, sometimes victim. Gradually he gets blacker as his lover gets whiter; at the end, his lover seems to be Satan offering the world to him. Karl chooses the everyday life of a black man in London, seemingly happier than he was before.

The scenario here is somewhat compromised by the fierceness of the visions of the past; Moorcock's anticolonialism makes Twain's modest and genteel by comparison. Further, a character named Karl Glogauer appears in *Behold the Man*, in which travel to the past dooms him to a meaningless death, trapped in the very Christ that has brought him back. Still, it seems clear that seeing the past without illusion is meant, in *Breakfast in the Ruins*, to be not only an educational experience (for Karl and for the reader) but an integrating one. Identifying with the oppressed rather than with the oppressors, turning down the Tempter's offer of Empire, the black Karl whom we see at the end, while he seems to have nothing more on his mind than getting down a modest bet and buying a suit, is clearly a more complete human being than the infantile and dilettante Karl of the book's beginning.

In the work of Pirandello, as we have noted before, confusion of eras of time, of sanity and madness (*Henry IV*), of the fictional and the factual (*Six Characters in Search of an Author*), and of the relationships between cause and effect (*It Is So!* [*If You Think So*]), all of which have their analogs in the physics of our time, become symbols for things falling apart, the center not holding, the loss of faith in progress, in society, in God. In the twentieth century, we are inclined to give a similar reading to *King Lear*, in which, it seems to us, the storm in Act III is not only an echo of the storms in Lear's mind, Lear's family, and Lear's kingdom, but a Nothing-Storm that threatens not only the balance of nature, but Nature Herself. The *nothing* that is repeated throughout the play seems an echo back from the twentieth century: *our nada which art in nada, nada be thy name*—except that in *Lear* there is no clean and well-lighted place.

Order of a sort, to be sure, is restored after the catastrophe; but of the troika attempting to unite the tripartite state, Kent is apparently dying and Albany and Edgar, while they may no longer be credulous weaklings, are pale shadows of past majesty. The end of an age has come:

> The oldest hath borne most; we that are young
> Shall never see so much, nor live so long.

For Aldiss in *Frankenstein Unbound* and *The Eighty-Minute Hour*, for Fred Hoyle in *October the First Is Too Late*, for Trevor Hoyle in the *Q Trilogy*, for Murray Leinster in "Sidewise in Time," and for Gordon Dickson in *Time Storm*, the temporal storm serves a similar apocalyptic function. In this well-used vision, the space-time fabric itself is torn asunder, more often than not by the work of humans, as if nature herself were recoiling in horror. The vision is medieval, recalling Dante's system in which, as the downflung Satan approached the Earth, the Earth herself drew away in horror, creating the enormous funnel-shaped pit of Hell, covered with a thin crust, on which fallen humanity must live. In *The Eighty-Minute Hour*, Aldiss calls it (33) "the ultimate in pollution . . . mankind's pollution of the whole continuum."

In the hands of an Aldiss, this scenario predictably gives us a no-win future (or past, or Paratime), during which, however, the individual may demonstrate some courage, some dignity, and some wit. *The Eighty-Minute Hour*, a bit like some of the work of Philip K. Dick, shows this being done by those who are "knowledgeable—or courageous—enough to tread [the] paths of madness"

(13)—which seems an analog for SF writers. The "general wish to get to hell out of a loused-up present" takes us back to some of the motives of the nostalgics.

In the hands of Murray Leinster, or of Robert Adams, the time storm may result in no more than well- or badly done chronopera. But for Gordon Dickson, whose optimism, while not fatuous, is greater than that of Aldiss, the apocalyptic time storm turns out, ultimately, to be redemptive, and the hero goes through changes, and comes to conclusions, much like those of Anderson's dancer from Atlantis. Once again, we get the nods in the direction of the honorable ancestors: Dickson's hero begins in his present as a Yankeeish sort of figure; after the time storm hits, the name of his leopard companion, Sunday, recalls both Crusoe's Friday and Hank Morgan's Sandy. The time storm seems to be sweeping all of space and time; in the here-and-now of *Time Storm*, it manifests itself as mistwalls which separate different eras. Most human beings vanish; those who remain, folk from different eras, attempt to understand and to correct what is happening. Dickson explicitly equates the time storm to inner individual struggles:

. . . the fight to understand, and be understood by everyone else in the face of the equally strong need to be yourself and yourself only. . . . The storm within . . . the time storm without is its analogy . . . because both storms are the result of conflict between two things that ought to be working together. (408–409)

This perception—and human love—prove to be sufficiently redemptive to straighten things out, both in the individual psyche and in the universe as a whole.

SUMMARY

Science fiction began as something done part-time by writers who saw themselves, and were seen, as part of the mainstream. Shelley, and Poe, and Verne, and Twain, and Wells all wrote quite as much mundane fiction as they did SF. Through the period of ghettoization, mainstream writers like Huxley and Orwell continued to do so. Mainstreamers doing fiction of travel to the past tended to use that mechanism to address mainstream concerns—the breakdown of values, the loss of center, the alienation of the individual in a mass society, the illusory nature of progress—and so did the occasional pulp story by folk like Campbell or Simak. Like most other mainstream SF, these stories of travel to the past were likely to end in alienation and defeat, or in highly qualified and compromised and obviously temporary victories.

The pulp tradition which begins in the 1920s tends, rather, early on to focus on adventure and on the technological solution of puzzles, a trend which begins with de Camp and is still going strong with Frankowski. Here, more often than not, the story ends with the traveler the victor (wherever he began, whether as citizen or as stranger) and history set going right again.

The tradition begun by Hale's "Hands Off" was, however, too obvious and too strong to lie long dormant, wherefore we shortly find in the pulp tradition a multitude of temporal lawmen taking up arms against outlaws who would use the past as their Dodge City, placing the whole present in imminent danger of extinction. As chronopera-ish as this scenario is, it leads us back to the concerns of the mainstream, picking up impetus as the New Wave rolls in in the 1960s and 1970s: is the present of the human race worth saving? can anyone know for sure what is going on? are we, after all, Leopold Blooms simple-mindedly trudging in unheroic tracks which are burlesque imitations of the heroics of the past? if, as Einstein feared, God plays dice with the universe, and if Hawking is right and nothing is impossible, is there any reality from which to be alienated? if God is dead, is everything permitted—not only to humankind, but to the universe itself?

The possibilities of the literature of travel to the past, then, are many and varied, and yet all curiously related: from chronopera to imperialistic triumph to existential isolation to a strange sort of transtemporal redemption. These possibilities have proved rich enough, over the past hundred years, to overcome all the intellectual and emotional difficulties of such travel up the line.

It is the peculiar genius of *A Connecticut Yankee in King Arthur's Court* that it has one foot in the mainstream, one foot in the ghetto to come, and—standing at the beginning of its own tradition—manages to touch at, or imply, or discuss, most of the concerns of the literature for a hundred years to come.

Chapter 8

STEPCHILDREN OF THE YANKEE

Papa . . . is as much a Pholosopher than as any thing I think, I think he could have done a great deal in that direction if he had studied while young, for he seems to enjoy reasoning out things, no matter what; in a great many such directions, he has greater ability than in the gifts which have made him famous.

—Susy Clemens

As Brian Aldiss points out in *Trillion Year Spree*, at the same time Mary Shelley was writing *The Last Man*, cholera was sweeping across Europe and Asia: in 1818, India; in 1819, Burma; in 1820, Siam; in 1822, southern Russia; in 1830, Moscow. By 1831, five years after the publication of Shelley's book, it was in London. Shelley, Aldiss says,

was hardly doing more than issuing a symbolic representation, a psychic screening, of what was taking place in reality. In that, at least, she was setting an example to be followed by the swarming SF scribes of the twentieth century. (50)

In her introduction to *Left Hand of Darkness* reprinted in *The Language of the Night*, Ursula Le Guin says very much the same thing:

This book is not about the future. Yes, it begins by announcing that it's set in the "Ekumenical Year 1490–97," but surely you don't *believe* that? . . . I am not predicting, or prescribing. I am describing. I am describing certain aspects of psychological reality in the novelist's way, which is by inventing elaborately circumstantial lies. (155–59)

"The future," she says, "in fiction, is a metaphor."

The past, I say, in science fiction, is also a metaphor.

Both those statements quite obviously need a bit of qualification. Sometimes, to be sure, when we write or read or think about SF which takes place in the future, we are doing a pretty straightforward thing, that thing which most non-SF readers think we do all the time: thinking about the future. We know that tomorrow is unlikely to be like today, and we wonder and we fear and we anticipate and we hope. Since we have been human, we have always been engineers of a sort: we are a wonderful pair of hands driven by a forebrain which not only remembers the past and contemplates the present but anticipates the future and is fueled by a stomach that can digest damn near anything. So in SF sometimes we wonder about our future science and our future engineering and our future cuisine and the impacts they will have on our future consciousness and our future societies: and then the future is not just a metaphor.

Similarly, in SF about the past, sometimes we contemplate the engineering and the science and the consciousness and the societies of the past and dramatize all those things by confronting them with a present-day knowledge and consciousness; and then the past is not just a metaphor.

But more often than not Aldiss and LeGuin and I are right: the future and the past are primarily metaphors, or perhaps distorting glasses through which we view our own lives and our own concerns and our own hopes and our own fears, all at a safer distance and with a larger perspective than we can manage by looking straight at them.

That means, then, that in fiction of travel to the past we are often symbolically engaged in the business of confronting our memories of the past with our present actualities; our uncomfortable and unfamiliar present with our unknown and threatening and promising future; our childhood with our adulthood; our adulthood with our old age; our America with our Europe; our Third World with our First World; our country with our city; our handicrafts with our high technology; our East with our West; our South with our North; and our fears with our hopes.

But these are the matters of all of science fiction; and the more we look at SF as a whole, the more echoes of this little sub-subgenre—travel to the past—we hear there. In Aldiss' *Non-Stop* and in Heinlein's *Universe* and in Harry Harrison's *Captive Universe* we are presented with a people surrounded by a technology they do not even know exists which is carrying them all unknowing to a destination they know not of; all three of these books deal with generational starships in which civilization has been lost and even the knowledge that there is more to the universe than The Ship is gone.

To be sure, this scenario is an appropriate and obvious treatment of our present situation on Starship Earth as we swirl through space-time: surrounded by technology most of us do not understand, heading toward a future none of us can foresee, aware that *what it is all for* is less apparent to us than to our more ignorant ancestors, we deplete the slender resources we have in squabbling over minuscule territories and ridicule or punish all those who would assert that any interests can exist outside those of The Ship.

But the humans in these ships in these novels are also very like our ancestors living in squalor among the ruins of the Roman Empire, convinced that the Pont du Gard at Nîmes must have been built by gods or demons, since obviously no humans could have accomplished such a thing. And they are like the inhabitants of Twain's Camelot faced with the technology of the Yankee, awed and superstitious and forced to acknowledge him as a master magician, almost a demigod. Whenever high tech confronts low tech, we have an echo of the *Yankee*.

In Anderson's *High Crusade*, low tech confronts high tech without benefit of time travel, and we have a replay of "The Man Who Came Early" in other terms. In Asimov's *Foundation*, knowledge of the engineering arts persists on Terminus (which plays Ireland to the Galaxy's Roman Empire) as the rest of the Empire slowly collapses, and the First Foundation is thereby enabled to play Hank Morgan to the rest of humanity. In Anderson's "Longest Voyage," humans on an Earth-sized world orbiting a gas giant have slipped back to a Renaissance level of technology; and the heroes, local would-be Magellans, meeting a wrecked spaceman, reject his potential gifts of technological breakthroughs in order not to lose the pleasure of making their own discoveries.

Such rejection of the technology of would-be Yankees is a familiar theme in science fiction. John D. MacDonald's 1951 story "Susceptibility" can stand for many others: a colony planted by a high-tech civilization is visited by an agent of the government, who finds that they are operating on a nineteenth-century level, using axes to chop down trees to heat their houses instead of using heat units, raising natural foods instead of using synthesizers, and the like. One field station is still operating, but the colonists use it as a penal colony. "But . . . ," says the field agent, "anybody who lives here can have every last thing they want." "Exactly," says the colonist (212). The field agent, of course, falls in love with the colonist and with the planet's low-tech lifestyle and goes over the hill; and again we are reminded of Jack Finney's Si Morley in *Time and Again*.

But the confrontation of superior technology with less advanced technology is not the only SF scenario which echoes the *Yankee* tradition: in Fredric Brown's "Letter to a Phoenix," the narrator, some 180,000 years old, has had his metabolism slowed in an atomic accident so that he doesn't sleep for thirty years and then, Arthur-like, has to hole up somewhere and sleep for fifteen. The human race, it develops, blows itself back into the Stone Age every ten or fifteen thousand years, reaching out to other stars or even other galaxies in the periods between; and only this boom-and-bust cycle keeps it from deteriorating and dying like all the rest of the intelligent races of the universe. Obviously, the narrator is often a Yankee-figure during low-tech periods: he has also become something of a political philosopher, wryly observing—in a line that combines the cynicism of a Twain with the optimism of a Heinlein—that "only insanity is divine. Only the mad destroy themselves and all they have wrought. And only the phoenix lives forever" (191).

On the other hand, another Wandering Jew figure—only 438 years old, thanks to a potion of Ambrose Pare's—in Gerald Kersh's "Whatever Happened to

Corporal Cuckoo?'' finds himself not a Yankee figure but rather an echo of the man who came early:

... in five hundred years you'd have more than you could spend. But how about me? All I'm fit for is to be in the army. I don't give a damn for philosophy, and all that stuff. It don't mean a thing to me. I'm no wiser now than I was when I was thirty. I never did go in for reading, and all that stuff, and I never will.... (99)

It took me nearly a hundred years to learn to write my name, and four hundred years to get to be a corporal.... And it took will power, at that! (111)

Cuckoo has the secret of perpetual youth and life, but—being as out of his time as The Man Who Came Early was out of his—he is *nithing*: ''There they are, making fortunes out of soap and toothpaste, and here I am, with something in my pocket to keep you young and healthy forever....'' And he can do nothing with it.

Any number of innumerable postholocaust stories, in which the survivors, armed like Robinson Crusoe only with what they can scavenge and with what they carry in their heads, attempt to survive or to prevail over the enemy, are echoes of the *Yankee*, except that the technologically impoverished society is in the future instead of the past. And any number of future histories which are replays of past history, like Asimov's *Foundation*, show us the past being played out in the future.

The themes which we have established in travel to the past, then, are found throughout science fiction; but just as the concerns of travel to the past are the concerns of SF, so are many of them the concerns of mainstream fiction, both that regarded, or disregarded, as ''popular'' and that which has been academically canonized.

Begin with a popular author, Stephen King, who has never written fiction of travel to the past, who, indeed, has only occasionally cruised the borders of science fiction itself. And yet, in book after book, we find stepchildren of the Yankee. When, in *Carrie*, the victimized heroine uses her paranormal powers to bring chaos into the town which has tormented her, we get this: ''Carrie hath murdered time'' (221). In *Christine*, in a ride in the haunted car ''we went back in time'' and had a partial vision of the car's past (415). In *Cujo*, King notes that ''the only place to run from the future is into the past'' (91). The frame of ''The Breathing Method'' is in a parallel universe. The hero of *The Dead Zone*, gifted and cursed with prophetic powers, asks the question we have posed to godlike time travelers: ''If you could jump into a time machine and go back to 1932, would you kill Hitler?'' (327).

In *Pet Sematary*, burial in a mana-ridden location reverses entropy, though, as so often happens when one messes with time, that turns out not to be such a good idea; in *The Shining*, it is an old hotel in the Rockies which possesses the mana which enables many pasts to invade the present. *The Talisman* gives us two parallel universes, one less technologically sophisticated than the other. In *The Stand* we are reminded of the triumph of Merlin's magic over Morgan's technology: in the fight against embodied entropy (403) some sorts of nonrational approaches may be necessary (472). *Thinner* is about curses and their victims, and the results of the curses are all either like getting younger or like going back in time, down the evolutionary scale: getting thinner, contracting acne, reverting to lizardry.

In his novel *It*, however, King comes closest to Anderson's dancer from Atlantis. "It," a malignant entity which periodically emerges to do mindless killings throughout the village, may remind us on one level of Fredric Brown's human race, which goes mad every so often in an apparent desire to return all creation to primal chaos. "It" most often appears as a clown: "Get back to your circus," we remember the Yankee saying, "or I'll report you." In the context of our discussion, you will remember, the circus is on one level the harmless foolery which takes in even the canny Huck Finn; on another, the reality which strips itself of costume after costume, rather like Melville's confidence man, until the existence of all objective truth is in doubt; on still another, the madhouse which is the whole world of humans and perhaps the whole creation.

This clown kills folks, the more brutally the better, and he has a particular taste for the young, the alienated, and the innocent. A group of youthful misfits faces off against "it" and sends it back into hibernation. After their temporary victory, they make a pact to the effect that, should "it" emerge again, they will reunite to fight the next battle.

They grow into middle age before "it" returns; and when it does, they come back together, some wealthy and successful, others humble and struggling, but all of them basically decent people. Not without wounds, and not without deaths, they eventually prevail, but only because in the fight against what is apparently an entropic principle they have managed to evoke a contrary force, which appears in the form of a turtle. The mills of God grind slowly, perhaps; or perhaps this is the turtle on which stand the four elephants which support the cosmos.

King has always been clever at evoking the ordinary, the small-town, the familiar, and then injecting the horrid into it; but in many of his novels, I think, his intellectual vision wavers. In *The Shining*, for example, the whole haunting of the hotel may be "real," *or* it may simply be an illusion brought on in the boy's mind by the psychotic behavior of his father; everything is nicely balanced, Henry James fashion, until the last pages of the book, where the attacks of animal-shaped plants make it impossible to sustain the balance. *The Stand* begins as a straightforward postholocaust book; even the complication of the wise black seer does not warp the frame; but when the opposing forces take on Satanic and supernatural dimensions, we begin to wonder whether we are still in the same novel. Shorter and more tightly focused, *Carrie* and *'Salem's Lot* are aesthetically the most satisfying of King's early works.

In *It*, however, King appears to be going for the fence, to be trying for a major horror story which will also be a work of art. What he does is juxtapose the stories of the two fights with "it," telling a bit of one fight in childhood and then a bit of the other in adulthood. With great skill he plays the two narratives off against each other, with the effect that two battles appear to be going on at the same time; and it is clear that in the final fight it is the children who come to the aid of the adults they have become, the past which is able to aid the present. Children do not have the power to kill "it"; adults have neither the innocence nor the blind determination to do so. Only by successful integration of child and adult, that is to say past and present, and only by the force not only of courage but also of long-term love, can the force of entropy be faced and overcome.

Turning to literature of the academic canon, we note that we have already described Joyce's *Finnegans Wake* as literature of Great Time; that *Remembrance of Things Past* is a time trip on its own terms; we might further note Faulkner's Quentin Compson's unsuccessful attempt to demythologize Southern history so that he can live with it; and we might remember the end of Thomas Wolfe's "Lost Boy," in which the narrator, returned to the house in which his brother died, finally recaptures the vision of the past in which he was a small child and his brother was kind and loving to him. There is sadness in that vision; for the narrator, having once captured the past for a moment, knows that it is now gone forever; when understanding arrives, the mystery departs. The illusion may have given more pain than the truth; but likely it was more beautiful. In his notes to *The Majesty of the Blues*, Wynton Marsalis says, "What you must do is endure the pain of coming to grips with your origins and your identity. Then your direction is absolutely clear."

A long way back in this book, I said that Paratime, stretched just a bit, could cover all of literature and account for anything. I seem to be in danger of doing the same thing for the themes of the *Yankee* and its successors, and with good reason: all narrative art, and much of pictoral art, is either the mythologization or the demythologization of the past, or both at once. As we saw in "Vintage Season," art involves both approach and distance, both human involvement and godlike distance. So does technology. So does science. All of us are made up of minds that contemplate and hands that touch; all of us are distant relations of the Connecticut Yankee.

Chapter 9

OF TIME AND THE RIVER

Diese umfall is auf der Mississippi vorgenkommen.

—Mark Twain

Now, by long and devious route, winding like the very Mississippi, we come to the end and ask again the questions we posed at the beginning:

1. Why did the idea of travel to the past, and the attempt to change that past with hindsight and technology, first appear in America?
2. Why in 1889?
3. Why in the work of Mark Twain?
4. And, given all that can be said against its plausibility, what is it doing not only *in* SF, but all over it?

From time to time, throughout our meanderings, I have suggested partial answers to some of these questions, which it might be well now to recall:

1. In his debunkings of the reactionary medievalism of Scott and others, Twain constantly confronts bogus nostalgia with a contemporary consciousness, which he does again when he sends Morgan to Arthur's court.
2. As belief in progress fades, the future is not only vast but distasteful; and the impulse to avoid it draws the consciousness to the past.
3. Americans have a peculiar tendency to identify past, present, and future time with location; as one travels to the past in space, one can generate the idea of doing so in time; and Mark Twain was ideally situated, midway in two past-future geographic continua, to give utterance to such a concept.

4. America is to Europe as child is to parent, and as the present is to the past: both these relationships were in a condition of peculiar strain at the end of the nineteenth century, and therefore both attraction and repulsion were at a high level.

5. The literature of travel to the past has a place in science fiction, in spite of its intrinsic implausibility, because its central tensions are the same tensions—expressed more nakedly—which generate the central energies of science fiction.

6. The figure of the time traveler appeals to the artist as a distorted reflection of himself, desperately needing the experience of the Other as material, just as desperately needing to distance himself psychologically from that same Other.

7. The hero of fiction is nearly always a freedom-seeker; and in Twain's day, the places on this earth where one might escape to freedom were becoming fewer and fewer. (Further, to gain freedom, Rhodes-like, by taking away the freedom of others, was for Twain not an acceptable choice.) In later SF, freedom may be sought off-planet, an option only marginally available to Twain in 1889. If one may not flee prison in space, one may do so in time.

8. The steamship made the nineteenth century the first great age of tourism; with weaponry, it became the great and ambiguous age of modern imperialism. The time traveler, caught in the moral crack between respect for native humanity and appreciation of technological progress, reflects the moral dilemmas of the tourist and of the imperialist.

9. The incestuous themes of the stories of Faust, Prometheus, and Frankenstein find fertile ground in the psyche of Mark Twain, who satirizes them on one level and accepts them on another; and these ambiguous attitudes find reinforcement in the *Matière de Bretagne* into which Twain projects his would-be Faust.

SCIENCE FICTION REDEFINED

Now, perhaps, we are ready to make a definition of science fiction which can include travel to the past, even though such travel savors mightily on the fantastic. Science fiction *begins with a slice of history*—most often future, sometimes present, sometimes past. "Past history" and "present history" are clear enough; but how are we to define "future history," which seems a contradiction in terms?

One of the ways in which SF differs from fantasy and resembles the mainstream is that the connection between the there-and-then and the here-and-now is always clear: in early SF, the connection is, as we have made clear, usually an explicit one. In more recent SF, accepted conventions and increased reader sophistication make those connections more and more implied rather than explicit; but they are still clear. *The Galactic Empire was falling*, says Asimov, and we are quite clear that somewhere in our future humankind has developed not only interstellar travel, but FTL travel and superior forms of communication; that prices have come down enough, and enough new sources of energy have been developed, so that interstellar trade is profitable; that weapons of war have been enormously developed; and so on. There is a credible history implied, then, between our place and time and the place and time of the SF narrative.

Fantasy needs no such connection. To be sure, Middle Earth seems to be our

Earth, and the time of *Lord of the Rings* seems to be somewhere in our distant past; moreover, the humans in Tolkiens' books seem our ancestors, more or less, and the nonhumans seem to have died out or abandoned the planet. But in spite of the massive documentation of the history of Middle Earth, there is no way we can connect it to "our" history; there is no way we can say, "This seems to have happened in 5,000 B.C., or 10,000 B.C., or whatever." SF, then, is rooted in the idea of history as is mainstream fiction, and as fantasy is not.

Into this more-or-less credible history, the SF narrative injects a more-or-less credible variable. (The *more-or-lesses* simply recognize the fact that some SF is more SF than other SF, that there is a hard core.) These variables tend to come in standard packages:

1. The new (at least new to us in our here-and-now experience) piece of technology. This is the most common. Suppose medical practice improves so that we can all live to be 200; suppose an FTL drive is developed; suppose we get serious about orbital solar collectors; suppose computers develop their own independent creativity; and so on.

2. The new (qualified as above) scientific idea or observation. Suppose genetic experimenting gives us a truly androgynous human race; suppose life develops on a planet of much higher temperature, or gravity, or atmospheric pressure; suppose life develops in a ring of gas surrounding a star; suppose a planet with a year which lasts several thousand of our years; suppose a planet which will support a race of winged sophonts.

3. The idea—scientific, social, or religious—which is not new to us, but which is used differently from the way we use it, or which is extended in ways we do not extend it, or which is put into a new context. Suppose a religious despotism (not a new idea, surely) becomes possessed of more-than-modern computer power; suppose a group like the Hansa takes over interstellar trade; suppose a future dictator who keeps a stable of vegetable corpses to provide him with organ transplants.

Notice that earlier science fiction tends to deal with one variable at a time (the Martians land; a time machine is developed; the United States develops a fascistic system), while later SF tends to stack several into one work (organ transplants are perfected; TV scrutiny of the world is available to a dictator; a physician, by means of implants, can be tuned directly to his patient; and so on, from Silverberg's *Shadrach in the Furnace*.)

Having injected this variable, or these variables, into a historical setting, the writer can then do several things with the result: (1) use it as a setting for a tale of adventure (Doc Smith); (2) investigate the effects of this idea on society (Asimov); (3) examine the insights which would result, and their effects on the psyche of the individual (Pohl's "Day Million"); (4) construct a cautionary warning (Heinlein, "If This Goes On . . . "); (5) build an analog to our here-and-now which will give the reader insights not otherwise available (Le Guin, *The Left Hand of Darkness*). Or several or all of the above. And what happens should follow reasonably, in cause-and-effect fashion, from the given history and the given variable.

We have, then, a plausible history injected with a plausible variable, with a plausible working-out of the results. A *Gedankenexperiment*, in fact, turned to the uses of fiction. Most such fiction, as we have noted, takes place in some hypothetical future; and the farther the future, the more plausible it is to assert large and fundamental change. In very-near-future fiction, we often get stuff which can pass for mainstream fiction, like the novels of Tom Clancy; in a-bit-farther-future, the cities-in-a-skyscraper of Robert Silverberg; in far-future fiction, silicon-based intelligence (computers, robots) supplanting carbon-based intelligence (you and me), hardware and software outlasting wetware.

If the writer turns this technique to the past, what we get is the whole family of the Connecticut Yankee. The traveler to the past injects new ideas into a known history, and that history is either changed for the better, or altered for the worse, or not affected at all. The method by which this is accomplished is, granted, fantastic; but the process, the basic recipe, is the same as for fiction of the future, except that it operates in a history which is known to us. Clearly, parallel histories may be justified in like manner: *if* Mohammed had been converted to Christianity, or *if* Richard the Lion-Hearted had lived to be old, or *if* Shakespeare had been an historian, then these and these and these results would logically follow.

THE *YANKEE* REAPPRAISED

That the *Yankee*, like all the best of Twain's long fiction, is not a "perfect novel" cannot be disputed. Like *Huckleberry Finn*, it has far too many places where the mask of the narrator slips and reveals one of the Twains behind it. Furthermore, it is not subject to the sort of interpretation which is clear and apparently without self-contradiction. The *Yankee*, like Twain himself, is both western and eastern, northern and southern, American and European. It is suspicious of progress and devoted to it; it is in love with and afraid of technology; it is ancient and childlike, venerable and childish. Almost anything one chooses to say about Twain can be shown to be true in one place or another. More of the resulting contradictions than usual were crowded into the *Yankee*; but a lot of them had been evident in Twain's first real book, *Innocents Abroad*.

It is useful to remember that Twain published *The Prince and the Pauper* in 1882, then *Life on the Mississippi* in 1883, then *Huckleberry Finn* in 1885, and finally the *Yankee* in 1889. As we have noted, one understands the *Yankee* better by dipping into the earlier books; as we have also noted, the first and last of the four tend to be greatly underestimated by most critics, the *Prince* being dismissed as puerile romanticizing and the *Yankee* being seen as demonstrating either Twain's inability to appreciate the knightly virtues or the triumph of farce over satire. Both estimations, in my judgment, fall short of the truth.

In *The Prince and the Pauper*, Edward, Prince of Wales, is a Tom Sawyer before his time and out of his place. He believes the books. He is a person of romantic ideals, however mistaken he may be about the details: a good kid, as

Tom is a good kid. Tom Canty, on the other hand, is a Huck Finn, a practical person who is willing to tolerate Tom's beloved books, but who, when the chips are down, will use the Great Seal to crack nuts with. His father is an echo of Pap Finn; and his good father, Henry VIII, is as uncomprehending of his real needs as Judge Thatcher is of those of Huck.

The Yankee is a well-grown-up Huck Finn. To be sure, he has adjusted to the routine of an urbanized life and a factory job; but he has the same wry pragmatism which characterizes Tom Canty and Huck. His reaction to wearing armor is very much of a piece with Huck's confrontation with the frontier nobility represented by the Shepherdsons and the Grangerfords. His identifying with the most oppressed classes of sixth-century society is like the revelations which come to Edward-as-Tom-Canty and like the moral development of Huck with respect to slavery. His recognition that, *in spite of* worldly honors and noble lineage, a man may nevertheless truly be a man, is like Huck's admiration for Colonel Sherburn facing the mob. And there is fine satisfaction in the fact that Miles Herndon, Hank Morgan, and Mark Twain all sit in the presence of the Sovereign of England.

In a way, *The Prince and the Pauper* is too *much* of a novel; it has a beginning, and a middle, and an end, and they all come so pat as to make the reader wary. Mawkish, we say, Hollywoodish; at least we do until Twain kills off Edward and his kinder, gentler England. *Huckleberry Finn* is perhaps not *enough* of a novel; it not only begins but also ends *in medias res*, like the *Iliad*, after a Tom Sawyer intrusion which has given critics fits and material ever since. Whatever else one may say about the *Yankee*, it could not have begun before it begins; and there is nothing anticipated, nothing yet-to-be-delivered, after its end, which is appropriate, inevitable, and uncontrived.

Now, that fact is passing strange, given that the novel deals with travel in time, which fact one would have thought would have given the writer a completely open-ended perspective on time and space. It is as though Twain had to burst the bounds of time in order to come to a satisfying finality, neither the dying fall of *Huckleberry Finn* nor the melodrama of *The Prince and the Pauper*.

Ironic, that: because satisfying conclusions are rare in serious modern literature, as they are in our century itself. And yet the Twain of the *Yankee* has anticipated our century in a number of important ways. Not only—as we have documented at perhaps unwonted length—have his ideas sired a whole host of SF time travel stories and novels, but his ideas strangely anticipate not only those of Freud and Einstein, but also those of Proust and Joyce. Without a whole new conception of time, neither of the latter would have written as they did.

Since Newton, time and space had been absolute: "Absolute, true and mathematical time of itself, and from its own nature flows equally without regard to anything external." Ole Christensen Roemer had already, in 1676, proved that the speed of light was finite. Absolute time was destroyed by the Michelson-Morley experiment of 1887, which showed that the ether did not exist and that the speed of light plus any other speed gives the speed of light. (The career of that extraordinary man, Albert Abraham Michelson, keeps touching Twain's in a fashion which is outrageously coincidental: as a four-year-old, he moved in 1856 to Calaveras County, where his father opened a store; in 1869, he moved to Virginia City, where Twain had been a newspaperman in 1862; in 1901, both he and Twain got honorary doctorates from Yale; and, more than any others, it was his experiments which brought about a whole new perception of light, space, and time.)

By 1909 when he wrote "Letters from the Earth," Mark Twain was well aware of the speed of light; having fun with the six-day creation, he notes that the newly created stars would not have done the Earth much good for some little time:

It is quite manifest that [God] believed his fresh-made skies were diamond-sown with those myriads of twinkling stars the moment his first day's sun sank below the horizon; whereas, in fact not a single star winked in that black vault until three years and a half after that memorable week's formidable industries had been completed. Then one star appeared, all solitary and alone, and began to blink. Three years later another one appeared. The two blinked together for more than four years before a third joined them. ...At the end of a thousand years not enough stars were yet visible to make a show. (413–14)

Twain has some of the details wrong, but no matter; it is clear that in 1909 he understands the finite nature of the speed of light, and the impossibility of clearly defining simultaneity. But whether, by 1889, he had heard of the Michelson-Morley experiment two years before is another question; it seems unlikely in the extreme. Even had he, that he would therefrom draw a concept of time in which one could travel would be unlikelier still. If the speed of light is finite, we reason, then nature does not define any two events as simultaneous; and that opens up a whole new way of thinking about the flow of time. All that can be said is that, as the time Twain was composing the *Yankee*, ideas about time were undergoing change; and that such change made the conceptualization of travel to the past more likely than did the old ideas about the subject.

As we deal with Twain's anticipation of Einstein, so must we with his Freudian anticipations. Of the Oedipal qualities of travel to the past it is almost certain Twain consciously recognized nothing. Neither his upbringing nor his education would have fitted him for such speculation. But just as, quite by chance, Twain was admirably placed in geography to look at the future with one eye and the past with the other, just so in his psychic life, as we have noted, do we find the elements which, combined with the Oedipal quality of the Arthurian legend, bring the pre-Freudian mix to critical mass. It is only in the later SF fiction of travel to the past that its Oedipal nature becomes overt. The *Yankee* is explicit enough in many ways, Heaven knows; but what it implies and what it fore-shadows are more impressive still.

HANK MORGAN AND THE MISSISSIPPI RIVER COMMISSION

When we have put all our answers and speculations together, however, some-how they still don't spell *Yankee*. They account for a good deal of the idea structure, and they lay a good deal of the groundwork, but they still come short of accounting for the beginning of a whole new idea in literature in the hands of Mark Twain in 1889.

In his notes to his daughter's biography of him, Twain notes that in 1884 he drove pegs into the ground around his house:

Each peg represented an English monarch and the date of his accession. The space between pegs was measured off with a tapeline, and each foot of it covered a year of a reign. William the Conqueror stood in front of the house; 21 feet away stood the peg of William Rufus; 13 feet from that one stood the first Henry's peg; 35 feet beyond it stood Stephen's peg—and so on. One could stand near the Conqueror and have all English history skeletonized and land-marked and mile-posted under his eye. (224)

I like the picture of Mark Twain standing near the Conqueror and looking over centuries of English history as the little girls ran from peg to peg, now forward toward Victoria, now backward toward 1066, doubtless sometimes taking short-cuts, say, from the nineteenth century to the Middle Ages.

That image may have helped Twain develop the idea of the *Yankee*; we know from Suzy's text that he was still playing with dates with his children two years later in 1886, when he had been making notes preparatory to the writing of that book for maybe a year, maybe two. We also know that in his old age, compiling his *Autobiography*, he allowed himself to wander about his own past like a Connecticut Yankee with a time machine:

Finally . . . in 1904, I hit upon the right way to do an Autobiography: Start it at no particular time of your life; wander at your own free will all over your life; talk only about the thing which interests you for the moment; drop it the moment its interest threatens to pale, and turn your talk upon the new and more interesting thing that has intruded itself into your mind meantime.

Also, make the narrative a combined Diary *and* Autobiography. In this way you have the vivid thing of the present to make a contrast with memories of like things in the past, and these contrasts have a charm which is all their own. (193)

Obeying his own dictum, Twain has put these introductory remarks into the middle of his book. The propensity of a restless mind to violate conventional notions of chronology may be noted throughout Twain's work, and that too may have helped contribute to the genesis of the *Yankee*.

But is that enough, or does travel to the past have even earlier roots in Twain's life and thought?

For what I take to be an answer, we must go back to the river. There are only two American authors who come readily to mind who have been riverboat pilots:

the other is Richard Bissell, who, like Twain, seems never quite to quit the river. If, as Paine thought (122), Twain was always writing about the river, then maybe Twain's Mississippi will serve as an idea source for travel to the past. "Time is a river," is a statement so old that one one can plumb its source or document its repetitions: we hear it from Heraclitus, from Augustine, and from John D. MacDonald. "Who," Asimov asks in "The Winds of Change" (265), "was the first human being, or hominid, that suddenly grasped the manner in which the river of time carried him from the dim past into the dim future, and wondered if it might be dammed or diverted?" The answer to the first part of that question is lost in the mists of antiquity; the answer to the second part seems to be "Mark Twain."

"A river, a very big and powerful river," says T. S. Eliot in his introduction to *Huckleberry Finn*, "is the only natural force that can totally determine the course of human peregrination . . . a treacherous and capricious dictator" (Norton *Finn*, 324). Like time itself, we would say. If time were like a sea, or a prairie, or a mountain range, then the traveler would have some choice as to how he would range. But time is a river. Let Eliot go on about the Mississippi:

At one season, it may move sluggishly in a channel so narrow that . . . one can hardly believe that it has travelled already for hundreds of miles, and has yet many hundreds of miles to go; at another season, it may obliterate the low Illinois shore to a horizon of water, while in its bed it runs with a speed such that no man or beast can survive in it. . . . The river is never wholly chartable; it changes its pace, it shifts its channel, unaccountably. . . . (324–25)

One could rewrite this passage, substituting *time* for *the river*, and have a near-echo of what people have been saying about time for centuries. Sometimes it moves fast, sometimes slowly; sometimes the choices of passage are great, for the river is wide, but sometimes there is no choice at all; and sometimes time, like the river, will kill you.

But you do not merely see the River, you do not merely become acquainted with it through the senses: you experience the River. Mark Twain, in his later years of success and fame, referred to his early life as a steamboat pilot as the happiest he had known. With all allowance for the illusions of age, we can agree that those years were the years in which he was most fully alive. . . . In the pilot's daily struggle with the River . . . he absorbed knowledge of which, as an artist, he later made use. (326)

Those last lines are crucial to this last portion of my argument; for not only did Twain grow up on the river, and work on the river, but *he was of the first generation to whom it was a matter of course that one might sail up the river as well as down it*. Before his time, one made a raft, floated it down to New Orleans, broke it up and sold the timbers, and walked home. Or one could pole a keelboat from New Orleans to Louisville in four laborious months. But by 1817, a steamboat could mount the river to St. Louis; and two years before

Twain's birth, there were 230 steamboats engaged in commerce on the river, and the New Orleans–Louisville trip took six days. A riverboat pilot, then, might, in the space of two weeks, go down the river and return, and find that river changed.

And, as we say, Twain is the only major author in history to have been a steamboat pilot on a great river, to have steamed upstream as well as down as a matter of making a living. Reread *Life on the Mississippi* and *Huckleberry Finn*, and then see if what Eliot says of that river does not mirror the nature of time, as the human sees it during his brief life:

In its beginning, it is not yet the River; in its end, it is no longer the River. . . . At what point in its course does the Mississippi become what the Mississippi *means*? It is both one and many. . . . And at the end it merely disappears among its deltas: it is no longer there, but it is still where it was, hundreds of miles to the North. (327)

Grant, if you will, that Eliot is writing out of a consciousness sixty years after that of Mark Twain as he wrote the *Yankee*; but permit me to doubt that in that passage Eliot is discussing time travel. The passage deals with the resemblance of *Huckleberry Finn*, in its beginning and end, to the river itself. But, given our concerns, we may also see how very much the river, as characterized by Eliot, is like time itself as seen through the *Yankee*.

Here we are, in the easy delta of the present, not knowing whether we are still in the river or at the beginning of the Gulf, with no idea of where the main channel is, or whether we are in it; but a thousand miles upstream, the river is as we saw it a thousand miles ago, clear and defined *and still there*. And with a steamboat, we can go back there in a matter of days.

If we may now become explicit about the identification of the River with time, not only is the past still there, but it is mutable. Indeed, if the past is the Upper Mississippi, it is, as Twain makes plain in *Life on the Mississippi*, forever*more* mutable:

Here was a piece of river which was all down in my book, but I could make neither head nor tail of it (VII). . . . If you will take the longest street in New York, and travel up and down it, conning its features patiently until you know every house and window and door and lamp-post and big and little sign by heart. . . . Next, if you will take half of the signs in that long street, and *change their places* once a month . . . you will understand what is required of a pilot's peerless memory by the fickle Mississippi (XIII).

It would be like having to learn not only one history, with every hero and date and battle exactly right, but a whole series of adjoining histories in nearby Paratime: not only what happened in this continuum, but all the might-haves in continua nearby.

Coincidentally, and parenthetically, note how much the relationship between the riverboat pilot and the riverboat captain is like that between the Boss and the King:

The captain could stand . . . in the pomp of a very brief authority . . . and then that skipper's reign was over. The moment that the boat was under way . . . [the pilot] could do with her exactly as he pleased, run her when and whither he chose, and tie her up to the bank whenever his judgment said that course was best. His movements were entirely free; he consulted no one, he received commands from nobody, he promptly resented even the merest suggestions. . . . So here was . . . a king without a keeper, an absolute monarch who was absolute in sober truth and not by a fiction of words . . . I think pilots were about the only people I ever knew who failed to show, in some degree, embarrassment in the presence of travelling foreign princes. But then, people in one's own grade of life are not usually embarrassing objects. (XIV)

The Boss of Chapter VIII of the *Yankee* is in that passage, in embryo.

Huck and Jim drift downstream on their river much as all of us drift in time, barely conscious of miles or days drifting away, passing crucial nexi all unknowing, as they pass Cairo, conscious of that passage only when the Cairos are gone beyond reclaiming. The inexorable passage of the river, like that of time, carries Jim deeper and deeper into a bondage which he fears but which he does not know for a long time is around him. All of us have been Sold Down the River. The current separates Jim, as it does us, from work, home, children. If for Huck the river affords a bogus death, it also separates him—blessedly—from his father, whom the river likewise kills.

At the end of the book, Huck and Jim leave the river to seek freedom in other directions. If the ending grates, then this is part of the reason: the narrative would not support a continuation of the symbolism, which would demand that Huck and Jim continue to drift, past New Orleans, through the delta, out onto the Gulf of Mexico, never again to be seen by mortal men.

But if the river is the passage of time, in *Huckleberry Finn* it also has aspects of Great Time, the absence of the passage of time. As Lauriat Lane, Jr., says (Norton *Finn*, 369–70), the journey has a metaphysical quality. The journeyer seems to have lost contact with reality and real time; and on the raft, Huck and Jim are as naked as souls in a medieval Last Judgment. R. W. Stallman sees the river (Norton *Finn*, 384–87) as the representation of conscience, spiritual integrity, baptism and rebirth, and the meeting with one's true self: in short, that Great Time which is the wellspring of all truth and virtue. And Great Time is another way to the past, as Huck's river is a way to Noah's ark (IX) and to Eden.

But leave that; Great Time has always been there in our human consciousness. Come back to the Mississippi as time flow, the upriver as early time, downriver as later. Come back to Twain the pilot, steaming upstream to find an Upper Mississippi unlike the one he had seen before. Above all, come back to the incredibly meandering course of much of that river, and the fact that Twain the pilot knew full well that one may, in many spots, leave the river, hike overland a half-mile, and find oneself twenty miles upriver. Can any purely spatial image be more suggestive of travel to the past?

If the river changes itself constantly, then can humans change the river? In

1878, the Army Corps of Engineers began to try. In *Life on the Mississippi*, Mark Twain seems to have mixed feelings about their efforts. His Uncle Mumford has an opinion (XXVIII) which is much of a piece with Twain's final verdict in the *Yankee* about the likelihood of a time traveler's being able to control the flow of history:

You turn one of those little European rivers over to this [United States River] Commission, with its hard bottom and clear water, and it would be just a holiday job for them to wall it, and pile it, and dike it, and tame it down, and boss it around, and make it go wherever they wanted it to, and stay where they put it, and do just as they said, every time. But this ain't that kind of a river. They have started in here with big confidence, and the best intentions in the world; but they are going to get left. What does Ecclesiastes vii. 13 say? Says enough to knock *their* little game galley-west, don't it?

("Consider the work of God: for who can make that straight, which He hath made crooked?") And furthermore, Mumford says, even if the engineers *could* do it, the result would be awful. By the time there are no boats left on the river at all, the Commission will, he says,

have the whole thing all reorganized, and dredged out, and fenced in, and tidied up, to a degree that will make navigation just simply perfect, and absolutely safe and profitable; and all the days will be Sundays, and all the mates will be Sunday-school suWHAT-*in-the-nation-you-fooling-around-there-for, you sons of unrighteousness, heirs of perdition! Going to be a* YEAR *getting that hogshead ashore*?

Improbably enough, Uncle Mumford is Isaac Asimov writing *The End of Eternity*: monkey with the past and, at best, you will make no dent at all, but at worst, you will succeed and bring about a brave new world in which you could not live and breathe as a Connecticut Yankee, or as an entrepreneur, or as a steamboat pilot. Plato could not have survived in his Republic, supposing him unlucky enough to bring it about instead of merely talking about it

There it is, then: travel to the past all there in potential in the Mississippi River, waiting to be fished out by any upstream-churning pilot who might later be lucky enough to visit Europe, and contemplate imperialism in the Pacific, and fret over the many identities that can be housed in one bosom, and read Malory.

Once again, a fine and circular irony: the very technology which makes it possible to steam up the river and invent the Yankee's sort of time travel is the technology which gives the Yankee his edge in the past. The steamboat is itself a time machine. Inventing the machine, we invent the idea of the accessibility of the past; accessing the past in fiction, we take the machine with us. Using the machine in the past, we destroy the past and the past destroys the machine, returning us to the century which developed the machine in the first place.

The raft of Huck and Jim flows naturally along with the river, day by day and mile by mile, as the river gets bigger and more complex and takes one deeper and deeper toward that land from which there is no return. What happens on shore during that journey gets more and more absurd, finally revealed as the fictitious and purposeless games of Tom Sawyer.

But a steamboat might head into the current and, as long as fuel lasted, match its speed with that of the current and stay abreast of a given spot on shore for a long time. Give it a bit more steam, and it could go happily upstream. Give the pilot, the Boss, the powers of the Mississippi River Commission, and he might even make a valiant attempt to change the course of the river.

As we have seen, whether or no that would be a good idea admits of some debate. However, not only would the attempt be heroic, but the temptation of that attempt would be well-nigh irresistible for any engineer. A brash and confident and ignorant engineer like Morgan might fail; a more modest and calculating and sophisticated engineer like Padway might succeed. Or, like the engineers in *The Dancer from Atlantis*, one might find, bafflingly enough, that what one did upstream was already part of what was going on downstream.

In any case, the journey and the attempt would doubtless prove instructive. Likely enough, the conclusion of a wise man might be that of Huck Finn: that the only way to beat the River is to leave it. Light out for the territory.

Dante would have agreed.

WORKS CITED

Abbott, Edwin A. *Flatland: A Romance of Many Dimensions.* New York: Dover, 1952.

Adams, Robert. *Castaways in Time.* New York: Signet, 1979. There are several sequels.

Alcock, Leslie. *Arthur's Britain: History and Archaeology* A.D. *367–634.* Harmondsworth, England: Penguin, 1973.

Aldiss, Brian W. *Cryptozoic!* New York: Signet, 1973.

———. *The Eighty-Minute Hour.* London: Pan, 1975.

———. *Frankenstein Unbound.* Greenwich, Conn.: Fawcett/Crest, 1975.

———. "Judas Danced." In *No Time Like Tomorrow.*

———. *Non-Stop.* London: Faber, 1958.

———. "Not for an Age." In *Who Can Replace A Man?*

———. *No Time Like Tomorrow.* New York: Signet, 1959.

———. "Poor Little Warrior!" In *Who Can Replace A Man?*

———. *Science Fiction Art.* New York: Bounty Books, 1975.

———. "The Sterile Millennia." In *Galaxies Like Grains of Sand.* New York: Signet, 1960.

———. "T." In *No Time Like Tomorrow.*

———. *Trillion Year Spree.* London: Gollancz 1986.

———. *Who Can Replace a Man?* New York: Signet, 1975.

"An Anachronism, or Missing One's Coach." *Dublin University Magazine*, 1838. Cited by Pinkerton.

Anderson, Poul. *The Best of Poul Anderson.* Introduction by Barry N. Malzberg. New York: Pocket Books, 1976.

———. *The Corridors of Time.* New York: Berkley, 1978.

———. "The Creation of Imaginary Worlds." In *Science Fiction Today and Tomorrow*, edited by Reginald Bretnor.

———. *The Dancer from Atlantis*. New York: Signet, 1972.

———. *Dialogue with Darkness*. New York: Tor, 1985.

———. "The Discovery of the Past." In *Past Times*.

———. *The Earth Book of Stormgate*. New York: Berkley, 1979.

———. "Gibraltar Falls." In *The Guardians of Time*.

———. *The Guardians of Time*. With an Afterword by Sandra Miesel. New York: Tor/Pinnacle, 1981.

———. *The High Crusade*. New York: Manor, 1975.

———. *The Horn of Time*. Boston: Gregg Press, 1978.

———. "The Little Monster." In *Past Times*.

———. "The Longest Voyage." In *The Best of Poul Anderson*.

———. "The Man Who Came Early." In *The Horn of Time*.

———. *A Midsummer Tempest*. New York: Doubleday, 1974.

———. "My Object All Sublime." In *The Best of Poul Anderson*.

———. *Past Times*. New York: Tor, 1984.

———. *Seven Conquests*. New York: Collier Books, 1970.

———. *There Will Be Time*. New York: Signet, 1973.

———. "Time Heals." In *Dialogue with Darkness*.

———. "Time Patrol." In *The Guardians of Time*.

———. *War of the Wing-Men*. New York: Ace, 1958.

———. "Wildcat." In *Seven Conquests*.

Ashe, Geoffrey. *The Discovery of King Arthur*. In association with Debrett's Peerage. New York: Henry Holt, 1985.

Asimov, Isaac. *The Bicentennial Man and Other Stories*. New York: Fawcett/Crest, 1976.

———. *Buy Jupiter and Other Stories*. Greenwich, Conn.: Fawcett/Crest, 1975.

———. "The Cosmic Corkscrew." Asimov's first story, which was never published and has been lost. Described in his introduction to *The Early Asimov, Book One*.

———. "The Dead Past." In *Earth Is Room Enough*.

———. *The Early Asimov: Book One*. Greenwich, Conn.: Fawcett/Crest, 1972.

———. *The Early Asimov: Book Two*. Greenwich, Conn.: Fawcett/Crest, 1972.

———. *Earth Is Room Enough*. Greenwich, Conn.: Fawcett/Crest, 1957.

———. *The End of Eternity*. Greenwich, Conn.: Fawcett/Crest, 1971.

———. "Fair Exchange?" In *The Winds of Change and Other Stories*.

———. *The Foundation Trilogy*. New York: Equinox, 1974.

———. "The Good Old Days." *IASFM*, April 1989.

———. "The Last Question." In *Opus 100*.

———. *Nightfall and Other Stories*. Greenwich, Conn.: Fawcett/Crest, 1970.

———. *Nine Tomorrows*. Garden City, N.Y.: Doubleday, 1959.

———. *Only a Trillion*. New York: Abelard-Schuman, 1957.

———. *Opus 100*. New York: Dell, 1970.

———. "The Ugly Little Boy." In *Nine Tomorrows*.

———. "The Winds of Change." In *The Winds of Change and Other Stories*.

———. *The Winds of Change and Other Stories*. New York: Ballantine/Del Rey, 1982.

Asimov, Isaac, ed. *Before the Golden Age: Book 3*. Greenwich, Conn.: Fawcett/Crest, 1975.

Ballard, J. G. "The Gentle Assassin." In *The Day of Forever*. London: Panther, 1967.

Baring-Gould, William S. *Sherlock Holmes of Baker Street: A Life of the World's First Consulting Detective*. New York: Clarkson N. Potter, 1962.

Bayley, Barrington J. *Collision Course*. New York: DAW, 1973.

———. *The Fall of Chronopolis*. New York: DAW, 1974.

Bellamy, Edward. *Equality*. New York: Appleton, 1897.

———. *Looking Backward 2000–1887*. Boston: Ticknor, 1888.

Benford, Gregory. *Timescape*. New York: Pocket Books, 1981.

Bester, Alfred. "Hobson's Choice." In *Starburst*. New York: Signet, 1958.

———. "The Men Who Murdered Mohammed." In *The Dark Side of the Earth*. New York: New American Library, 1964.

Bilenkin, Dmitri. "The Uncertainty Principle." In *The Uncertainty Principle*. Translated from the Russian by Antonina W. Bouis; introduction by Theodore Sturgeon. New York and London: Collier/Macmillan, 1978.

Bishop, Michael. *No Enemy but Time*. New York: Timescape/Pocket, 1983.

Blish, James. *Cities in Flight*. New York: Avon, 1970.

Boucher, Anthony, ed. *The Best from Fantasy and Science Fiction, Fifth Series*. Garden City, N.Y.: Doubleday, 1956.

Bradbury, Ray. "The Dragon." In *A Medicine for Melancholy*.

———. "The Exiles." In *R Is for Rocket*.

———. "Forever and the Earth." In *Long After Midnight*. New York: Bantam, 1978.

———. "The Fox and the Forest." In *The Illustrated Man*. New York: Bantam, 1965.

———. *I Sing the Body Electric*. New York: Knopf, 1969.

———. *A Medicine for Melancholy*. New York: Bantam, 1959.

———. "Night Meeting." In *The Martian Chronicles*. New York: Bantam, 1951.

———. *R Is for Rocket*. New York: Bantam, 1965.

———. "A Scent of Sarsaparilla." In *A Medicine for Melancholy*.

———. "A Sound of Thunder." In *R Is for Rocket*.

———. "Time in Thy Flight." In *S Is for Space*. New York: Bantam, 1976.

Bretnor, Reginald, ed. *Science Fiction Today and Tomorrow*. Baltimore: Penguin Books, 1975.

Brown, Fredric. *The Best of Fredric Brown*, edited by Robert Bloch. New York: Ballantine/Del Rey, 1977.

———. "The End." In *The Best of Fredric Brown*.

———. "Letter to a Phoenix." In *The Best of Fredric Brown*.

Brunner, John. *The Tides of Time*. New York: Ballantine/Del Rey, 1984.

Bulwer-Lytton, Sir Edward George Earle. *The Coming Race*. New York: George Routledge & Sons, 1874.

Burroughs, Edgar Rice. *A Princess of Mars*. Chicago: McClurg, 1917. First as "Under the Moons of Mars," in *All-Story Magazine*, 1912, as by Norman Bean.

Campbell, Joseph. *The Hero with a Thousand Faces*. Princeton, N.J.: Princeton University Press, 1968.

Card, Orson Scott. *Seventh Son*. New York: Tor, 1987.

Cartmill, Cleve. "Deadline." *ASF*, March 1944.

Chalker, Jack. *Downtiming the Night Side*. New York: Tor, 1985.

Chamberlain, Gordon B. *See* Charles G. Waugh.

Child, Francis James, ed. *The English and Scottish Popular Ballads*. 5 vols. New York: Dover, 1965.

Clarke, Arthur C. *The Fountains of Paradise*. New York and London: Harcourt Brace
     Jovanovich, 1979.
————. *2001: A Space Odyssey*. New York: Signet, 1968.
————. *2020: Odyssey Two*. New York: Ballantine/Del Rey, 1982.
Clemens, Susy. *Papa: An Intimate Biography of Mark Twain*. Edited with an introduction
     by Charles Neider. With a forward and commentary by her father. Garden City,
     N.Y.: Doubleday, 1985.
Clement, Hal. "The Creation of Imaginary Beings." In *Science Fiction Today and
     Tomorrow*, edited by Reginald Bretnor.
————. *Mission of Gravity*. New York: Doubleday, 1954.
Cowper, Richard. *Time Out of Mind*. New York: Pocket Books, 1981.
David, Peter. *Knight Life*. New York: Ace Fantasy/Berkley, 1987.
de Camp, L. Sprague. "Aristotle and the Gun." In *A Gun for Dinosaur and Other
     Imaginative Tales*. New York: Doubleday, 1977.
————. "Balsamo's Mirror." In *The Purple Pterodactyls: The Adventures of W. Wilson
     Newbury, Ensorcelled Financier*. New York: Ace, 1980.
————. "The Best-Laid Scheme." In *The Wheels of If*.
————. *The Best of L. Sprague de Camp*. New York: Ballantine, 1978.
————. *The Bronze God of Rhodes*. New York: Doubleday, 1960.
————. *The Dragon of the Ishtar Gate*. New York: Doubleday, 1961.
————. *An Elephant for Aristotle*. New York: Doubleday, 1958.
————. "A Gun for Dinosaur." In *The Best of L. Sprague de Camp*.
————. *Lest Darkness Fall*. New York: Pyramid, 1963.
————. *The Wheels of If*. Chicago: Shasta, 1948.
de Santillana, Giorgio, and Hertha von Dechend. *Hamlet's Mill: An Essay on Myth and
     the Frame of Time*. Boston: David R. Godine, 1977.
Defoe, Daniel. *The Life and Adventures of Robinson Crusoe*. Philadelphia: Jesper Hard-
     ing, 1847.
del Rey, Lester. "And It Comes Out Here." In *Mortals and Monsters*. New York:
     Ballantine, 1965.
Dick, Philip K. "Captive Market." In *The Preserving Machine*. New York: Ace, 1969.
————. *Martian Time-Slip*. New York: Ballantine, 1976.
————. *Now Wait for Last Year*. New York: MacFadden, 1968.
————. *The Three Stigmata of Palmer Eldritch*. New York: Manor, 1976.
————. *Ubik*. New York: Bantam, 1977.
Dickens, Charles. *A Christmas Carol. In Prose. Being a Ghost Story of Christmas*.
     London: Chapman and Hall, 1843.
Dickson, Gordon R. *Time Storm*. New York: Bantam, 1979.
Dille, Robert C., ed. *The Collected Works of Buck Rogers in the 25th Century*. Edgemont,
     Penn.: Chelsea House, 1969. The comic strip based on the Phil Nowlan stories
     and until 1939 written by him.
Doyle, Sir Arthur Conan. *The Lost World*. London: Hodder & Stoughton, 1912.
Drake, David. *Birds of Prey*. New York: Tor, 1984.
————. *Bridgehead*. New York: Tor, 1986.
Duffy, Maureen. *The Erotic World of Faery*. New York: Avon, 1972.
Edmondson, G. C. "The Misfit." In *Stranger Than You Think*.
————. *The Ship That Sailed the Time Stream*. New York: Ace, 1965. An Ace Double
     with *Stranger Than You Think*.

Eklund, Gordon. *Serving in Time*. Toronto: Laser Books, 1975.

Ensor, Allison R. Preface to the Norton *Yankee*.

Farley, Ralph Milne. "The Man Who Met Himself." In *The Omnibus of Time*.

————. *The Omnibus of Time*. Los Angeles: Fantasy, 1950.

————. "Rescue Into the Past." In *The Omnibus of Time*.

Farmer, Philip Jose. *Doc Savage: His Apocalyptic Life*. Garden City N.Y.: Doubleday, 1973.

————. "The Long Wet Purple Dream of Rip Van Winkle." In *The Purple Book*.

————. *The Other Log of Phileas Fogg*. New York: DAW, 1973.

————. *The Purple Book*. New York: Tor/Pinnacle, 1982.

————. *Tarzan Alive: A Definitive Biography of Lord Greystoke*. New York: Doubleday, 1982.

————. *Time's Last Gift*. New York: Ballantine/Del Rey, 1977.

————. *Venus on the Half-Shell*. As by Kilgore Trout. New York: Dell, 1975.

Finney, Jack. *About Time: Twelve Short Stories*. New York: Simon & Schuster, 1986.

————. "The Face in the Photo." In *About Time*.

————. *Forgotten News: The Crime of the Century and Other Lost Stories*. New York: Simon & Schuster, 1983.

————. "I Love Galesburg in the Springtime." In *About Time*.

————. "I'm Scared." In *About Time*.

————. "Of Missing Persons." In *About Time* and *The Third Level*.

————. "Second Chance." In *About Time* and *The Third Level*.

————. "Such Interesting Neighbors." In *About Time* and *The Third Level*.

————. "The Third Level." In *About Time* and *The Third Level*.

————. *The Third Level*. New York: Dell, 1959. Collection.

————. *Time and Again*. New York: Simon & Schuster, 1970.

————. "Where the Cluetts Are." In *About Time*.

Franklin, H. Bruce. *Future Perfect: American Science Fiction of the Nineteenth Century*. Revised edition. Oxford: Oxford University Press, 1978.

————. *Robert A. Heinlein: America as Science Fiction*. Oxford: Oxford University Press, 1980.

————. *War Stars: The Superweapon and the American Imagination*. New York and Oxford: Oxford University Press, 1988.

Frankowski, Leo. *The Cross-Time Engineer*. New York: Ballantine/Del Rey, 1986.

————. *The Flying Warlord*. New York: Ballantine/Del Rey, 1989.

————. *The High-Tech Knight*. New York: Ballantine/Del Rey, 1989.

————. *The Radiant Warrior*. New York: Ballantine/Del Rey, 1989.

Fraser, J. T. *Time, the Familiar Stranger*. Amherst: University of Massachusetts Press, 1987.

Gerrold, David. *The Man Who Folded Himself*. New York: Random House, 1973.

Gibbon, Edward. *The Decline and Fall of the Roman Empire*. New York: Heritage Press, 1946.

Gilbert, Sandra M., and Susan Gubar. *The Madwoman in the Attic: The Woman Writer and the Nineteenth-Century Literary Imagination*. New Haven: Yale University Press, 1979.

Ginsburg, Mirra, ed. and trans. *Last Door to AIYA: A Selection of the Best New Fiction from the Soviet Union*. New York: S. G. Phillips, 1968.

Girouard, Mark. *The Return to Camelot: Chivalry and the English Imagination*. New Haven and London: Yale University Press, 1981.

Goldsmith, Howard. "The Proust Syndrome." In *Crisis*, edited by Roger Sherwood. New York: Nelson, 1974.

Green, Martin. *Dreams of Adventure, Deeds of Empire*. New York: Basic Books, 1979.

Grosser, Paul E., and Edwin G. Halperin. *Anti-Semitism*. Secaucus, N.J.: Citadel Press, n.d.

Gunn, James. *The Road to Science Fiction #3: From Heinlein to Here*. New York: New American Library, 1979.

Haiblum, Isidore. *Transfer to Yesterday*. New York: Ballantine, 1973.

Halasz, Nicholas. *Captain Dreyfus: The Story of a Mass Hysteria*. New York: Simon & Schuster, 1986.

Hale, Edward Everett. "Hands Off" In *Alternative Histories: Eleven Stories of the World as It Might Have Been*, edited by Charles G. Waugh and Martin H. Greenberg. First in *Harper's*, March 1881.

――――. "The Man Without a Country." In *The Atlantic Monthly*, 1863.

Harrison, Harry. *Captive Universe*. New York: Putnam, 1969.

――――. "The Time-Machined Saga." In *Analog*, March–May 1967. Book Title: *The Technicolor Time Machine*. New York: Doubleday, 1967.

Hawking, Stephen W. *A Brief History of Time: From the Big Bang to Black Holes*. Toronto, New York, etc.: Bantam, 1988.

Heinlein, Robert. "All You Zombies." In *The Unpleasant Profession of Jonathan Hoag*.

――――. "By His Bootstraps." In *The Menace from Earth*.

――――. *The Cat Who Walks Through Walls*. New York: Putnam, 1985.

――――. *Citizen of the Galaxy*. New York: Scribner's, 1957.

――――. *The Door into Summer*. New York: Signet, 1957.

――――. *Double Star*. New York: Doubleday, 1956.

――――. *Farnham's Freehold*. New York: Putnam, 1964.

――――. *Friday*. New York: Holt, Rinehart and Winston, 1982.

――――. "If This Goes On . . . " In *Revolt in 2100*. New York: Signet, 1953.

――――. *I Will Fear No Evil*. New York: Putnam, 1970.

――――. *Job: A Comedy of Justice*: New York: Ballantine/Del Rey, 1984.

――――. *The Menace from Earth*. New York: Gnome, 1959.

――――. *The Number of the Beast*. New York: Fawcett Columbine, 1980.

――――. *The Puppet Masters*. New York: Doubleday, 1951.

――――. "They." In *The Unpleasant Profession of Jonathan Hoag*.

――――. *Time Enough for Love*. New York: Putnam, 1973.

――――. *Universe*. New York: Dell, 1951.

――――. *The Unpleasant Profession of Jonathan Hoag*. New York: Gnome, 1959.

Hogan, James P. *The Proteus Operation*. New York: Bantam, 1986.

Holmes, Oliver Wendell. "The Old Man Dreams." In *The Writings of Oliver Wendell Holmes*, XII, 9. Cambridge, Mass.: Riverside Press, 1891.

Hoyle, Fred. *October the First Is Too Late*. New York: Fawcett/Crest, 1968.

Hoyle, Trevor. *The Gods Look Down*. New York: Ace, 1982.

――――. *Seeking the Mythical Future*. New York: Ace, 1982.

――――. *Through the Eye of Time*. New York: Ace, 1982. With the two books above, this makes up *The Q Trilogy*.

Huxley, Aldous. *Brave New World*. New York: Bantam, 1968.

Irving, Washington. "Rip Van Winkle." In *The Legend of Sleepy Hollow and Other Stories*. New York: Washington Square Press, 1962.

Janes, Julian. *The Origin of Consciousness in the Breakdown of the Bicameral Mind*. Boston: Houghton Mifflin, 1976.

Kaplan, Justin. Introduction to the Penguin *Yankee*.

————. *Mr. Clemens and Mark Twain*. New York: Simon & Schuster, 1966.

Kelley, Leo P. *Time Rogue*. New York: Lancer, 1970.

Kenney, Alice P. "Yankees in Camelot: the Democratization of Chivalry in James Russell Lowell, Mark Twain, and Edward Arlington Robinson." *Studies in Medievalism*, 1, No. 2 (Spring 1982).

Kersh, Gerald. "Whatever Happened to Corporal Cuckoo?" In *Star Science Fiction Stories No. 3*, edited by Frederik Pohl. New York: Ballantine, 1962.

Ketterer, David. *New Worlds for Old: The Apocalyptic Imagination, Science Fiction, and American Literature*. Garden City, N.Y.: Anchor/Doubleday, 1974.

King, Stephen. "The Breathing Method." In *Different Seasons*.

————. *Carrie*. New York: Signet, 1975.

————. *Christine*. New York: Signet, 1983.

————. *Cujo*. New York: Signet, 1982.

————. *The Dead Zone*. New York: Signet, 1980.

————. *Different Seasons*. New York: Signet, 1983.

————. *It*. New York: Signet, 1987.

————. *Pet Sematary*. New York: Signet, 1984.

————. *'Salem's Lot*. New York: Signet, 1976.

————. *The Shining*. New York: Signet, 1978.

————. *The Stand*. New York: Signet, 1980.

————. *The Talisman* (with Peter Straub). New York: Berkley, 1985.

————. *Thinner* (as Richard Bachman). New York: Signet, 1985.

Klein, Gerald. *The Day Before Tomorrow*. New York: DAW, 1972.

Knight, Damon. "Beachcomber." In *In Deep*. First in *Imagination*, 1952.

————. *The Best of Damon Knight*. New York: Doubleday, 1976.

————. *In Deep*. New York: Manor, 1972.

————. "Time Enough." In *The Best of Damon Knight*.

————. "You're Another." In *The Best from Fantasy and Science Fiction, Fifth Series*, edited by Anthony Boucher.

Knight, Damon, ed. *Turning Points: Essays on the Art of Science Fiction*. New York &c: Harper & Row 1977.

Langford, Michele K., ed. *Contours of the Fantastic: Selected Essays from the Eighth International Conference on the Fantastic in the Arts*. Westport, Conn.: Greenwood, 1990.

Le Guin, Ursula K. *The Dispossessed: An Abiguous Utopia*. New York: Avon, 1974.

————. "April in Paris." In *The Wind's Twelve Quarters*.

————. *The Language of the Night*. New York: G. P. Putnam's Sons, 1979.

————. *The Left Hand of Darkness*. New York: Ace, 1969.

————. *Rocannon's World*. New York: Ace, 1966.

————. "Semley's Necklace." In *The Wind's Twelve Quarters*. First in *Amazing* 1964 as "The Dowry of the Angyar." Later as the first chapter of *Rocannon's World*.

————. *The Wind's Twelve Quarters*. New York: Bantam, 1976.

Leinster, Murray. *The Best of Murray Leinster*. New York: Ballantine/Del Rey, 1978.

————. "Sidewise in Time." In *The Best of Murray Leinster*. First in *ASF* 1934.

Levine, George, and U. C. Knoepflmacher, eds. *The Endurance of Frankenstein*. Berkeley: University of California Press, 1979.

Lewis, C. S. "On Science Fiction." In *Turning Points*, edited by Damon Knight.

London, Jack. *The Iron Heel*. Westport, Conn.: Lawrence Hill & Co., 1980. First published in 1908.

Lugard, Flora Louise Shaw. "Cecil Rhodes." *Encyclopedia Brittanica*, 11th ed.

MacDonald, John D. "Half-Past Eternity." In *Other Times, Other Worlds*.

————. *Other Times, Other Worlds*. New York: Fawcett, 1978.

————. "Susceptibility." In *Other Times, Other Worlds*.

MacKaye, Harold Steele. *The Panchronicon*. New York: Charles Scribner's Sons, 1904.

McLaughlin, Dean. "Hawk Among the Sparrows." In *Hawk Among the Sparrows*. New York: Scribners, 1976.

Malory, Sir Thomas. *Le Morte d'Arthur*. Edited by Janet Cowen. 2 vols. Harmondsworth, England: Penguin, 1981.

Malzberg, Barry. *The Engines of the Night: Science Fiction in the Eighties*. New York: Doubleday, 1982.

Marsalis, Wynton. Quoted by Stanley Crouch in his liner notes for *The Majesty of the Blues*. CBS Records, 1989.

Mathews, Richard. *Aldiss Unbound: The Science Fiction of Brian W. Aldiss*. Volume IX in the Milford Series: Popular Writers of Today. San Bernadino, CA: The Borgo Press, 1977.

May, Julian. *The Adversary*. Boston: Houghton Mifflin, 1982.

————. *The Golden Torc*. Boston: Houghton Mifflin, 1982.

————. *The Many-Colored Land*. Boston: Houghton Mifflin, 1981.

————. *The Nonborn King*. Boston: Houghton Mifflin, 1983.

————. *A Pliocene Companion*. Boston: Houghton Mifflin, 1984. The above four novels make up *The Saga of Pliocene Exile*, for which *A Pliocene Companion* is a guidebook.

Meredith, Richard C. *At the Narrow Passage*. New York: Playboy Press, 1976. Vol. 1 of *The Timeliner Trilogy*.

————. *No Brother, No Friend*. New York: Playboy Press, 1979. Vol. 2 of *The Timeliner Trilogy*.

————. *Run, Come See Jerusalem!* New York: Ballantine, 1976.

————. *Vestiges of Time*. New York: Playboy Press, 1976. Vol. 3 of *The Timeliner Trilogy*.

Mitchell, Edwin Page. "The Clock That Went Backward." In *The Crystal Man*.

————. *The Crystal Man*. Collected and with a biographical perspective by Sam Moskowitz. Garden City, N.Y.: Doubleday, 1973.

Mitchell, Kirk. *Never the Twain*. New York: Ace, 1987.

Moglen, Helen. *Charlotte Bronte: The Self Conceived*. New York: Norton, 1976. Cited by Gilbert & Gubar.

Moorcock, Michael. *An Alien Heat*. New York: Harper and Row, 1972. Vol. 1 of *The Dancers at the End of Time*.

————. *Behold the Man*. New York: Holt, Rinehart, 1971.

————. *Breakfast in the Ruins*. New York: Avon, 1980.

————. *Dying for Tomorrow*. New York: DAW, 1978.

———. *The End of All Songs*. New York: Harper & Row, 1976. Vol. 3 of *The Dancers at the End of Time*.

———. *The Hollow Lands*. New York: Harper & Row, 1974. Vol. 2 of *The Dancers at the End of Time*.

Moore, C. L., and Henry Kuttner (as Lawrence O'Donnell). "Vintage Season." In *The Science Fiction Hall of Fame, Vol. IIA*, edited by Ben Bova. First in *ASF* 1946.

Moore, Ward. *Bring the Jubilee*. New York: Farrar Straus, 1953.

Moskowitz, Sam. "Lost Giant of American Science Fiction: A Biographical Perspective." In Edwin Mitchell, *The Crystal Man*.

Neider, Charles. See Susy Clemens.

Nichols, Peter, ed. *The Science Fiction Encyclopedia*. New York: Doubleday, 1979.

Niven, Larry, *All the Myriad Ways*. New York: Ballantine, 1981.

———. *Ringworld*. New York: Ballantine/Del Rey, 1970.

———. "The Theory and Practice of Time Travel." In *All the Myriad Ways*.

Nowlan, Philip. "Armageddon, 2419 A.D." *Amazing*, August 1928. First Buck Rogers story. See Robert C. Dille.

Oppolzer, Theodore Ritter von. *Canon of Eclipses*. Owen Gingerich, trans. New York: Dover, 1962.

Orwell, George. *Down and Out in Paris and London*. New York: Harper, 1933.

Paine, Albert Bigelow. See *Mark Twain's Autobiography*.

Patrouch, Joseph F., Jr. *The Science Fiction of Isaac Asimov*. Garden City N.Y.: Doubleday, 1974.

Paul, Terri. "The Worm Ouroboros: Time Travel, Imagination, and Entropy." *Extrapolation* 24, No. 3 (Fall 1983).

Paulos, John Allen. *Innumeracy: Mathematical Illiteracy and Its Consequences*. New York: Hill & Wang, 1988.

Pinkerton, Jan. "Backward Time Travel, Alternate Universes, and Edward Everett Hale." *Extrapolation* 20, No. 2 (Summer 1979).

Piper, H. Beam. *Lord Kalvan of Otherwhen*. New York: Ace, 1965.

———. *Paratime*. New York: Ace, 1981.

———. "Time and Time Again." In *The Worlds of H. Beam Piper*.

———. *The Worlds of H. Beam Piper*. Edited by John F. Carr. New York: Ace, 1983.

Pirandello, Luigi. *Naked Masks: Five Plays by Luigi Pirandello*. Edited by Eric Bentley. New York: E. P. Dutton, 1952.

Poe, Edgar Allan. "A Tale of the Ragged Mountains." *Godey's Lady's Book*, April 1844.

Pohl, Frederik. *Alternating Currents*. New York: Ballantine, 1969.

———. *The Annals of the Heechee*. New York: Ballantine/Del Rey, 1987.

———. *The Coming of the Quantum Cats*. New York: Bantam, 1986.

———. "Day Million." In *The Road to Science Fiction #3*, edited by James Gunn.

———. "The Deadly Mission of Phineas Snodgrass." In *In the Problem Pit*.

———. *In the Problem Pit*. New York: Bantam, 1976. Collection.

———. "Let the Ants Try." In *Alternating Currents*.

Pohl, Frederik, and Jack Williamson. *Wall Around a Star*. New York: Ballantine/Del Rey, 1983.

Poleshchuk, A. "Homer's Secret." In *Last Door to AIYA: A Selection of the Best New Science Fiction from the Soviet Union*. Edited and translated by Mirra Ginsburg.

Pournelle, Jerry. *A Step Farther Out*. New York: Ace, 1979.

Priestley, J. B. *Man's Time*. London: Crescent Books, 1964.

Rabelais, François. *The Complete Works of Rabelais*. Translated by Jacques leClerc. New York: Modern Library, n.d.

Reynolds, Mack. *Equality: In the Year 2000*. New York: Ace, 1977.

———. *Looking Backward, From the Year 2000*. New York: Ace, 1973.

Roberts, Keith. "Weinachtsabend." In *The Grain Kings*. London: Hutchinson, 1976.

Rose, Mark. *Alien Encounters: Anatomy of Science Fiction*. Cambridge: Harvard University Press, 1971.

Saberhagen, Fred. *A Century of Progress*. New York: Tor, 1983.

Shelley, Mary. *Frankenstein*. New York: Bantam, 1967.

———. *The Last Man*. London: Grey Walls, 1954.

Sherred, T. L. "E for Effort." In *First Person, Peculiar*. New York: Ballantine, 1972.

Silverberg, Robert. *Shadrach in the Furnace*. Indianapolis: Bobbs Merrill, 1976.

———. *Up the Line*. New York: Ballantine, 1969.

Simak, Clifford D. *All the Traps of Earth and Other Stories*. Garden City, N.Y.: Doubleday, 1962.

———. "The Big Front Yard." In *Skirmish: The Great Short Fiction of Clifford D. Simak*. New York: Berkley, 1977.

———. *Mastodonia*. New York: Ballantine/Del Rey, 1978.

———. *Our Children's Children*. New York: G. P. Putnam's Sons, 1974.

———. "Project Mastodon." In *All the Traps of Earth and Other Stories*.

———. *Time and Again*. New York: Ace, 1951.

Smith, Curtis C., ed. *Twentieth-Century Science-Fiction Writers*. 2d ed. Chicago and London: St. James Press, 1986.

Smith, E. E. "Doc." In *The Skylark of Space*. New York: Pyramid, 1958.

Stableford, Brian. "The British and American Traditions of Speculative Fiction." In *Contours of the Fantastic*, edited by Michele K. Langford.

———. *Scientific Romance in Britain*. London: Fourth Estate, 1985.

———. "Utopias." In *Science Fiction Encyclopedia*, edited by Peter Nichols.

Stapledon, Olaf. *Star Maker*. Harmondsworth, England: Penguin, 1973.

Suvin, Darko. "Victorian Science Fiction, 1871–85: the Rise of the Alternative History Sub-Genre." *Science Fiction Studies* 10 (1983).

Tenn, William. "Brooklyn Project." In *The Road to Science Fiction #3: From Heinlein to Here*, edited by James Gunn.

Tennyson, Alfred. *Idylls of the King and a Selection of Poems*. New York: Signet, 1961. Includes "Locksley Hall."

"Thomas Rymer." Ballad No. 37 in *The English and Scottish Popular Ballads* by Francis James Child. New York: Dover Books, 1965. Vol. 1.

Tolkien, J.R.R. *The Lord of the Rings*. Boston: Houghton Mifflin, 1978. 3 vols.

Tuck, Donald H., compiler. *The Encyclopedia of Science Fiction and Fantasy: Through 1968*. 2 vols. Chicago: Advent, 1974.

Twain, Mark. *Adventures of Huckleberry Finn. An Annotated Text: Backgrounds and Sources: Essays in Criticism*. Edited by Sculley Bradley, Richmond Croom Beatty, and E. Hudson Long. New York: W. W. Norton, 1961.

———. *A Connecticut Yankee at King Arthur's Court*. Edited and with an introduction by Justin Kaplan. Uses the text of the first English edition [*A Yankee at the Court of King Arthur*. London: Chatto and Windus, 1889]. Harmondsworth, England: Penguin Books, 1979.

————. *A Connecticut Yankee in King Arthur's Court*. The Iowa Center for Textual Studies *Works of Mark Twain*. Edited by Bernard L. Stein with an introduction by Henry Nash Smith. Berkeley, Los Angeles, London: University of California Press, 1979.

————. *A Connecticut Yankee in King Arthur's Court*. Afterword by Edmund Reiss. New York: Signet, 1963.

————. *Following the Equator*. Hartford: American Publishing Company, 1897.

————. *The Innocents Abroad: or The New Pilgrims' Progress. Being Some Account of the Steamship Quaker City's Pleasure Excursion to Europe and the Holy Land*. Introduction by Edward Wagenknecht. New York: The Heritage Press, 1962. Originally Hartford: American Publishing Company, 1869.

————. "Letters from the Earth." In *What Is Man? and Other Philosophical Writings*.

————. *Life on the Mississippi*. New York: Bantam, 1981. Originally Harper, 1896.

————. *Mark Twain-Howells Letters*. Edited by Henry Nash Smith and William M. Gibson. Cambridge, Mass.: Harvard University Press, 1960.

————. *Mark Twain's Autobiography*. With an Introduction by Albert Bigelow Paine. 2 vols. New York and London: Harper & Brothers, 1924.

————. *Mark Twain's Letters*. Edited by Albert Bigelow Paine. New York and London: Harper and Brothers, 1917.

————. *Mark Twain's Notebooks and Journals*. Volume I (1855–1873) edited by Frederick Anderson, Michael B. Frank, and Kenneth M. Sanderson. Berkeley, etc.: University of California Press, 1975. Volume II (1877–1883) edited by Frederick Anderson, Lin Salamo, and Bernard L. Stein. Berkeley, etc.: University of California Press, 1975. Volume III (1883–1891), editors and publisher as for Volume II, 1979.

————. "A Medieval Romance." In *Sketches New and Old*.

————. *The Mysterious Stranger and Other Stories*. New York: Signet, 1962.

————. *Personal Recollections of Joan of Arc*. New York: Harper and Brothers, 1896.

————. *The Prince and the Pauper*. Edited by Victor Fischer and Lin Salamo with the assistance of Mary Jane Jones. Berkeley, etc.: Iowa CTS/University of California Press, 1979. Originally published in Boston by Osgood and in London by Chatto and Windus, 1881.

————. *Sketches New and Old*. New York and London: Harper and Brothers, 1903.

————. *The $30,000 Bequest and Other Stories*. New York and London: Harper and Brothers, 1903.

————. *What Is Man? and Other Philosophical Writings*. Edited by Paul Baender. The Iowa Center for Textual Studies *Works of Mark Twain*. Berkeley, etc.: University of California Press, 1973.

Uttley, Alison. *A Traveler in Time*. New York: G. P. Putnam's Sons, 1940.

Verne, Jules. *Twenty Thousand Leagues under the Sea*. New York: Bantam, 1962.

Vonnegut, Kurt. *Slaughterhouse Five: or, The Children's Crusade*. New York: Delacorte, 1969.

Waugh, Charles G., and Martin H. Greenberg, eds. *Alternative Histories: Eleven Stories of the World as It Might Have Been*. Afterword by Gordon B. Chamberlain. Bibliography of Alternative History by Barton C. Hacker and Gordon B. Chamberlain. New York and London: Garland, 1986.

Weisinger, Mort. "Thompson's Time-Traveling Theory." *Fantasy Magazine*, January 1937.

Wells, H. G. "The Chronic Argonauts." *Science Schools Journal*, 1888. An earlier version of *The Time Machine*.

————. *The Island of Doctor Moreau*. New York: Stone and Kimball, 1896.

————. *The Time Machine: An Invention*. New York: Holt, 1895.

————. *The War of the Worlds*. New York: Harper, 1898.

Williamson, Jack. *The Legion of Time*. Reading, Pa.: Fantasy Press, 1952.

Wilt, Judith. "*Frankenstein* as Mystery Play." In *The Endurance of Frankenstein*, edited by George Levine and U. C. Knoepflmacher. Berkeley: University of California Press, 1979.

Wolf, Fred Alan. *Parallel Universes: The Search for Other Worlds*. New York: Simon & Schuster, 1988.

Zamiatin, Eugene. *We*. Translated and with a foreword by Gregory Zilboorg. Introduction by Peter Rudy. Preface by Marc Slonim. New York: E. P. Dutton, 1924.

INDEX

About the Author

BUD FOOTE is Associate Professor of English at Georgia Institute of Technology. He contributed an essay to *Contours of the Fantastic* (Greenwood Press, 1990). He has reviewed books for *National Observer* and was science fiction columnist for the *Detroit News*.